The End of Empire

The End of Empire

The Cyprus Emergency:
A Soldier's Story

Martin Bell

Pen & Sword
MILITARY

First published in Great Britain in 2015 by
Pen & Sword Military
an imprint of
Pen & Sword Books Ltd
47 Church Street
Barnsley
South Yorkshire
S70 2AS

ISBN 978 1 47384 818 4

A CIP catalogue record for this book is available from the British
Library

Typeset in Ehrhardt by
Mac Style Ltd, Bridlington, East Yorkshire
Printed and bound in the UK by CPI Group (UK) Ltd,
Croydon, CRO 4YY

Pen & Sword Books Ltd incorporates the imprints of Pen & Sword
Archaeology, Atlas, Aviation, Battleground, Discovery, Family
History, History, Maritime, Military, Naval, Politics, Railways, Select,
Transport, True Crime, and Fiction, Frontline Books, Leo Cooper,
Praetorian Press, Seaforth Publishing and Wharncliffe.

For a complete list of Pen & Sword titles please contact
PEN & SWORD BOOKS LIMITED
47 Church Street, Barnsley, South Yorkshire, S70 2AS, England
E-mail: enquiries@pen-and-sword.co.uk
Website: www.pen-and-sword.co.uk

Contents

List of Illustrations

Corporal Martin Bell, 1959.

The author's letters from Cyprus and the chocolate box in which they were kept.

Regimental Scrapbook.

The author in the regimental archives.

Lieutenant Colonel Arthur Campbell MC.

1st Battalion marching into Kykko Camp, Nicosia, May 1957.

Soldiers of D Company searching a bus watched by the Commander-in-Chief Middle East Land Forces.

Turkish Cypriot demonstration in Nicosia, July 1958.

Governor Sir Hugh Foot inspects the Battalion, August 1958.

Governor Sir John Harding with the Intelligence Section, 1957.

'The General laughs with RSM Gingell and CSM Evans.'

The Keep, all that remains of Gibraltar Barracks, Bury St Edmunds.

Regimental skiffle group.

The Commanding Officer, Lieutenant Colonel Silvanus 'Bertie' Bevan (left).

Band and Drums beating retreat, March 1959.

Governor Harding and soldiers of the Regiment in riot gear, 1957.

Soldiers of the Regiment escorting demonstrators in Nicosia, October 1958.

Drumhead service.

Soldiers of C Company searched by their own officers outside Kykko Monastery in the presence of a monk, September 1958.

Newspaper cuttings from the time of the Cyprus Emergency.

Preface and Acknowledgements

For this rather unexpected book I am indebted to my mother and father for keeping the letters that I sent from Cyprus as a serving soldier more than fifty years ago; to Merita Zhubi for finding them; to my sisters Anthea and Sylvia; to the Suffolk County Records Office in Bury St Edmunds; to the Trustees of the Museum of the Suffolk Regiment; and to the Suffolk Concert Band.

Books take on a life of their own. What started as a personal reminiscence has turned into a narrative of the last two years of one of the British Army's great regiments of the line: its culture and character, its operations, its personalities and its codes of conduct, speech and dress. It had served for more than 270 years before I joined it; I was hardly its most proficient soldier, as the Regimental Sergeant Major never tired of reminding me; but shortly after my demob it marched off parade and was gone for ever. It deserves to be well remembered.

The story is told from an unreservedly other ranks' perspective; no disrespect is intended, except where it is, to the distinguished and gallant officers whom I met along the way.

I am grateful for the erudition of Dr Piers Brendon, author of *The Decline and Fall of the British Empire*, who ploughed this furrow before me; and for the advice of an old soldier, Major John Benjamin of the Royal Signals.

I am also indebted to Panayiotis Michael and other former detainees of the British for their recollections of Operation Matchbox in July 1958, in which I was among the soldiers rounding them up and giving them grief.

The National Archives at Kew proved to be a treasure-house of recently declassified documents, including the file on Matchbox. This revealed that the island-wide round-up of EOKA suspects had gone ahead despite the strong opposition of the Governor Sir Hugh Foot, who was in theory the colony's Commander-in-Chief. Other files disclosed an extensive breakdown of military discipline in Famagusta in October 1958. Operationally the Governor was in office but not in power.

The Regiment's outstanding soldier was Lieutenant Colonel Arthur Campbell MC. His book about the campaign, *Flaming Cassock*, was commissioned by one Governor of Cyprus and then suppressed by the next. It has been my privilege, with the help of some friends, to rescue it from oblivion. The inch-thick sheaf of documents about its suppression, also declassified, is an eloquent expression of the colonial mind-set of the time. The island belonged not to us but to its people.

And most of all I am grateful to Second Lieutenant (later Brigadier) Charles Barnes my Intelligence Officer, to the formidable Regimental Sergeant Majors Gingell and Hazelwood, to Colonel Pat Hopper, Brigadier Bill Deller, Brigadier Tony Calder, Lieutenant Alfred Waller, Lance Corporal Dave Pygall of Watford FC, the Orderly Room clerks and all the men of the Suffolk Regiment, the 12th of Foot, with whom I am proud to have served. This book is for them.

Martin Bell
London, 2014

The Suffolk Regiment 1957–1959

The regimental office and veranda
Were no place for the casual bystander,
With beltless soldiers frog-marched in
On charges of indiscipline
And corporals and other rankers
Busted and given two weeks' jankers;
The 12th of Foot on active service
Dealt harshly with the frail and nervous
Except the officers, those precious beauties,
Whose only punishment was weekend duties.
And so by means both military and marvellous
We lived up to our ancient motto *Stabilis*.

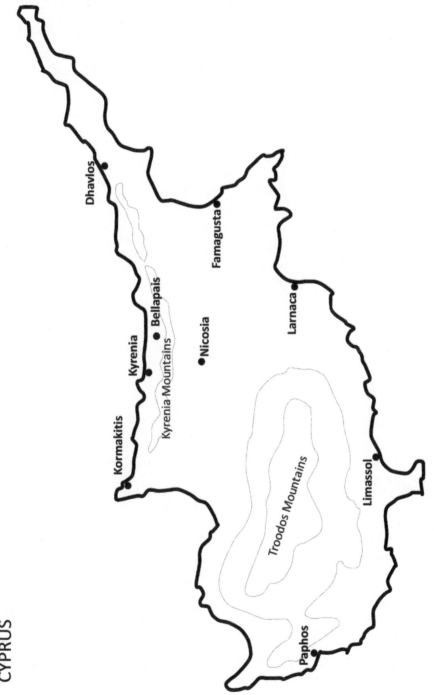

CYPRUS

Dhavlos

Famagusta

Bellapais

Kyrenia

Nicosia

Larnaca

Kyrenia Mountains

Kormakitis

Troodos Mountains

Limassol

Paphos

Chapter 1

Destination Cyprus

T he British acquired Cyprus from Turkey, not as a colony but as a protectorate, in 1878. It was a diplomatic *coup de main* by the Prime Minister Benjamin Disraeli. Queen Victoria congratulated him: 'The High and Low are delighted,' she wrote, 'except Mr Gladstone, who is frantic.' So began a period of British rule, paternalistic rather than energetic, that lasted for eighty-two years. The island became a full crown colony in 1925 and an important military base for what was still a far-flung Empire. It slept in the sun for many years, receiving little attention from the outside world, including the colonial power itself, until a crowd of Greek Cypriots rioted and burned down Government House in 1931. The people of Cyprus were made to pay for its rebuilding out of their taxes. Greek Cypriots served loyally for the British in the Second World War, and in Palestine. Between 1940 and 1950 there was even a Cyprus Regiment, whose muleteers were the first colonial troops on the Western Front. Cypriots hoped that their loyalty would help them achieve independence after the war. It did not. The British did not believe that Greek Cypriots had either the will or the capacity for a violent uprising.

In a referendum organised by the Orthodox Church in 1950 and boycotted by the Turkish minority, 95.7 per cent of Greek Cypriots voted for *Enosis*, union with Greece. The British, who would not compromise on sovereignty, ignored it. The alternatives were continuing British rule or armed rebellion – or both, which was what actually happened.

Cyprus in the 1950s was still a British colony and, for half the decade, an island of peace in the turbulent Middle East. It was offshore of Arabs and Israelis. Its population of some 550,000 was 80 per cent Greek and 18 per cent Turkish, with smaller minorities of Maronites and Armenians. The tranquillity – what the poet and novelist Lawrence Durrell called 'the quietness and certainty of ordered ways and familiar rhythms' – did not last, however. On 1 April 1955 the Greek insurgents of EOKA, the National Organisation of Cypriot Fighters, began a campaign of armed resistance to British rule. They attacked targets in Famagusta, Larnaca and Limassol. They blew up the radio station in Nicosia. Their stated aim was *Enosis*. The colonial authorities were caught by surprise, wrong-footed and unprepared. The security forces were slow to respond. Their peacetime chain of command was just not up to it. Durrell was at the time the Governor's press adviser. He wrote 'The days passed in purposeless riots and the screaming of demagogues and commentators, and the nights were busy with the crash of broken glass and the spiteful detonation of small grenades'. He described the violence as a 'feast of unreason'.

The British, for whom the island was strategically important, were determined to hold on to it at all costs and put the rebellion down. They would no sooner decolonise Cyprus than Gibraltar. They appointed a military governor. They introduced emergency measures including detention without trial, the death sentence for bearing arms and the most severe press censorship ever imposed in one of the Queen's dominions. They also mounted a military campaign against the EOKA fighters, led by Colonel Grivas, whose hard core in the mountains never amounted to more than 200 men.

In terms of the balance of forces it was a mismatch. Troops poured into the island, battalion after battalion, until they numbered some 35,000. In January 1956 alone, five new infantry battalions joined the order of battle, backed up by the Royal Horse Guards with their armoured reconnaissance vehicles. Nineteen major units were committed to the campaign at its height. We had a big army then, close to 400,000 strong, about half of whom were national servicemen conscripted for two years. It was like a national press-gang on a massive scale. Six thousand young men were called up at a time, always on a Thursday, giving them perhaps the weekend to adjust to the shock of it. Some never did so. It is estimated that over the years of National Service 140 of them took their own lives.

Field Marshal Sir John Harding, Governor of Cyprus from 1955 to 1957, played an important part in this story. Before taking up the governorship (which by his own account he did reluctantly), he was Chief of the Imperial General Staff. In this capacity as head of the armed forces, his last big argument with the Government in 1955, which he won, was about the length of National Service. He wanted to keep it at two years for reasons of military efficiency. The Government wished to reduce it to 18 months for reasons of political expediency. We were not aware of it at the time, but his digging-in of the heels on this issue had a considerable impact on us conscripts. So did the severity of his policies in Cyprus.

The Army then, rather more than today, was recruited county by county. Most counties had their own regiment and some had several, so when I was 18 years old and living in Suffolk my draft notice duly arrived in a brown envelope. Brown envelopes were to play an important part in my life. I was called to the colours and overnight became Private 23398941 Bell M of The Suffolk Regiment. (No soldier ever forgets his Army number.) I had no choice in the matter and it did not occur to me to dodge the draft. It was something expected of all of us in passing from boyhood to manhood. We did not know much about rights in those days but we surely knew about obligations.

My experience was not unique. Between 1945 and 1960, when National Service ended, there were more than a million peacetime conscripts like me. But it was *exceptional* – unlike anything we had done before or would ever do again. I had just been accepted by King's College Cambridge. I had the choice of doing the studying first and the soldiering later. I decided to get the hard part over and done with, little knowing that National Service was about to end anyway. The beginning of wisdom is to know how much you don't know. Soldiering taught me how much I did not know.

I had (and still have) no regrets. Up till then I had hardly travelled abroad and had not done much in life but study Latin, mow the lawn and pass a few exams. The Army was different – *very* different. It was only in the uniform of a private soldier that I looked up from my books and started to learn about life. It shook me up and took me to Cyprus on active service, in the year after the Suez fiasco. The Cyprus emergency was equally part of the retreat from Empire, but we did not know that at the time. It was the Army's defining commitment and point of main effort. It was, in military terms, the place to be. And The Suffolk Regiment was there. Its 1st (and only operational) Battalion had been serving in Cyprus since the year after the rebellion began – and one after another the drafts of new recruits were flown out to join it after basic training in Bury St Edmunds.

What followed changed me and many others and had a huge impact on us at the time – but in view of all that happened in my life later (I became a broadcaster, a war reporter and an MP), I would have forgotten most of it had I not made a discovery in my attic more than half a century later. There in an old chocolate box lay more than 100 letters that I had written from the island to my parents and my twin sister Sylvia between October 1957 and May 1959. I wrote at least one a week and thought they had been lost, but there they were, some still in their envelopes with threepenny stamps on them, as fresh on the page as if I had written them yesterday. And in legible handwriting too. I called them News from Nowhere.

I was not a reporter then, but they were reports of a sort, first-hand impressions, some of them now acutely embarrassing, which told what it felt like – if not how it was, at least how it seemed – to be a conscripted soldier at the time. Some are tinged with home-sickness. Others tell a story of riots and road blocks and curfews and cordons and searches and of a strategy that ultimately failed. The futility of it all was slow to dawn. There was no 'spin' on the letters, except a wish to assure my family that I was not in any real danger. Because we were not technically at war (although sometimes it seemed so), the Army applied no censorship to them. Nor was anything military self-censored, except a falling-out with the Regimental Sergeant Major. And when they sounded pessimistic, as they tended to do when I was on guard duty, I warned the family to take no notice of them. As I re-read them all those years later, they unlocked a further store of memories, from basic training to the flies round the latrines to the name of the long-serving Post Corporal. They also encouraged me to fill in some gaps with lessons learned and information not then available, some of it from old Top Secret files declassified between 2012 and 2014 and stored in the National Archives. This was at last a time of demystification. The files were still in the original folders, some with the Governor's signature on them and, having come from the old Colonial Office, they were held in the category of 'migrated documents'. A few have been 'redacted', with diplomatically sensitive passages removed, but even the censorship has been inconsistent, and most have survived intact.

We have finally reached a point where the truth really can be told about this distant conflict. We have lessons to learn from it, and it is beyond due time to do so. What follows is an attempt to tell it, both personally and historically, and to draw some conclusions from it. I was politically unaware at the time to an extreme degree. If there were a way of disowning one's younger self I would most cheerfully do so. It is clear to me now that as this young man became a much older man, he changed into someone else along the way. But I have not censored out, or even 'redacted', my most mindless and vacuous comments, which dismay me today and for which I can only apologise. Here are some of them.

> We had a panic on here last week after the Wogs had attempted to blow up the radio station.
>
> I was put on guard and on guard I stayed. We have two or three coils of barbed wire around the camp, as much to keep us in as to keep the Wogs out.
>
> Beirut is a very queer place, much more oriental and Woggish than Nicosia.

A casual racism pervaded the Army of the time, an all-white conscript army which served overseas yet showed little interest in other countries and cultures. I clearly shared it. I was literate but barely half-educated. Only occasionally, and towards the end of the tour of duty, did I try to distance myself.

> Bellapais is the most beautiful village on the island. All the rest of them are brown, dusty and insanitary – in fact what the Army calls 'Woggish'.

I even made my first attempt at political analysis of the situation around me. After all, I was supposed to be in Intelligence. There was always a peace plan or proposed constitution, usually framed in terms that were bound to be rejected by one side or the other, or simultaneously by both. While the Government was trying to suppress a rebellion, it did not wish to be seen to be operating in a political vacuum. So a number of offers were laid on the table, in the hope of halting what Lawrence Durrell called 'the deathward drift of affairs on the island'. None of the proposals did. Even in Intelligence – perhaps *especially* in Intelligence – we had remarkably little idea of what was going on around us. My own assessment was typically myopic.

People here are hoping that the new proposals by the British Government are so unacceptable to the terrorists as to bring them out into the open. At the moment they can remain in their hide-outs for months on end with never a chance of detection. And quite apart from the excitement of operations, it might help us to get home earlier if the terrorists can be winkled out.

It didn't work out like that. We know so much more now than we did then about what happened and how. We also learned about ourselves and how little the blind application of force can accomplish. The lessons still apply.

It was another world then and another Army. It was also the way we were. The past, they say, is another country. It is sometimes worth revisiting.

Chapter 2

Gibraltar Barracks

I even got the date wrong. For many years I misremembered that I was called up on 18 June 1957. In fact it was a few days earlier, on the 13th, that I slipped nervously through the gate of Gibraltar Barracks in Bury St Edmunds. Not that it mattered to anyone but me, but it was the start of an extraordinary experience. For two years, like all conscripts, I was where I did not want to be and doing what I did not want to do. Unless we were physically unfit or could show that we were conscientious objectors, we had no choice in the matter. I was in neither category, so I went ahead with it with little idea of what was involved. Once through the gate, however, it seemed that the only human right we were left with was the right to be drilled and shouted at. For the first time in our lives we were totally *unfree*. Some of it was utterly miserable and some of it, to our surprise, was on the sunny side of tolerable. It changed me completely and did me some good. It was the best education I ever had, better even than the three years at King's College Cambridge which came next.

Gibraltar Barracks was no ivory tower, but the Victorian red-brick depot and training base of The Suffolk Regiment, the 12th of Foot in the original order of battle. It stood four-square and forbidding between the Newmarket Road and the Ipswich to Cambridge railway line. Its ten-foot-high walls made it look like a prison, which from our point of view was exactly what it was; and we were just at the start of serving our two-year sentences, with no remission for good behaviour. I was among a draft of forty recruits, mainly from Suffolk but some from Essex, Hertfordshire and the suburbs of London, whom the permanent staff had to turn into soldiers in ten weeks of basic training. (It seemed much longer.) They did this by shouting at us. Everyone who had the right to shout at us did so, from the parade ground to the Quartermaster's store. These included the Regimental Sergeant Major

(RSM), the Quartermaster Sergeant, the Provost Sergeant and most of all the Platoon Sergeant 'Mac' Sennett.

'Private Bell,' he would bark, 'you are a horrible little man. What are you?'

'A horrible little man,' I dutifully replied, since one's faults are usually more obvious to others than to oneself. And so he went on down the line of Suffolk's finest. I remember naively wondering why he could not be more *polite*. I had expected to be shouted at on the parade ground, but not while trying on a pair of army boots. I could not see the point of it.

As we filed into the regimental gym for the first time, he singled out the college boys, of whom I was one, for special attention. 'You there!' he exclaimed, scowling fiercely, 'You are a college boy, aren't you? I can spot a college boy by just by lookin' at 'im'. The college boys were those with one or two A levels to their name.

The uniform that we wore was the old scratchy battledress of *Dad's Army*. It bore a flash on the right sleeve in the regimental colours of red and yellow. The cap badge design was of a castle and key. The socks were grey. The towels and the underwear were green. So was the groundsheet or poncho, which could either be slept on or worn (it had a head-sized hole in the middle). The gym shorts were dark blue. It occurred to me that the reason none of the kit was white was so that, if by misfortune we ever found ourselves on a battlefield, we would have nothing to surrender with.

We painted stones and bollards. We cleaned windows. We peeled potatoes. We applied a hot spoon to our boots before polishing them and we polished them until we could shave in our reflections in them. We scrubbed our webbing with Blanco and polished our brasses with Brasso: Blanco and Brasso were our new best friends. We folded our sheets and blankets into rectangular bed packs which were critically appraised by Sergeant Sennett after Reveille every morning. We waited on the officers on one of their dinner nights. (They too wore red and yellow.) We fired our rifles, the old bolt-action Lee-Enfields, on the range. Afterwards we cleaned them, until the barrels gleamed, with an oily rag and a weighted device known as a pull-through. We could name all the parts, like the point of balance and the upper sling swivel and the lower sling swivel and band. We threw dummy grenades and then (with some trepidation) real ones. We charged a sack-cloth enemy yelling like banshees and with bayonets fixed. We were even shown how to twist the blade in the sack–cloth enemy's body. We disassembled and reassembled the Bren light machine gun and the Sterling sub–machine gun. We learned battlefield first aid and field craft, which is the art of staying alive in dangerous places (and turned out later to be quite useful to me). We calculated distances to bushy-topped trees. We trained and retrained until we dropped, from Reveille to Retreat until Lights Out. There were bugle calls for everything. We studied the military scriptures, Queen's Regulations and Staff Duties in the Field. We learned about military discipline, which was inescapably all around us. We shouldered arms and ordered arms and reversed arms and ported arms and presented arms. And we drilled on the parade ground as if our lives depended on it, which I suppose in a sense they did. The art of soldiering is to survive one's orders without actually disobeying them. The purpose of drill is to train the soldier in the habit of reflexive obedience: today on the parade ground, and tomorrow on the battlefield. Only a fool, or a soldier under orders, would obediently go 'over the top' into machine-gun fire and probable death.

There was a classroom too, whose windows I cleaned tearfully one day. Being new to the Army, which did its own housekeeping, I was slow to understand what window-cleaning had to do with soldiering. The classroom was a wooden hut in which we learned a highly selective version of military history. The officers taught us about the Regiment's victories but not its defeats. There was no mention of the 2nd Battalion being all but wiped out in the retreat from Mons at Le Cateau on 26 August 1914. Of its established strength of 998 at the start of the day, only 111 answered the roll call at the end. Two officers were left out of twenty-five. The Commanding Officer, Lieutenant Colonel Brett, was one of the first to be killed. The extreme sacrifice was unnecessary. As the Germans advanced the Battalion believed it was under orders to hold its ground at all costs. But the Corps Commander, General Sir Horace Smith-Dorrien, wrote later 'Someone, certainly not I, ordered that on no account were the Suffolks to retire … It was never my intention that any troops should be ordered to fight to the last.' Frontline soldiers dodge the bullets: their generals dodge the blame.

It was as if the defeats were erased like the battalions. As we prepared to receive our marching orders for Cyprus there was no mention either of the 4th and 5th Battalions which went down in the surrender of Singapore to the Japanese in 1942. (More than half a century later, on 9 March 2000, I held an Adjournment Debate in the House of Commons on their behalf.)

One of our most unfortunate officers was Brigadier E. H. W. Backhouse, later Colonel of the Regiment. As a young subaltern he was badly wounded at Le Cateau and spent the rest of the First World War in a German prison camp. Then, after landing in Singapore in the Second World War in February 1942, he spent three and a half years in a Japanese prison camp. So much of soldiering is a roll of the dice.

The Adjutant impressed us with our good fortune in serving in the ranks of the most exemplary regiment the Army had ever known. No less an authority than Field Marshal Sir Claude Auchinleck (later, in his retirement, one of my neighbours and my father's drinking companion in Suffolk) described it as 'a very fine regiment'. Its 2nd Battalion had served under him in India, where it was finally disbanded in 1947.

As we were about to join the 1st Battalion on active service in Cyprus, we were also briefed on the situation there and our task of bringing peace to the people by defeating the terrorists of EOKA whose campaign had begun two years earlier. In January 1957 the Suffolks had ambushed and killed one of its top military commanders, Markos Drakos. On Good Friday 1957 near Lefka they had captured an armed group led by Georghios Demetriou, who surrendered to a corporal and sergeant of Support Company (a photograph shows the group displayed like trophies on the ground with the soldiers standing proudly over them). Before deployment to Cyprus, the Battalion had completed a successful three-year tour of duty in Malaya. We were not as fashionable as the Cavalry or Guards, but we reckoned that we were good at what we did: we were the counter-insurgency specialists and made well aware of it. In March 1957 the EOKA second-in-command, Grigoris Afxentiou, had also been killed by the British after an informer betrayed his hiding place near Machairas Monastery in the Troodos Mountains. Great things were expected of us. The total defeat of EOKA was thought to be not only possible but imminent. We did things by the book in those days. There was a sequence of military instructions known as Mission, Execution, Administration and Logistics. Victory over EOKA was our mission, surely worth the battle honour which would be the Regiment's last.

Towards the end of basic training in Bury St Edmunds, I was despatched by rail warrant to Westbury in Wiltshire, to take the officer selection test, the War Office Selection Board (WOSB), and find out if I had the makings of an officer in me. It soon became clear that I did not. When I failed the intelligence test I was ordered by the presiding Brigadier, who thought I should have done better, to take it again – and I failed it again. It was the first of life's hurdles that I fell at. I was used to passing exams, not failing them, and felt very sore about it. It was not that I fancied the rank and the privileges, but I felt I had let myself down. Many years later Brigadier Robin Searby of the 9th/12th Lancers, who after service in Bosnia reformed the officer selection process, looked up my record in the card index at Westbury and mused 'Was the nation robbed of the services of a great general?' Not even I think of an adequate second lieutenant.

When the ten weeks of basic training were over, we had a passing-out parade, with a band, on the RSM's sacred square in Gibraltar Barracks. It was not actually a square but a rectangle of hard-pounded tarmac sloping gently uphill from the Keep. The families were invited. My father, who was a peaceable man, was among the lookers-on. I disliked marching except when there was a band – and with a band, like most soldiers, I marched three inches taller. It was in the blood on the other side of the family: my maternal grandfather, Lieutenant W. J. Gibson, was Director of Music of the Band of The Life Guards in the 1920s. When the parade was over the Platoon Sergeant graciously told us we were no longer the total shambles he had started out with. In fact, we were almost soldiers. The emphasis was on the *almost*.

My father Adrian Bell, who was both an author and a farmer, wrote in his weekly column in the *Eastern Daily Press* that he had been many times in Bury St Edmunds cattle market but he had never before set foot in its barracks. And he was impressed by what he saw. 'Through its gates pass young civilians who within ten weeks become platoons of soldiers drilled to move as one man. Their trousers have knife edge creases ... the thought was in my mind, either it was a hell of a waste of time or the brilliant buckles and boot-toes were symbolical of something else, not seen ... A few officers and sergeants on these squares had twice created an amateur army and that had saved us, starting from the basic act of making a man shine his boots until he could see his face in them. Who are we, then, to question the fact that there must be something important in shining boots? I glance at my own boots and feel a little bit ashamed of them'. [*Eastern Daily Press*, 31 August 1957] I loved my father, the most admirable and eloquent of men. I would not see him again for nearly two years. The hardest part of soldiering was not the discipline but the enforced separation from family life.

Since it was by then September, I took my twin sister to the *Last Night of the Proms* at the Royal Albert Hall, with Sir Malcolm Sargent conducting. (It was my season for sergeants of one sort or another.) I wore with pride my battledress uniform, complete with its red and yellow flash and its knife-edge creases, and felt I was doing my bit for Queen and country. We left for Cyprus the next week.

For the journey one of the draft, Private Lamont from Lowestoft, was made up temporarily to lance corporal so that someone should be in authority in case of a mutiny. Being an ambitious young man, I had rather fancied this mini-promotion myself; but the officers were concerned that the college boys, being over-educated, might turn into barrack-room lawyers. Besides, there were two Private Bells on the draft. Alan Bell from Thorpe Morieux near Lavenham was Bell 940. I was Bell 941. The Army did things by numbers.

We went to London on Saturday and stayed the night at Woolwich Arsenal, which is a massive place. Sunday morning we spent getting organised and at 8.30 in the evening we left for Southend Airport. We flew in a four-engined DC4. Our plane left about 1 and we had an hour's stop in Malta at 7. We arrived in Cyprus about 2 and ever since then have been pushed about.

Chapter 3

On Active Service

Kykko Camp was just down the road from the airport. The Battalion had arrived there from its previous base in Xeros five months before we did: and being of the Regiment, it did not just arrive, it marched in ceremonially in columns of three, the officers at the head of each company and the sergeants behind. The event is recorded in the regimental archive. The Brigadier took the salute as the Band and Drums played the regimental quick march *Speed the Plough*, and three of the rifle companies in their starched khaki drill uniforms wheeled smartly past the Guard Room into their new home. The fourth company must have been the Advance Party: it is one of the long traditions of the Army that battalions never relocate without an Advance Party. Otherwise, how would they know where they were going, especially if their officers were leading them? When we followed on in early October, jet-lagged (or rather prop-lagged) and just a bit apprehensive, it did not seem much of a home. And the Band did not play us in. I wrote:

> The camp is a large expanse of ugly and unprepossessing ground, such as is suitable for military purposes only, row upon row of very utilitarian tents, bleached white in the sun, occasional tin huts and illimitable wastes of barbed wire.

It was like landing on the Red Planet. As we deplaned the red earth smelt bitter-sweet after a shower, which was not enough, however, to settle the dust. It reminded me instantly of Sergeant Sennett, for had he not told us repeatedly that we too were a shower? I was to spend the next 20 months in a tent where the only air-conditioning was the wind blowing through it, mixed sometimes with dust and sometimes with rain. It cured me of camping fever for a lifetime. I have never voluntarily slept under canvas since. My first letter home as a dog-tired young soldier was pencilled faintly on lined paper, after my only pen had been broken when I hit the ground hard during training. I was doing my best not to be miserable. Everyone felt sorry for the new recruits, the ones with the most 'days to do', especially the new recruits themselves. The letter was barely legible.

> I have just spent my first day here and as a result am covered in dust, not that the work itself was dirty: it was merely sorting out thousands of used rounds of ammunition, but our whole camp is built on and covered in red dust, even our sheets and blankets are impregnated with it.

We twenty half-trained young soldiers were posted initially to A (Training) Company. With basic training behind us, we still had more of the same ahead. The course would not begin until the rest of the draft had caught up with us. Until then, there were fatigues. There were always fatigues.

> On the first day we did fatigues for five and a half hours, and the rest of the time was ours except for a kit inspection. Yesterday we spent the morning digging trenches around tents so that when the rains come and water comes off the roof it will have somewhere to flow to. We did the same for an hour this morning. On both occasions it was a pick and shovel job in bone-hard ground and very blistering on the hands … I will make a crude attempt at a plan of the camp on the next page.

And so I did. It was my second letter home and probably revealed more about me than it did about the camp. The primitive map shows four lines of eight tents – one of them marked 'trench which I helped to dig' with stores and offices at the end of each line. Another is marked 'M. Bell, his tent'. Beyond the tents lie the ablutions and latrines 'sanitary arrangements of which the less said the better'. Near the northern perimeter of the camp stands the 'cookhouse, complete with authentic smell' and beside it the NAAFI (the other ranks' watering hole), 'much patronised'. The plan shows without comment the axis of authority, the Officers' Mess at one end of the camp and the Battalion's offices at the other. Near the main (and only) gate stands the 'regimental flag-pole, very important' and a 'guard box, as used in concentration camps'.

More revealing was my idea of the world beyond the wire. The main road outside the Guard Room is shown with an arrow pointing west 'to the airport (London Road)' and an arrow pointing east 'to Nicosia, and the Wogs'. A third arrow points north 'to the hills', the Kyrenia Mountains. And still, since the rest of the draft had by now caught up with us, the NCOs of A (Training) Company drilled us and dragooned us and drove us on.

We are training as hard as we can go – fooling about with Bren guns and mortars and grenades, taking them to bits and putting them together again, firing and cleaning them. Besides weapon training we are treated to a fair number of lectures, which offer an excellent opportunity to go to sleep, but are actually quite interesting about EOKA and their weapons and such things as ambushes and patrols. According to him [the instructing Major] the fact that the Cypriots only attack when they have the advantages of numbers and surprise shows that they are 'yellow': I call it only sensible. We finish about five, after which I spend two and a half hours cleaning my kit for muster parade the next morning.

The Army's training manual concluded 'It must be remembered that the Cypriot people have, because of their geographical position, been struggling against foreign administrations since earliest times, and are crafty in the extreme. Airs of injured innocence and the like should not be taken notice of, nor anything allowed to impede a complete and thorough search.' The manual urged us, on operations and patrols, to be in a state of constant alertness. It added: 'Troops are only really alert when they are (i) genuinely interested or (ii) frightened.' And when we came to think of it there was plenty out there to frighten us.

I realised that for the first time in my life I had an *enemy*, in the sense of someone who might rather have liked to kill me. I had no wish to kill him at all. If I had met Colonel Grivas I would have preferred to shake his hand and ask after his family. EOKA's armoury was smuggled, stolen or home-made. They were short of heavy weapons and ammunition. By mid-campaign in

March 1957 they were reckoned by Army Intelligence to have no more than seven light machine guns, thirty-two sub-machine guns, thirty-five rifles and 670 shotguns. The sources of many of these weapons were the security forces themselves. Colonel Grivas wrote in his diary 'The theft of Bren guns was a windfall, but I lack the ammunition to exploit them'. His men were expert in making pipe bombs using explosives pilfered from one of the island's mines.

Our training ranged from cordons and searches to crawling around cradling a Bren gun among rocks and thistles as an introduction to field craft, Cyprus-style. We should have had fine views of the Kyrenia Mountains to the north and the Troodos Mountains to the south, except that we were too close to the ground to appreciate them. The training was recruit-unfriendly: 70 per cent of it was on weapon handling. With the whole island as its training ground, the Army improvised a rifle range ten miles from Nicosia, where a river bed ran through a deep ravine. It was raining of course: it is one of the traditions of military life that it always rains during training. We took up our firing positions on one side of the ravine and let loose with live rounds at the other. The rifles kicked back at the shoulder. It was called the recoil. I wrote:

> The only snag is that we have to spoil the scenery by shooting bullets at it.

All this was done with the old .303 Lee-Enfield, the infantry's mainstay through two world wars and beyond. Only in January 1958 were we finally issued with the new Belgian-designed but British-made self-loading rifle (SLR). We liked the idea of not being killed while we were bruising our fingers trying to load the five-round clip which fed into the ten-round magazine of the Lee-Enfield. The RSM did not approve at all, because a parade is a performance, and the new rifle was shorter and harder to drill with than the old one. The soldier could not slope arms with it so easily, nor present arms so smartly, nor order arms with such a convincing clatter. These were the parade ground's defining moments. It was important for good order and military discipline that the sounds should be exactly synchronised. Only then was the RSM satisfied. There was a legend in the Battalion that when we did it right, just once and only once on the hard red earth of the parade ground, he very nearly smiled.

Having mastered the basics we then went on to advanced infantry training. I passed the tests and surprised myself by being rated as 'skilled' on the Sterling sub-machine gun. It may be that I cheated a bit. The tests were marked on a points system, and it fell to me as a college boy to add up the scores on forms that looked remarkably like the old milk returns on my father's dairy farm.

We then had to learn the anti-riot drills, which were entirely new to us. We came from a quiet corner of England. We had never known rioters in Suffolk (not even in Ipswich), but we were aware there were plenty in Cyprus. And so there were, both Greeks and Turks. The timing was perfect, for much rioting lay in store for us. The island's pressure cooker was near boiling point. Because the police were demoralised, it was left to barely qualified soldiers to take their place in crowd control, to uncertain effect. We were training for what the Labour MP Lena Jeger called 'intolerably abhorrent tasks, really the worst kind of police work'. [*Hansard*, 21 December 1956] The drills, like everything else, were done by the book.

> It entails much cleaning of equipment and polishing up of drill, since it is reckoned that if the rioters see a highly disciplined force marching towards them with brasses gleaming they will disperse at once. It is surprisingly complicated and consists of two squads armed with stone-age weapons (batons and shields), two stretcher-bearers, two people to put out barbed wire, two others carrying a banner inscribed 'disperse or we fire' in three languages and five riflemen. All I have to do is to stand at the side of the riot squad and fire at anyone who tries to throw bombs from the roof-tops.

One of the photographs of the time shows us on parade with rifles in one hand and riot shields in the other. This was unrealistic. It takes two hands to fire a rifle, or even to drill with one. We were not three-handed soldiers.

Our orders were the same since Governor Harding's Instruction No 1 of October 1955. We were to ignore the flying of flags, the painting of slogans or other 'child-like activities'. But if we found our way obstructed by barricades covered by stone-throwers we were to close with and disperse our assailants. If attacked, even by superior forces, we were to fight it out. Were we not soldiers of the Suffolk Regiment, the celebrated 12th of Foot? Retreat was out of the question. Our instructions included the following: 'If you are attacked with arms or explosives, shoot the attackers at once, wherever you are.'

The drills were identical in all of Britain's small wars. In Aden ten years later, the languages were English and Arabic, but the warning was the same. The 'disperse or we fire' banners were even deployed by our successors of The Royal Anglian Regiment in Londonderry and Belfast during the Troubles that I later reported on. It was rumoured, but never confirmed, that some of the tattered old banners unfurled in Northern Ireland were still in Arabic, which would have confused the hell out of the rioters in the Bogside. The operation in Derry was called Operation Banner.

Most of the letters from this period are intact, but one survives as a single intriguing page.

> I am one of the few people outside the Officers' Mess who knows the rule. We are not supposed to have any matches for a month.

I have no idea what the mystery rule was. And the ban on matches seems odd, since the NAAFI especially was a heavy smoking environment and the cry of 'crash the ash' (pass the cigarettes) would regularly resound through the fumes. It was more likely connected to a rumoured deployment to the mountains, where forest fires were a hazard. A wind-whipped fire in June 1956 killed thirteen British soldiers, including five from our neighbours the Royal Norfolks, during Operation Lucky Alphonse. EOKA was blamed for starting the fire, but it could as well have been natural causes, a misdirected mortar round or the result of an attempt to burn the enemy out of his hide-outs.

For all of us in A Company, the month of extended training was a period of bad weather, home-sickness and maximum military misery, for which we were paid 28 shillings a week, to go up to 35 shillings after six months' service; and for some it was about to get worse.

In matters of the heart I was a late starter and had no girlfriend. But many of the others had. Some had become engaged, and even married, just before call-up. There were no phone calls home and of course no internet to maintain contact between the soldier and his loved ones. There was only the British Forces Post Office (ours was BFPO 53). The postman, Corporal Whiffen, the longest-serving man in the Battalion, had thoroughly earned his British Empire Medal in ensuring that the mail got through. In a matter of weeks the 'Dear John' letters started arriving, from girls who were not willing to wait for two years and had found someone else. The Army was very good on compassionate cases, as I discovered doing my shifts one night in six as Duty Clerk. If you wanted to get a pair of boots re-studded it could take three weeks, but if something serious happened at home, like the death of a parent, you would be repatriated within 24 hours. However, being jilted by a girlfriend did not qualify. The NAAFI took on the air of a funeral parlour. Never before in my short and sheltered life had I seen grown men crying into their beer. In the hit single of the time the Everly Brothers sang how they felt:

> 'Bye bye love,
> Bye bye happiness
> Hello loneliness,
> I think I'm gonna cry.'

Elvis Presley's *Heartbreak Hotel* was another favourite.

The mother of a national serviceman wrote to one of our officers: 'Dear Sir, please forgive the liberty of writing to you, but I am faced with a very awkward situation. My son is serving in your unit at present. His twin sister Barbara is getting married on April 4, and I would appreciate it if my son could possibly get home, as I have no one in the family to give her away.' Her request was not successful.

For my own part I was still unhappy about failing the officer selection test during basic training – a serious case of a young man's wounded pride – and learned that I could re-take it if I wished. So I wrote to my father:

> Would you feel less like disowning a son who is a second lieutenant than one who is a common private? Not very well put, I'm afraid, but what

I'm getting at is that, since everyone else around Beccles seems to have passed, would you feel happier if I did? Though if the trouble starts again – and every officer on the island is sure that it will – I may get just as much fun as an intelligence clerk.

To my father, who was a sensible and unmilitary man – just too young for one world war, just too old for the other, and as a farmer in a reserved occupation – it made no difference at all. But what on earth was I doing (especially in view of my later life) looking for *fun* in a war zone? It seemed a strange aberration. It still does. It may have been because the Regiment's senior and middle-ranking officers had served in the Second World War, and we conscripts felt envious of their 'sharp end' experience. The prospect of endless parades was unappealing. Only 15 per cent of conscripts were posted abroad on active service: I was in that lucky or unlucky minority.

As to operations and deployments and whatever the immediate future might hold for us, we were kept entirely in the dark and fed on rumours. The Army's idea of a communications policy was to bark orders at us.

One of the things I like least about the Army is having to depend for information on rumours at third hand … We are living on rumours at the moment and little else. According to the aforesaid rumours, Cyprus is becoming the main panic station of the Middle East. Three battalions have been put on immediate standby to go to the Lebanon.

Nothing came of the rumours of course. Nothing ever did, especially the persistent rumour that we would be sent home early as a gesture of political goodwill and to prepare for the forthcoming amalgamation with some lesser regiment from Norfolk. What we knew for sure was that, with the extra training finished, we would be posted elsewhere in the Battalion. We draftees then had an interview with the Adjutant to ask – or more likely be told – what our postings would be. It must have been a very short interview, since there were forty of us and only one of him. The options were to join one of the three rifle companies (Bravo, Charlie and Delta), Support Company (mortars, anti-tank guns and machine guns) or Headquarters Company. As there was not much use for mortars and anti-tank guns in crowd control and internal security, Support Company functioned as a fourth rifle company. I was attached to a rifle company for a while and decided that, given the choice, it was not for me.

The life of a rifleman out here is most unenviable.

They are now coming to the end of a month of solid guards of police stations, power stations, detention camps and the like; all of which, in so far as I can gather, is a very depressing way to spend one's time, especially as some of the more fortunate units on the island are presently conducting a most interesting operation near Limassol.

We college boys liked the look of Headquarters Company. It had an outstanding Officer Commanding in Major John Fisher-Hoch, a man so civilised that I often wondered, though I never dared ask him, what on earth he was doing in the Army. He went on to play a part in the final and magnificently illustrated version of the regimental history. His HQ Company offered some relatively restful alternatives to riot duty, like becoming a clerk in the Orderly Room, which was the Battalion's office and I thought a bit unadventurous. I sought a compromise by joining the Intelligence Section: not too arduous, I thought, but with a bit of real-world soldiering on the side. Even then I was blessed, or cursed, with a low boredom threshold.

And so it came to pass. My posting as a clerk in the Intelligence Section was announced in Battalion Orders Part One (not to be confused with Battalion Orders Part Two), but delayed for operational reasons as we practised our riot-control procedures one more time. The period of relative calm was ending. The Nicosia garrison had to be ready for anything, and even the freshly-trained recruits, if not yet attached to one of the rifle companies, were formed into special riot squads. It was the Army, not the police, who would be deployed to deal with the rioters. We would do what we were ordered to do but were totally unqualified for. Since we understood neither their cause nor their language, there was no buffer between us but violence, theirs and ours: it was a hopeless interface and an unavoidable collision. One of our generals wrote later 'The soldier had to be continuously employed in police patrolling and crowd control, a task for which he was neither intended nor trained'. Amen to that. It was one of the reasons why the counter-insurgency failed.

The brass hats in charge of the security forces have become even more jumpy than usual. On Monday 28 [October] the Greeks stage a big celebration to commemorate their resistance to Mussolini during the war. On the very next day the Turks put on a similar exhibition in aid of their Independence Day, or something futile like that. The upshot of these communal carouses is that riots are expected.

Why I thought Independence Day 'futile' I can neither remember nor imagine. Kykko Camp was like an island within an island. I showed remarkably little interest in the world beyond its gates. And yet I was about to serve in *Intelligence*. In which case, Heaven help the Army – and Heaven help me.

What we had no idea of, because there was no way of knowing, was that our arrival in Cyprus coincided with the time when events were going (to use an old Army phrase) 'pear-shaped'. The former Governor, Field Marshal Sir John Harding, had just departed; but the Acting Governor George Sinclair, who was very much his disciple, was urging the reintroduction of repressive measures in the weeks before the arrival of the new Governor Sir Hugh Foot, who was known to be more liberal and open to compromise. EOKA was thought to be using a ceasefire to prepare a new offensive. Sinclair wrote to the Colonial Office on 24 November 1957, 'EOKA has seized the initiative from us. This has been made easier for them by our own reluctance to take full-scale and effective counter-measures.' And he wrote to Harding 'I no longer see any likelihood of avoiding a second head-on clash with EOKA. In these circumstances I believe that the sooner we stop the present drift and resume the initiative against EOKA the better … I believe that we shall move have to move very, very quickly.' [FCO Archive 141/4422]

This was deliberately pre-emptive. The new Governor's peace-seeking policy was undermined even before he set foot on the island. The Acting Governor then became his Deputy. The disagreements between them were never resolved. The conflict was about to resume. It was at this point that, in the innocence of untested youth, I joined the Battalion's Intelligence Section.

Chapter 4

Intelligence Section

I had been a soldier for almost five months. The Intelligence Section was housed in half a Nissen hut with a tin roof next to the office of the second-in-command. The office had no air-conditioning even in the hottest weather, but it did have a slow-turning fan and half a veranda. The section's established strength was an officer, a sergeant, two or three interpreters and two clerks, of whom I was one. Every infantry battalion had such a section. It was supposed to be the brains of the outfit, an outreach sub-unit, to gather useful intelligence and point the rifle companies in the right direction. Whether it actually did so was highly questionable. But I was lucky with my timing. The Intelligence Officer, or IO, had just been jilted by his girlfriend (another of those Dear John letters). So, to forget his sorrows like a French *legionnaire*, he lost himself in his work and took us on constant and busy patrols from the city to the foothills of the Troodos Mountains, which had just been added to our operational area. She would never know it, but the IO's ex-girlfriend did us a favour. I often wondered what became of her. Lieutenant Morriss's ex-girlfriend, where are you now? Why did you so heartlessly turn him down? And is it true that you eventually married the Adjutant? I wrote:

We paid visits to the odd spots where the Battalion had a guard, e.g. the explosives dump of the local mining company, and a very small and lonely power station that must have expended all the electricity it produced to light up the iron fence at night to deter invaders.

Our keen patrol was entirely Intelligence Section: the IO, his batman, an interpreter, the other clerk and myself, and turned out to be unexpectedly restful. All we did was to jump aboard the Land Rover and set out on a tour of four or five villages between Nicosia and Morphou. We didn't spend long in any one place, but just ambled around the village or wandered into its coffee shop, looking misleadingly forbidding with machine-guns at the ready. The owner of the coffee shop, who is known to the security forces as the ring-leader of the local EOKA organisation, let us have the coffee free of charge, so I reckon I have benefited to the extent of 35 mils (seven pence) from EOKA funds.

The idea behind this exhibition was to show the locals that we were alert. (Trouble was expected because of the murder of a Turk in that area earlier in the week.) As usual, of course, no trouble materialised. I don't suppose it ever will, but I do wish the authorities would stop panicking.

I was wrong. The authorities were right to be concerned, if not to panic. Communal tensions were rising. One of our most frequent destinations was Eliophotes, a small Turkish village surrounded by much larger Greek villages south west of Nicosia. The Turks were afraid of attack and annihilation. Their political leader Dr Kuchuk cabled the Governor on 6 December 1957 'Immediate steps must be taken to arm Turkish villagers and provide them with necessary measures of security'. Foot, who was touring the hinterland at the time, reported to London that the Turks were angry and resentful. [FCO Archive 141/4422] We took coffee with the mukhtar, the head man, and assured him that we were there to protect them. I don't think he believed us. The security forces' grip was loosening. The villagers were not driven out but eventually fled of their own accord. Ethnic cleansing had not yet been coined as a term – that came later, in the Balkans – but the reality of it was imminent. A *de facto* partition of the island was already beginning, in the summer of 1958, as Greeks and Turks separated themselves from each other. It was the start of a long and irreversible process. The Turks had their own quarter of Nicosia, as well as some of its suburbs, but withdrew from isolated and outlying villages.

Outside the towns, where the only really bad feeling between the two communities exists, the Greeks and Turks just sit in their villages racked by fears that they are about to be attacked: they even post sentries at night, armed with sticks and cudgels and any old iron.

It was a rare moment of excitement in the foothills of the Troodos Mountains in December 1957 when we were on patrol and the new Governor, Sir Hugh Foot, sped past us in his armoured limousine, followed by a sleek vehicle containing 'sinister Special Branch types'. I never related to the Special Branch types. In my letters home I always described them as sinister. It must have been their dark glasses (the RSM had views on dark glasses: he did not approve of them). The lives of the sinister Special Branch types seemed so much easier than ours. What we did not know was that the Governor had been warned against making this inaugural tour by the District Commissioner of Limassol on the grounds that he would not meet 'anybody worthwhile'. This was because the Colonial Office had stated that the change of governors did not mean a change of policy (which of course it did – that was the whole point of it); so he was boycotted by the Greek Cypriot leaders. One of them, the Mayor of Nicosia, was overheard to say 'we definitely must obey what Grivas says'. It was not a good time to be cooperating with the British, and an inauspicious beginning for the new Governor. The difficulties that he faced were overwhelming. The Suffolk Regiment's Land Rover, covered with the dust of his cavalcade, then proceeded to the nearest village coffee shop; and whether or not we met 'anybody worthwhile', we certainly met a lot of Greek coffee drinkers (all men of course: the women were either in the fields or making the coffee). The conversation followed an invariable pattern, as we and the locals talked past each other through the interpreter. It was an exercise in mutual mystification.

> On the one hand the poor IO is trying to keep to the relevant topics, such as whether or not Makarios should return, and on the other hand the Oldest Inhabitant (OI) is refusing to be dragged into politics and expounding eloquently on the subject of water supplies and drains, as if we were the District Commissioner and his staff. Things finally reached a point where we had to make our excuses and leave, or be shown by the OI (not to be confused with the IO) where his house was falling down. We left.

The garrison may have been strong in numbers, but the Intelligence Section was not. Having fallen out with the CO who required one office move too many, the lovelorn and disaffected Intelligence Officer applied for a transfer to one of the rifle companies. He was worried even in those days about redundancy, and that having first been jilted by his girlfriend he might next be jilted by the Army. In addition to which, he fell out with the Commanding Officer.

> What made Mr Morriss pack up his goods and chattels and depart was the idiocy of the CO, who decided to move the Intelligence Section into another office. This so grieved the IO – who has already had to supervise three such upheavals since we came to this camp – that he has asked at once for a transfer.

For a while we were given a part-time replacement in Lieutenant Mike Askins, who was also Assistant Adjutant. (Not a top-of-the-heap job: the Adjutant shuffled paper for the CO and the Assistant Adjutant shuffled paper for the Adjutant.) The other clerk, Private Hodgkinson (a.k.a. 'Hodge'), also applied for a transfer following a long-running feud with the Sergeant. We could have made a TV sit-com out of the comings and goings in the Intelligence Section, so various was the cast of characters and so much at odds with each other. The Sergeant, who was a bit full of himself, had wished to become an instructor at Sandhurst, but joined one of the rifle companies instead. I was as unimpressed by him as he was by me.

> Any enterprising officer cadet would make mincemeat out of him.

Thus our numbers were greatly reduced.

> When I first jumped upon this particular band-wagon it consisted of an Intelligence Officer, a sergeant and two clerks. It now consists of half an IO and me.

From time to time, whatever the state of alert in Nicosia, we had to show that we were ready for European warfare. So to prepare ourselves to face the armies of the Warsaw Pact we went on manoeuvres in wild country near

Dhavlos on the north coast. Sergeant Pocock, the Intelligence Sergeant, had not yet left us.

Had I packed the correcting ink? Had I put in a map sheet of Nicosia? Did I know where the rubbers were? Had we got any paraffin for the hurricane lamps? And so on. The Sergeant's immediate and involuntary action on being told to do anything by the IO is to pass the buck to one of us overworked clerks and then stamp and storm like an aspiring Hitler if one job on a list of 20 fails to be completed to his satisfaction. However, after a time one learns to ride the storm of a sergeant's wrath, so I take no notice.

I actually missed the Sergeant when he was gone. With his talent for making mountains out of molehills he kept us busy. The Suffolk Regiment did not enjoy tranquillity.

We trundled in to this part of the world with as much noise as possible, and the Army is capable of making quite a lot. Ever since then the Battalion has been living in chaos, with everyone swearing at everyone else.

Even in the late 1950s the coast of Cyprus was already in the eye of property speculators. In the middle of the training area there stood a derelict hotel. The other ranks were under canvas in bivouacs. The officers, with a weather eye on the gathering clouds, saw to it that they did better.

The hotel, having been requisitioned by the Army to relieve the sufferings of its officers, has been ruined. But the scenery around it remains lovely. It is a nice change to wake up and find the sea on our doorstep – assuming we had a doorstep, which we haven't.

We were playing some sort of NATO-related war game, the Blue side against the Red, with the Suffolks taking on the forces of the Duke of Dhavlos, nefarious allies of the Warsaw Pact who were actually one of our own platoons. The Intelligence Section stayed out of the way and practised its compass work and map-reading with an uphill trek to a Crusader castle, followed by lunch. It was more like an outing than an exercise. So defective was my compass work that when I took a back bearing to find out where I was it told me I was in the middle of the sea. Even the next year, at the height of the conflict between the Army and the EOKA guerrillas, we had to pretend that we were trained for European warfare. But the three-week exercise was cut short when rain stopped play. It was a feature of NATO war games, wherever they were held, that they were invariably rained on, and so it was with 'Exercise Mountain Goat'. The Army has a phrase that 'any fool can be uncomfortable'. But first the comfort-free bivouacs were washed away, then the Company Headquarters tent, until we finished up crowded into two Nissen huts, which showed what size we were reduced to and how little the Warsaw Pact had to fear from Headquarters Company of the 1st Battalion of The Suffolk Regiment. The Commanding Officer, who characteristically left his second-in-command, Major Malcolm Dewar, to run the exercise, turned up in the nick of time to cut it short.

> It rained when we were lying in our bivouacs which was never for long, as we had to be up at 5.30 every morning, and it rained as I was sitting on top of a mountain – quite a sharp one too – trying to pick out the enemy with my binoculars and eventually it rained so hard that the whole exercise was called off a day early … The CO who, like all good men and true, values his comforts, decided that it would be a good thing if the Battalion returned to camp instead of remaining in Dhavlos and getting pneumonia all round.

After that we thought more fondly of the camp. It seemed that we were fair-weather soldiers. But whatever the weather, and especially on security duties, the Army's way of doing business was to hurry up and wait. We spent months on standby for commotions that were increasingly likely to occur. Instead of exercises there would be operations, with a real enemy to defeat, armed and dangerous.

Chapter 5

Riot Duty

A s the National Service years rolled on, the situation in Cyprus worsened dramatically. The Suffolk Regiment was caught up in the middle of it. From that point on the soldiering seemed more purposeful and I complained less. I took National Service literally and supposed that what we were doing was somehow in the service of the nation. The Intelligence Section was supposed to be the Battalion's eyes and ears. I wrote:

> Somebody in high places has got hold of the notion that (a) there is going to be a 'solution' to the Cyprus problem announced early this week and that (b) the Greeks aren't going to like it. Thus from Monday we are confined to camp. A special force has been formed to deal with riots at the detention camp [Kokkinotrimithia], and the Int Section has to stand by with all its maps and battle-boards and instruments of war. Besides which a camp has been cleared, presumably for an influx of a new battalion; and on Monday the Turks stage yet another of their processions – this time in commemoration of Turkish Cypriot Youth Day (not to be confused with Turkish Youth Day or Turkish Cypriot Children's Day, both of which have special panic-days of their own).

The Governor, Sir Hugh Foot, was not a military man like his predecessor Sir John Harding, but a conciliator and peace-seeker. The colonial hard-liners called him 'Pussyfoot'. He toured the island on foot and on horseback. He shook hands. He lit candles in churches. He visited coffee shops. He was determined to meet as many people as possible (whether or not they were 'worthwhile'), to break with the past and make a new start. On Christmas Eve 1957 he ordered the release of 100 Greek Cypriot detainees. He described himself as both a friend and a servant of the people. He had served in the British colonies for thirty years. He was no stranger to Cyprus. He knew the ground and had previously been Colonial Secretary, the island's senior civil servant, between 1943 and 1945. Those were quieter times on the island, if not beyond. The *Cyprus Mail* welcomed him with the headline 'I come back as your friend'. He said 'Cyprus cannot be condemned to a future of hate and fear. The people of this lovely island must one day again work and live together in peace and respect and tolerance and happiness'. [FCO Archive 141/3939] Instead, a period of ceasefire ended and EOKA resumed its island-wide offensive.

In April 1958, after fifty bomb explosions in ten days and on his own initiative, the Governor wrote secretly to the EOKA leader Colonel Grivas asking for a personal meeting to urge him to save the people of Cyprus from disaster by abandoning the campaign of sabotage and violence. Foot said he would come alone and unarmed and for that day the EOKA leader would face no threat of arrest. The letter reached Grivas after ten days and at the second attempt. His response was to leak it to the press by way of the American Embassy. The Governor then had to draft a hasty telegram – it survives in the archive as an old-fashioned strip of words ripped off the machine and pasted on to paper – to an alarmed Colonial Office: 'It will show I meant what I said when I stated that I was prepared to do anything I could to prevent the tragedy which violence will bring.' The Secretary of State for the Colonies, Alan Lennox-Boyd, was unsympathetic. He was an MP from his party's imperialist and right wing, which was why he held the colonial portfolio, to reassure the others. He wrote back 'I am very sorry to disappoint you, but for reasons I can elaborate to you when next we meet I cannot, repeat not, possibly authorise publication of text of letter or any reference to its having been sent.' [Colonial Office Archive 967/346] In the aftermath of its Suez debacle the Conservative Government was sensitive to any perceived sign of weakness.

In the rush of events that came upon us the Governor's instinct was to allow what I called 'folkloric' or national demonstrations by Greeks and Turks, one after the other, whenever possible. He saw them as a sort of safety valve.

He says that these two days provide a chance for the peaceful political development of Cyprus – which has been said many times before and invariably been disappointed. Hope springs eternal …

Our principal vantage-point was the Central Police Station, on the edge of the Turkish Quarter of Nicosia, setting up our maps and battle-boards amid much military bustle in a first-floor office, where we were quite literally above the fray, but only just above it. The Governor visited us there one day and the Turks, who knew he was present, held a noisy demonstration outside to demand partition. Beneath us lay the notorious 'Murder Mile' of Ledra Street and the inter-communal boundary which we called the Mason-Dixon Line. The Army had taken over from the law and was in process of taking over from the police, not only because of its manpower and firepower but because elements of the police had become intimidated and ineffective. I dossed down in a sleeping bag in a former police office and ate in what was once a lawyers' conference room. The police radios were better than ours, and by listening in to their networks we could actually find out what was going on, especially after an unexpected upgrade of their communications.

We have now moved into a new operations room in the police station, next door to a super-colossal and entirely new police ops room which really looks like something out of an exaggerated American film of the Battle of Britain: maps, boards, telephones, models, wirelesses and generally facilities to control a revolution throughout empires.

Equally to the point, when the rains came, the stone-built police station was a better place to be than a leaky and windswept army tent.

I paid a fleeting visit to my tent this morning and found it receiving a good rinsing out, running water and all mod cons.

I sent a letter to my sister:

I am writing in the Central Police Station in Nicosia from a perch in a window overlooking the Turkish part of Murder Mile. This is normally the most pleasant and picturesque of streets but now it doesn't look at its best. The curfew is on, the street is partitioned with barbed wire, and the Suffolks are patrolling the roadway looking very purposeful and melodramatic in their riot kit consisting of weapons, steel helmets and respirators (gas masks), with batons and shields in hand.

The respirators were protection against our own tear gas. The Central Police Station, which was my second home for long periods, was also my reading room in between riots and map-marking duties. By this time I had been in the Army long enough not to be over-awed by it. The subversive thought occurred to me that we might perhaps have been more effective if we spent less time on the parade ground and more in the streets and the mountains. Could we not sometimes have left the barbed wire at home? And how could we win people over by locking them up? My views of course were neither sought nor offered. One of the books sent to me in a comfort parcel from home was about the Crimean War, which from my Nicosia vantage-point in mid-emergency gave me an assuring sense of *déjà vu*.

I am greatly comforted to find that the present inefficiency of the British Army was not without parallel in the past.

Without much competition, after four months in the Intelligence Section, I took my first modest step up the promotion ladder. In February 1958 I became a lance corporal.

Life has been particularly easy since the benevolent authorities gave me my stripe: not that the extra three shillings and sixpence weekly fills the coffers to overflowing, but my duties are very light. Formerly I was being landed with a guard [duty] at least every ten days, but now the security of the camp has done without my assistance for more than a month. May the good work continue.

With the promotion, although I was only a lance corporal, came occasional weekend duties as Company Orderly Sergeant. The days in camp were punctuated by bugle calls. I had to be up early, raise the flag at Reveille, ensure that all were present and correct at guard mounting, and report in the evening that all but the guard were safely abed. Guard duty was also easier for a lance corporal. I used it mainly for writing letters.

I am permitted to sleep for the first half of the night, and for the second half have nothing more arduous to do than sit in a semi-heated guard room and every now and then wander out to wake up the duty cook or regimental policeman.

Then I got lucky again. For the last half of my military service an IO took over who was almost a friend, in so far as there could be a friendship across the Great Divide between officers and other ranks. He was Second Lieutenant Charles Barnes, a regular officer three years older than I was. The Army Chief of Staff complained that too often the newest subaltern, rather than someone more senior, became the Intelligence Officer, but in this case it worked to my advantage. The officers lived apart, of course, even on operations. But once, during an exercise in the Troodos Mountains, Charles Barnes astonished me by presenting me with a can of beer from the officers' tent. It was an act of kindness which I never forgot.

I really am extraordinarily lucky with my bosses. Though the Battalion is crawling with a large number of poor officers, the IOs seem to improve with every change. Second Lieutenant Barnes and I are hitting it off very well. We both suffer from the inconvenience of having two lieutenant colonels wandering about at all hours making the most impossible requests (or rather giving the most impossible orders).

Actually we respected one of the lieutenant colonels much more than the other. And the 'poor officers' comment was unfair even by my standards. Most of the officers were competent and better than I would have been had I passed the War Office Selection Board; but I suspect that I took a jaundiced view of them because of my failure to become one. It may be that I had a chip instead of a pip on my shoulder. I tried not to take an especially jaundiced view of the one recruit in our draft, Second Lieutenant Orr, who had passed the WOSB.

Under the new leadership as under the old one, it was not all office work and village patrols. Being proper soldiers, we went on route marches too, as tests of endurance and map-reading. The three-ton trucks would drop us on one hillside and make a 60-mile detour to pick us up 14 miles away on another. And arrogant as we were, we had much to learn from the locals, who knew their island so better than we did.

> The army mind, faced with the problem of finding the best way up a mountain, invariably elects to charge straight at it; the subtle Cypriots seek out meandering paths, which zig-zag about the mountain side with an even surface, exerting themselves much less and reaching the top more quickly. On the top of the mountain we found a Greek whose job it is to keep a look-out for forest fires. He most hospitably gave us water to drink and to wash in. I can't fathom these Greeks. We spend all our time deporting their nearest and dearest to detention camps and prisons, and all they do in return is offer us the fruits of their hospitality.

The emergency powers were draconian. They included arrest without warrant, imprisonment without trial, a life sentence for sabotage, corporal punishment for schoolboys who rioted and the death sentence for carrying weapons, and even for 'consorting with terrorists', as well as for murder. If two men were arrested together, one armed and the other not, they could both end up on the scaffold. Twenty-two Greek Cypriots were sentenced to death during the four years of the emergency. Thirteen were reprieved. The other nine were executed, all during Field Marshal Harding's governorship. The first, on 10 May 1956, was Michael Karaolis, hanged for the murder of a Greek Cypriot policeman. When his appeal was turned down by the Privy Council, Harding wrote to the Secretary of State: 'If we are to restore law and order here and bring about a solution to the Cyprus problem in keeping with our own interests, we have got to face all (repeat all) the consequences of firm government and see this business through.' He added a brisk hand-written note, following representations by the British Ambassador in Greece: 'Sir J. Harding regrets that he cannot allow the possibility of repercussions in Athens to affect his decision on the Karaolis case.' [Foreign Office Archive 371/123885] Colonel Grivas according to his diaries had planned a daring operation to save Karaolis by kidnapping a high British official in Nicosia. He called it his Plan D. For whatever reason it was not put into effect.

Others were killed haphazardly without being tried or sentenced. Young men who were suspected troublemakers were sometimes rounded up and transported to a remote location, from which they would have to walk home. The practice was known as 'bussing' and in one notorious case had tragic consequences (eight Greeks were killed by Turks in the Geunyeli massacre of January 1958). I convinced myself, against a mass of evidence to the contrary, that the emergency measures were working and that we were somehow winning the war against EOKA.

> Most of them [the Greeks], so far as I can gather, have had to suffer for so long and to so little purpose from road blocks and curfews and government restrictions that they have become rather peeved with EOKA for not allowing them to jog along in their usual pacific rut. My job does permit me to get some view, if an oblique one, of public opinion in our area at least. On most weeks we (an interpreter and myself, normally) go out to some village and do our best to get involved in an argument in the coffee shop. Last week we went to a particularly obscure little hamlet living off an oasis in the most arid country in Cyprus. There, of all places, we were treated to a learned denunciation of Marxism, in English, by the local schoolmaster. He took an unusually moderate view of union with Greece.

He had to be careful not to express it publicly, for not only the British but left-wing Greek Cypriots were targets for EOKA assassination squads. Grivas was determined, through a campaign of selective killings, to eliminate the Communists as a political entity; and he succeeded in doing so. At this point I still believed in the line put out in the Suffolk Regiment's tented academy of military science, also known as A (Training) Company:

> The nationalists, supposedly champions of liberty, have conspired to produce a situation in which there is no freedom of speech whatsoever.

The schoolmaster's lecture was a typical side-show. In 18 months in the Intelligence Section, patrolling and probing week in and week out, working the coffee shops and peering into candle-lit churches, I cannot recall coming up with a single piece of useful or usable intelligence. What we did find in plenty were leaflets.

No sooner had our Land Rover entered the village we were supposed to be prowling around, than we found it was ploughing through a small mountain of EOKA leaflets, which had obviously been distributed only a few minutes before we arrived. The Cypriots must be the most untidy people in the world. The vagabonds who produce these leaflets scatter them to the four winds in their hundreds, knowing full well that no one will ever pick them up for fear of being found with them in their possession. So it is left to us either to act as park keepers and pick them up ourselves or else turn the locals out of their coffee shops and get them to clean up their own horrible streets. After trying the first course for the first hundred or so leaflets and finding it a rather undignified sort of job, we soon switched to the second. Total bag must have been about 500 leaflets – which doesn't seem very much but looks an awful lot when scattered wholesale about the streets.

This was in early April 1958, and I am sure we drove back to camp with a feeling of having done a good day's work of intelligence-gathering. We were quite wrong of course. The so-called 'vagabonds' were getting the better of us in winning the people over. And by forcing them to clean their streets at gunpoint we were probably doing more to recruit for EOKA than to defeat it.

At the same time anti-EOKA leaflets were produced by a group of expatriates whose leader called himself 'Cromwell'. He was rumoured to be a soldier in the Royal Horse Guards, but this was never established. The leaflets urged a boycott of shops where the English signs had been removed: 'If you do not see the name of a shop, bar, café or hotel written in English, the owner of this shop is a collaborator of EOKA and he should be boycotted'. The organisation originally called itself AKOE, but changed its name to anti-EOKA when it learned that AKOE also stood for the Greek Homosexual Liberation Movement. The leaflets caused consternation in Government House, because Greek politicians saw them as black propaganda by the intelligence services. The intelligence operation was actually not that clever. I knew that because I was part of it.

Chapter 6

The Colonists

We lived and served apart from the people, in islands within an island. Kykko Camp was such an island. So were Army Headquarters Cyprus, HQ Middle East Land Forces, Government House itself and even the Ledra Palace Hotel. The symbol of our separate existence was the ubiquitous barbed wire. Three coils of it surrounded the camp. We took it with us on riot duty to close off streets. We took it with us on cordons and searches to make cages like sheep pens for holding people while checking their identities. We took it with us even on exercises because we never knew when it might come in handy. Along with the angle irons that held it down, heavy hammers for the angle irons and various other bits and pieces of hardware, it was what was known in the Army as *stores*. Barbed wire was the constant barrier between us and them, the soldiers and the people. We never overcame it.

We were even offered a booklet called *Know Your Cyprus*: 'If the villagers don't put out a mat with "Welcome" on it for you it's because the EOKA gangsters have frightened them out of it and so you don't get a chance to meet the people and see how they live. This booklet will tell you about the Cyprus villagers: read it when you're browned off: you'll find there's a lot more to Cyprus than you can see from the back of a truck.'

The officers of course were better briefed than we were – or were they? Looking back on the record I doubt it. At a Junior Leaders Course in April 1958 the subalterns were lectured by a colonial official who questioned the Greek Cypriots' moral and physical courage: 'There have been one or two who have been first class, but the majority have been very easily intimidated … They have been very easy subjects for terrorism and indoctrination.' He then added 'Of the situation before us, it is highly unlikely that anyone knows what it is.' And he was supposed to be the expert!

Behind the wire it was the colonial mind-set that surely doomed us to failure. We had little knowledge or understanding of the Cypriots we were dealing with, or their languages. That was a handicap from start to finish, as was the shortage of skilled interrogators. We in the Battalion should have done better, not least because of the three interpreters attached to the Intelligence Section. Two of them were Turkish Cypriots, Sami Hifzi and Mustafa Mahmoud, who dressed like country gentlemen and wore jackets and ties and waistcoats even in the hottest weather, became real friends and provided us with an insight into the character as well as the language of their community. The third, a Greek speaker, could not have been recruited locally or he would have been accused of being an informer and a traitor by the Greek community. He was Chris Dunkley, a Greek scholar and private soldier in the Intelligence Corps, about to go to Cambridge to study classics. He too knew the history and politics as well as the language. He outshone us all: he was tall and languid and very, very bright. He had a mind of his own and actually *liked* the Greeks. He came to us from his Greek course in an easy-going Intelligence Corps headquarters in Nicosia and had never before worked at the sharp end or even had to wear uniform on duty. He was in for a shock. Among the rank and file infantry and in his ill-fitting and bedraggled battledress he was not a happy camper.

> Thus he finds it rather hard to go out on wet road blocks, particularly as he had been on guard on Thursday night and on Friday night he went out with me to ambush a power station and lie in wait in some rather damp and draughty corn to blaze away at any masked men that might come our way with bombs in their hands. None came. The Greeks are rather good at avoiding ambushes.

The power station was the one we had visited with our first and lovelorn IO.

> It is an acting, probationary and inconsiderable power station, not actually worth blowing up.

Our success rate on these operations was so low that we calculated that if we laid a thousand ambushes the Greeks would run into only one of them.

I noted that Chris went through agonies of misery, especially when wet – and it seemed to us that the Commanding Officer ordered extra patrols and road blocks when the rains came.

> The powers-that-be decided not to indulge in patrols or any such picnics during the week, when the weather would have been ideal, but to save all the fun and games up for the weekend, with the result that the patrols and road block parties poured forth to inundate the countryside, only to get extremely wet and miserable. Some of them must be out there still, completely drenched.

These included the unfortunate Chris Dunkley. But when he got back he was, unlike the rest of us, willing to raise the awkward questions. One day on a Land Rover patrol, he asked one of the more approachable of the officers, our temporary IO Mike Askins, who was also a national serviceman, what on earth we were doing in Cyprus and why we were doing it. He did not believe in our mission on the island, saw no purpose to it and predicted that no good would come of it. The more we repressed the Greeks, the more they would turn against us or shower us with kindness. Or both.

In the Regiment's magazine I dared to describe the Intelligence Section as its 'last outpost of civilisation'. It was of course nothing of the kind. It was more like a cover organisation for spinning wheels and appearing to be busy while not actually doing much of any military value at all. The Army was expert at it even on the parade ground, where it was called 'marking time' (marching on the spot without going anywhere). The tasks were apparently wide-ranging. We issued maps. We talked in coffee shops. We circulated photographs of wanted men. We patrolled the hinterland. We searched buildings for leaflets and culverts for bombs. My only operational success to date was to find a small bundle of leaflets in a hole in the wall of an empty house.

> Now I shall become an even more ardent hole-explorer than ever. Leaflet hunting is very like fishing – at the slightest success one's hopes rise out of all proportion to one's chances.

We visited the cloisters and cells of a derelict monastery in the foothills and as usual gleaned no worthwhile information.

The monks had abandoned the place two years before, and I can't say I altogether blame them.

Most of all, we shuffled paper to an extent that even then seemed self-defeating. While pretending to be men of action, soldiers with the Queen's Commission have an extraordinary interest in pushing the paperwork. It denotes an ambition to go to Staff College and become staff officers, which is the path to high command. One of the things that I learned about officers, rather to my surprise, was that while singing the praises of teamwork they were also competing fiercely with each other. I wrote:

The various intelligence headquarters, of which there are a vast number all hopelessly un-coordinated, are grabbing the opportunity to unburden themselves of reams of instructions on everything from the correct size of ambush parties to ways and means of detecting false identity cards.

The paperwork also flowed outwards from the Intelligence Section. For bureaucratic purposes the Battalion capitalised itself as 1 SUFFOLK. Under this heading I pounded out sitreps (situation reports) and intsums (intelligence summaries) in such quantities that my hard-worked typewriter broke down and had to be repaired with the help of a shrewdly placed pin. If I had the choice between the parade ground and office, I would take the office and try to look like the busiest intelligence clerk in the history of the infantry. This was at the time of a Turkish uprising.

My work is increasing and multiplying like nobody's business – files to be made of all the villages in our area, lists of identity cards of wanted men to be typed out, and maps to be made up, torn apart, and marked – I find life very full and the time passing very quickly … Looking out of the window, I can see truckloads of bored soldiers armed with batons and shields waiting to descend like the Assyrian hordes on the Turks of

Nicosia. But, even from my knowledge of the Turks, I think that rain will stop play as far as rioting is concerned.

The fact that it was all for nothing had not yet occurred to me – and did not, until the end when it was too late.

The Intelligence Section also held the monopoly on the Battalion's maps and wax pencils and hard plastic covering, known as 'talc', to clip over the maps to be marked and re-marked as locations changed. This stuff was in short supply, leaving me in a favourable position when dealing with the company commanders. I actually became quite adept at putting up maps and marking them with operational boundaries and the appropriate symbols for battalions and companies and platoons, which won the approval of Lieutenant Colonel Arthur Campbell, who became the CO's deputy. For nearly two years, sticking pins in maps was what I did for a living. I tried to make an art form of it.

It gives a chap who can't paint or sculpt his one and only chance to give free rein to his artistic impulses.

And we owned an imposing map case, built for us by the Pioneer Sergeant. It opened on hinges to show two talc-covered maps, one large scale and one small, and closed like a briefcase to be taken on operations. It then became a battle map. It had a carrying handle and a sling. I would leave the camp with a rifle slung on one shoulder, the map case on the other – and a backpack. I felt like the very model of a modern intelligence clerk. I also learned that not all the officers were blessed with map-reading skills. If we were out on patrol and the lieutenant who was leading it said he was virtually certain that he knew where we were, it was a sure sign that we were lost. So I wrote the following:

> If you wish to avoid mishaps
> On a line of confrontation
> Just know that officers and maps
> Are a dangerous combination.

We also held the Battalion safe containing impressive-looking documents stamped in red and ranging from Confidential to Top Secret. The most sensitive of these was not about operations at all, but whether a certain NCO was entitled to all of the medals that he wore. It was the one advantage of having taken the WOSB: I came to the Battalion with the security clearance necessary when seeking the Queen's Commission.

And in an age long before PowerPoint, the officers needed help with their presentations. Towards the end of the emergency, Army HQ Cyprus decided that it needed to train a private soldier in the production of 'tactical sketches', whatever they were. I would have fancied the job myself, especially if fewer drill parades went with it, but by then I was a corporal.

> I have been painting posters. The officers hold periodic discussion groups and lectures and, being largely inarticulate themselves, they have to rely on posters displaying all sorts of details of army organisation to make their points ... I'll have to stop now – I've got my horrible posters to do. It's a pity that the Army doesn't have a union to control working hours. Still, in time I should become an expert poster-man.

I was much more respectful to them in public of course, especially the able but slightly raffish Signals Officer, and later Adjutant, Captain Pat Hopper. I corrected one of his signals about some dramatic events in Varosha near Famagusta in October 1958, because I thought it would improve the grammar. As a man of deeds rather than words, he was not the least bit interested in the grammar. He said 'The trouble with you, Corporal Bell, is that you think too much!' It was an unanswerable charge. I did then and still do. But not nearly enough about the questions raised by my Greek-speaking mate Chris Dunkley.

We also manned the 50 Brigade radio link. Every morning Brigade HQ would call up at 0900 hours for situation reports. Our call sign was Bravo 9 and I was Acorn Minor (the IO was Acorn). I pressed the transmit button and replied in my best officer-class tones 'November Tango Romeo' (nothing to report), unless there really was something to report, in which case a real officer, like Captain Hopper, would take over. I also complained that our office had become a public thoroughfare used by 'noisy signallers rushing in and out on mad errands'. The radio set should really have been in their office not ours. Or better still in a military museum.

All the Army's wirelesses are hopelessly antique. Some of them are even inscribed in Russian – they were originally made with a view to being distributed among the allies, as they were then. Now, some 14 years later, we still use them.

When the campaign was over, the inquests on it agreed that one of the great deficiencies was that the soldiers' radios were totally inadequate, especially at long range. The journalists' communications were so much better (as they still are) that HQ Cyprus was constantly being asked about events that it did not even know had occurred. The press was quick-footed: the chain of command was slow and cumbersome. The HF (high-frequency) radios were defective to the point of uselessness, because the static interference drowned out the signal, especially at night – and EOKA operated mainly under cover of darkness. We British were fighting deaf as well as blind.

I did my best to master the radio procedures, the phonetic alphabet from Alpha to Zulu (Baker had just been replaced by Bravo), and the call signs which coded the identities of commanding officers, adjutants and even intelligence clerks. For security reasons a town or village could not be named: it was always 'your location' or 'my location'. Message received and understood was 'Roger'. Message will be complied with was 'Wilco'. The Army of today still uses the NATO alphabet, but has dispensed with the old code words. It does perfectly well without Sunrays and Seagulls and Acorns. Their incongruity intrigued me, and years later I wrote a nostalgic tribute to them:

> When I served in the ranks the then CO
> Was known as Sunray on the radio,
> Which we who knew him thought inapposite,
> Since he was not conspicuously bright.
> The Adjutant was code-named Seagull,
> To which he was in literacy the equal.
> Lest our identities should be mistaken,

We in Intelligence were known as Acorn;
My military career was never finer
Than when I used the call sign 'Acorn Minor'
Yet from this acorn grew no mighty oak,
But just a wandering and insurgent bloke.

Chapter 7

Commanding Officer

My work in the Intelligence Section brought me into regular contact with the Battalion's Commanding Officer, Lieutenant Colonel Silvanus 'Bertie' Bevan. I was surely too harsh on him in my letters, in one of which I described him as 'the old fool who runs the Battalion'. As a young staff officer in 1944 he had served in Imphal during the battle for Burma with the 50th Indian Parachute Brigade when it was outflanked by the Japanese. He was not, however, in the thick of it but at rear headquarters. 'It was unnerving,' he wrote, 'listening to the radio traffic and being unable to help.' The Commanding General sent an order 'Fight your way out. Good luck'. Nine hundred men were lost as the Japanese advanced. It was a low point in the campaign. The Brigadier was relieved of his command and 'busted' to Major. Bertie Bevan returned to regimental duty.

In 1945 he was appointed Brigade Major to the 1st Parachute Brigade in Lincolnshire. It was a plum job but did not work out for him. The Paras were veterans of Arnhem, which he was not. He was a veteran of India, which they were not. Besides which, he was who he was. After four months the Brigadier called him in and said 'Bertie, one of us has to go and it won't be me!' Again he returned to regimental duty.

His appointment as Commanding Officer was controversial. He was not over-qualified except on the rifle ranges, where he was a crack shot. He had the support of his predecessor and of the Colonel of the Regiment, for they preferred one of their own to the indignity of having a CO imposed from outside. The Suffolks' next Commanding Officer presumptive, Major Charles Boycott – father of the journalist Rosie Boycott – had resigned from the Army unexpectedly, leaving a sudden and unwanted vacancy which had to be filled. Rosie, I wonder, did you know why he resigned, and what the consequences were for Private Bell and the rest of the Regiment's rank and file? And as a five-year-old, could you not have persuaded your father to stay just a little longer? There were those in the regimental family who suspected that Bertie Bevan was not up to it. He was therefore provided with able substitutes, Lieutenant Colonel Arthur Campbell and Major Malcolm Dewar. It seemed to us other ranks that the Battalion worked better with the deputies in charge.

> We have our second-in-command as acting CO – which promises much better for the success of the coming week.

It was most unusual for an infantry battalion to have two lieutenant colonels on its strength – and unfortunate, from an other-ranks' point of view, that the wrong one was in command. I regret that I did not admire the CO as much as I should have done; and I was probably closer to him than any other junior rank except his batman. One day in May 1958 I was pressed into service as his close protection. Usually he had a corporal to drive him even the walking distance from Battalion Headquarters to lunch in the Officers' Mess; but this time he insisted on driving himself.

> On Saturday night a patrol had stumbled upon 431 sticks of dynamite. So the next day the CO had to go out and congratulate everybody, with me as escort: so much for my peaceful Sunday morning. The CO himself, though rumoured to be humane on occasions, is generally the complete caricature of an army officer with several years' service in India, which indeed he has had. He is a great hulk of a man, with a body wrecked by years of over-indulgence in officers' messes and a mind completely gone to seed. He also has one of the loudest mouths in the whole of the Army, which he uses as a megaphone for a stock of military clichés (e.g. 'The main point that seems to emerge is this … '), which he manipulates in various permutations to convey one meaning or another. Our trip to the hills that morning was vastly amusing. For some reason he wished to talk about the Church while driving the Land Rover. Hence the oddest of monologues: 'My father I may say was a deeply religious man – GET OUT OF MY WAY YOU FAT WOG – … The main point that seems to emerge from a study of the Holy

Trinity is – YOU ARE A F****** F****** YOU ROAD HOG'. And so the great tirade went on.

He was no mean road hog himself.

Bertie Bevan was one of those men whose life story is best read between the lines. Although actually born in Nicosia itself, he was a true son of the Raj. His Vickers machine guns were carried by pack mules on the North West Frontier. He even described himself as a frontier wallah. (It was an age of wallahs: dhobi wallahs, char wallahs, frontier wallahs and even intelligence wallahs.) He qualified for one of the last Indian Service Medals ever struck: they were usually awarded for putting down native uprisings, in this case a mutiny in a Nepalese battalion in the frontier station of Kohat. He prided himself on having bagged three panthers near the garrison town of Mhow (Military Headquarters of War). (It has since been renamed.) He justified his big game hunting as a challenge to do something out of the ordinary. He blamed the scarcity of panthers on the poachers, not the hunters. He was out panther-hunting in September 1939 when his bearer, whom he had sent back to get some ice, brought him instead the news from the nearest station master that war with Germany had been declared. Somewhere out there were bigger game than panthers to be hunted.

That was how he came to know about internment. As a subaltern in 1939 he helped to establish the prison camp in Ahmednagar where 1,000 unfortunate Germans and Austrians living in India, mostly businessmen or Lutheran missionaries, were locked up for the duration of the war. It was not what he had joined the Army for, but one of his duties among the businessmen was to separate German and Austrian Jews from the others: another was to settle a dispute between rival Indian contractors for the camp's food supply. Although it was sited in an old infantry barracks, British combat rations (known as 'Compo') were not considered acceptable by the internees. No bratwurst, I suppose.

Commanding a battalion of his regiment is every infantry officer's ambition, as Field Marshal Harding himself wrote retrospectively (his was the Somerset Light Infantry), and Bertie Bevan was no exception. The circumstances of active service in Cyprus would have challenged the very best. A good CO does more than give orders; he has to know his soldiers individually and inspire them by example; and sometimes, on internal security, he has to discipline and restrain them too. In spite of him or because of him we were still a good and well-respected battalion.

Others took a more favourable view of Lieutenant Colonel Bevan than I did. He was duly awarded an OBE, which came up with the rations for a Commanding Officer in those days, unless vetoed by the Brigadier or the General in his chain of command. He was on good terms with both. Quite reasonably, he took the award as a sign that he had made a success of his time in the Battalion. The citation, endorsed by Major General Kendrew the General Officer Commanding, said of his soldiers 'They have invariably carried out their duties with efficiency and good humour, in spite of much provocation, at times, by Cypriot rioters. Colonel Bevan has trained his battalion to a very high standard indeed and has instilled a great sense of duty and tolerance into his officers and men'. It was quite an accolade, but we were probably more easy-going than he was. His Adjutant described him as a genuine if somewhat quaint character. 'He was inclined to be intolerant, as he readily admitted, but beneath a forbidding exterior there beat a soft heart.'

The legend of Fingers the goat confirms this. Unlike such regiments as The Royal Welch Fusiliers, The Suffolk Regiment did not possess a mascot. The Fusiliers' was a well-groomed goat with the rank of lance corporal; on one famous occasion it was 'busted' to private for head-butting a drummer. Animals were strictly forbidden inside our wire, but soldiers would always be soldiers. One day in November 1958 a lance corporal from C Company returned to the camp with an abandoned baby goat which he had found on operations. The goat, called Fingers, was successfully hidden for a while and fed on milk, until the day when it escaped and was discovered eating the Commanding Officer's roses. The Commanding Officer was not amused. The lance corporal was up on CO's orders immediately; but, so far from court-martialling the animal, Lieutenant Colonel Bevan allowed it to be adopted as C Company's official mascot, at least until the end of the tour when it could easily have blended into the scenery. In this way The Royal Welch Fusiliers were not the only regiment to get their goat. Fingers accompanied C Company even to the rifle range: the riflemen marched in columns of three with the goat following faithfully behind them. Always eccentric, the CO could also be magnanimous.

From my vantage-point in the other ranks I studied the officer class extensively. Having failed the selection test, I was especially interested in those around me who had passed it. What qualities did they have that I lacked? Self-confidence was clearly one of them. I was a shy young man and had led too sheltered a life. The officers had a born-to-rule air about them, a sense of entitlement, and seemed rather more men of the world. They were the British class system in uniform. Those whom I admired (unlike the CO) were the Intelligence Officer Second Lieutenant Barnes, the Adjutant Captain Pat Hopper, the OC Headquarters Company's Major John Fisher-Hoch and the CO's second-in-command the charismatic Lieutenant Colonel Arthur Campbell MC. Now *there* was a real soldier.

Chapter 8

Unintelligent Operations

O ne of the tasks of the Intelligence Section was to maintain a log book of incidents on operations and a scrap-book of press cuttings and photographs. Everything went by the book and was done by numbers: if we had been officially at war, which we were not, we would also have had to fill in a War Diary on army form C2118. The log book of incidents, which I largely wrote myself in the Central Police Station, has disappeared from the record. I suspect that I may have been ordered to burn it, along with much else, as we suspended operations and withdrew behind the wire in March and April 1959. The archive of photographs and press cuttings now lives in retirement, somewhat tattered, in the Suffolk County Records Office in Bury St Edmunds. I put it together with scissors, glue and scotch tape – the original pre-computer cut and paste. I did not do it very well, either: many of the photographs have come adrift from their moorings and have settled loosely, without dates or captions, between the back pages of the impressively-bound old ledger. I don't know why the cover was red and dark blue: it should have been regimentally red and yellow. The photographs, being old, are black and white. I wish there had been more of them, for they are the only visual record remaining of the Regiment's last stand. I should have done a better job than I did.

Most of the pictures are of parades and official visits, one after the other, as if these were our main occupations, as it sometimes seemed that they were. We were on every VIP's itinerary of camps that had to be visited; and every visit would include a parade at which the visitor took the salute as we all marched past. He would then address us from the saluting base and proceed to the Officers' and Sergeants' Messes. A typical caption reads 'The General laughs with RSM Gingell and CSM Evans'. The Regimental Sergeant Major may have laughed with the General, but I would swear on the Regimental Collect ('Oh God, our Rock and Fortress, uphold, we pray Thee ... ') that he never laughed with me. Rather he did the reverse. Happily, we were reconciled at a Royal Anglian Regiment event in Cambridgeshire many years later. When the Regimental Sergeant Majors changed half way through my tour of duty, I was spectacularly ungracious – and I now believe quite wrong – about the departing RSM, who had introduced some necessary discipline and sorted out the Sergeants' Mess when it badly needed sorting. I wrote:

He was gifted with a hideous grating voice, a sadistic mind and only one eye, which was very penetrating.

Nor had I seen the last of RSM Gingell. He would come back to haunt me later.

The file includes pictures of The Suffolk Regiment's skiffle group. It was the age of Lonnie Donegan and the Battalion had won not only the inter-services shooting championship but the inter-services skiffle championship too. There were unit competitions for everything from music to marksmanship. To its credit (or mine, since I compiled it) the scrap-book honours the other ranks as well as the officers. It includes a photograph of a Christmas party 'For Batmen, Signallers and Pay Clerks'. The officers still had batmen then (soldiers who were also servants) and I speculated wildly in the regimental magazine about some future army in which every soldier would be issued with his own batman. Because of the emergency we had two Christmas Days. One was on 25 December for half the Battalion and the other on 27 December for the other half. What we liked about it was that, just once a year, or actually twice on this occasion, we got a free film show (Orson Welles in *The Third Man*) and the officers served the other ranks. Somewhat the worse for wear from their own festivities, they poured a potion called 'gunfire', tea and neat rum in slapdash quantities, which I thought a foul mixture at the time, but rather warmed to as a pick-me-up in later conflicts. The Army was an environment high on alcohol. I heard later of a court-martial at which the absorption of eighteen pints at one sitting was described by the defending officer as 'normal social drinking'. I seem to have stuck mainly to fruit juice at the time, but have made up for it since.

One photograph which has mysteriously gone missing, and which I remember vividly, was of Headquarters Company under Major John Fisher-

Hoch marching on to the parade ground for a great parade in the summer of 1958. Everyone was out of step except Lance Corporal Bell. The Company Sergeant Major had some observations to make about that, which he felt it his duty to share with me. We marched traditionally, as soldiers do, with the officers in front and the sergeants behind – the officers to lead us and the sergeants to prevent us from deserting.

Some of the photographs were operational. One showed a soldier of D Company, screwdriver in hand and a visiting general looking on, searching a bus for hidden letters, weapons and explosives. Another showed a cordon and search of the Kykko Monastery annexe in Nicosia on 6 September 1958. The caption (which I must have written) reveals that C Company under Major Thursby found an EOKA banner, together with leaflets and other 'seditious literature'. (The Orthodox Church, led by Archbishop Makarios, was the spiritual and political seat of the revolt, and we could hardly have expected it to be neutral.) One of the more remarkable photographs showed the soldiers of C Company themselves, after the operation, formed up in open order and being searched by their officers in the presence of a monk, 'as a precaution against the publication of atrocity stories by the Greek Cypriot press'. Actually the Greek Cypriot press was severely censored, but Radio Athens was not, which the British accused of fomenting insurrection. Governor Harding said it had directed 'a steady stream of abuse and invective at the island, well calculated to alienate Greek Cypriots from their lawful government'. Radio Athens was therefore jammed from 5 March 1956 onwards. The jamming was expensive and technically difficult. And there was no blueprint for it: it had never been tried before. The Governor therefore appointed a Jamming Officer.

The conduct of British soldiers on operations was becoming an issue. The search of the monastery was repeated two weeks later. Churches and monasteries, far from being no-go areas, attracted the special attention of the security forces, including from time to time The Suffolk Regiment's Intelligence Section. The Army even issued a *monastery map* to point us in the direction of these seats of sedition. After one of the searches of Kykko Monastery it was alleged by the Greek Cypriots that the Archbishop's dog had gone missing. This caused some alarm at Battalion Headquarters because of the potential repercussions, which would not have been to the

Regiment's advantage. If the dog had indeed been abducted it was returned in short order to the Monastery. C Company already had a goat and had no need for a dog, even one owned and blessed by a Beatitude.

The possession of 'seditious material' was a criminal offence under the Government's Emergency Powers. On 3 June 1958 the Battalion Diary recorded 'Schoolmaster found in possession of EOKA leaflet. Fined £2 in special court'. A typical leaflet, which I picked up myself and sent home, was a primitive cartoon of a John Bull figure clutching three bags of cash and being challenged by an EOKA fighter with a sub-machine gun. The tents of a detention camp behind barbed wire stood in the background. The words beneath the cartoon were: 'The oppressor with our money makes his grip stronger every day and fills up his own belly. Sabotage the following English products as we order, EOKA.' There must have followed a list of the products to be boycotted, especially clothes. It was a political statement for the Greeks at the time, especially the young, not to be well dressed. It was fashionable to look scruffy in locally-made clothes. Self-determination began at home.

Not all the leaflets were pro-EOKA. There were Turkish ones too and some apparently by British expatriates.

> The leaflet racket has of late got completely out of hand. The various seditious organisations, of which there are scores, have vied with one another to produce longer, more violent leaflets for so long that the lunatic fringes have now joined in to turn confusion into havoc. Lately we have had leaflets urging the British not to buy the goods of 'pot-bellied, blood-sucking Greeks'. And last week another masterpiece (printed, significantly, on War Office paper) depicting Makarios with a Greek caption 'Begin the day with Gillette'. Whatever next?

I have wondered since, but was only just beginning to then, whether any of the black propaganda, the cordons and searches and confiscations and snatch patrols, the curfews and hot pursuits and baton charges, and the indiscriminate nature of most of them, did anything to advance the cause of a negotiated settlement. Probably not, but it was the way that we did things back then. It had worked before, in Malaya and Kenya, and was supposed to work again. The retreat from Empire was a long and disorderly process, something between a phased withdrawal and a scramble for the exit.

In October 1958, at the extreme point of the emergency, came the day of regime change at the top. Major General Sir Douglas Kendrew KCMG, CB, DSO and Three Bars was replaced as General Officer Commanding by Major General Sir Kenneth Darling GBE, KCB and DSO. Lance Corporal Bell, whose only decoration was one stripe on his arm, observed:

We have a new General, who goes by the unlikely name of Darling. He concentrates his energies on trying to give the impression that he will succeed where his predecessors failed. When they take over a job, all officers are infected with the new broom bug ... Having toured the district talking to the troops (including ourselves) about the efficiency of his new broom, he has achieved nothing except a great deal of unpopularity in the eyes of the *Daily Mirror*.

He brought in a new Head of Intelligence too, a British colonel of Polish origin with a sharp tongue and a short fuse. He was the sort of man who Gets Things Done.

Last week he assembled all the intelligence officers on the island for a convention. And while they cowered in submissive rows before him, he explained in the coarse language of his species exactly how he wanted things done: maps covered with plastic to denote one thing, with pins to denote another, with tracing paper to denote another, plus files, plus dossiers, plus other permutations of intelligence material in all its endless ramifications. He would personally pay visits to ops rooms all over the island, and would see to it that everything was just so, OR HEADS WOULD ROLL!

At which the Intelligence Officers quaked and trembled and made plans to prepare for the day of doom. They pinned their faith on the principle, 'Baffle them with bull', which means this: that if you cover enough map boards with enough maps, and enough maps with enough plastic and tracing paper, and enough plastic and tracing paper with enough pins, pencil marks, pen marks, diagrams and hieroglyphics, in all the colours of the rainbow and several more – then the Polish martinet will be so impressed by the general appearance of the thing that he will ignore its consequent inefficiency and uselessness.

General Darling wrote later: 'We started on a business as usual basis, and eventually when our fortunes did not prosper too well, radical measures to meet the emergency had to be undertaken ... The final round of the emergency [1958] was probably the most difficult of all, since it witnessed the outbreak of bitter inter-communal fighting to be followed quickly by what proved to be EOKA's final campaign of violence during a period of intense activity in the political field.' [Colonial Office Archive CO 226/1077]

On 14 October 1958 the Administrative Secretary, John Reddaway, advised General Darling on his plan for the defeat of EOKA: 'In my view there is no future in making things hot for the Greek Cypriots in general in the hope that they will then betray EOKA. Such attempts as have been made to do this in the past have failed. The man in the street either genuinely knows nothing of EOKA or is too terrified to tell what he does know. Moreover, it only makes enemies of people whom we must hope, in the end, to win back to cooperation and confidence.' [FCO Archive 141/4217] Reddaway later wrote a book called *Burdened with Cyprus*. General Darling took his advice.

As we surmised at the time, the new General was trying to distance himself as far and as fast as he could from the strategy of the old one. (The new Governor had done the same.) The standardisation of maps and operations rooms was just the start of it. His new broom swept widely. He revamped the intelligence services, making the Head of Special Branch the Director of Intelligence. He established a Battle School near Kyrenia to refine the tactics that he believed would finally defeat EOKA – 'The value of a well formed Battle School goes without question'. It would have a commandant, six instructors and a staff of ninety-nine (he must have been required by the War Office to keep it under 100). It would have separate officers' and sergeants' messes; that was also in the great tradition – officers and other ranks literally never messed with each other.

Most of all he ordered a major operational step-change, away from the big set-piece manoeuvres of the past to small-scale boots-on-the-ground operations conducted by specially-trained and highly skilled teams 'in which the officer content will be unusually high'. Selected units were ordered to form such teams, but it was late in the day, and much as we favoured officers going out on patrols, I never heard of it in the Suffolks during our time in Nicosia. The General was for ever bombarding commanding officers with such instructions, but ours was on his way out and we were probably exempted. The proposed actions by small patrols would not have been much use in dealing with major riots in the Old City, where the deployment of too small a force could become a provocation. In his Directive No 4 in December 1958 General Darling wrote 'I do not favour what may be termed large scale cordon and search operations ... These are necessarily clumsy operations, expensive in troops and inevitably give rise to all manner of charges relating to the behaviour and conduct of the security forces ... We shall defeat EOKA more by brains than by brawn. Intelligence is therefore the key to success'. He was still a believer, as they all were, in the doctrine of the knockout blow. Indeed, he thought the war was winnable *and that he could win it*. He wrote that late in the campaign in February 1959 'There is little doubt that we were in position to strike at the very top of EOKA which would have been, we believe, a mortal blow'. [FCO Archive 141/4459] When the final negotiations were in progress, the British believed they knew where Grivas was hiding. They had the house under surveillance and could have raided it. General Darling decided not to: 'I was quite clear in my mind that I was not prepared to risk a single British life in the process ... to have acted in this way at this time would have been irresponsible to a degree.' [John Reddaway, *Burdened with Cyprus*, Weidenfeld & Nicolson 1968, p. 70]

But by then the cordons and searches had done their damage. The hearts and minds campaign, in so far as there ever was one, had failed completely. In his final report, classified Secret, that he wrote in July 1959 'in the hope that the lessons of Cyprus will not be forgotten', General Darling conceded: 'EOKA was a highly organised underground movement, broadly based throughout the island and supported, either willingly or by compulsion, by almost the entire Greek Cypriot population in its anti-government activities.' (Colonial Office Archive 926/1077)

And so it came to pass as I foretold it. The knockout blow was never delivered. EOKA survived and prospered. And when the campaign was all over, and the emergency powers had failed, and the Independence settlement had collapsed, and its guarantees had proved worthless and the island was invaded and partitioned by the Turks, the outcome of failure had to be admitted. It was obvious even in our time. On 22 April 1959, when the Independence Agreements had been reached and we soldiers were still on the island, the Governor Sir Hugh Foot, wrote a perceptive memorandum in which he concluded: '*Without intelligence there is no hope.* The most obvious lesson of the emergency was that everything depended on intelligence. Our failure to destroy EOKA was largely a failure of intelligence.' [FCO Archive 141/4233]

General Darling himself looked back in regret and agreement: 'The question may be asked why, when EOKA was on the brink of defeat in March 1957, was the organisation able to stage such a spectacular recovery despite the fact that large forces and the formidable apparatus of Emergency Powers were at the disposal of the Government?' General Darling identified the summer of 1958, which was on the Suffolk Regiment's watch, but just before his own, as the time when the activities of EOKA really took root. We know from Top Secret intelligence documents, now declassified, that at about this time, and partly because of our repressive measures, it became harder to recruit agents and informers, and the flow of usable intelligence dried up. In November 1958 the Cyprus Local Intelligence Committee noted 'Agents are always difficult to find and enlist'. When the emergency began the Government of Cyprus had not a single high-level agent within the insurgency. Brigadier George Baker, the Chief of Staff, added in his report on the emergency 'Unless agents are recruited before terrorism starts, the chances if doing so afterwards are very slight'. We in the security forces were thus, at least in part, the authors of our own misfortunes.

It may be that military intelligence is a contradiction in terms. In the Cyprus emergency we were short of intelligence, in both its senses, at the time when we needed it most. Our attitude to the Greek and Turkish Cypriots, in whose interests we were supposed to be helping the civil power, was outstandingly dismissive. But it wasn't much friendlier to the soldiers of other regiments and corps. The Army is tribal and we were one of its tribes. We were especially unimpressed by the Grenadier Guards, who reinforced us one day at the Central Police Station in Nicosia. They held a drill parade in its courtyard. We thought that they were bonkers. I wrote:

They came tearing out here at a high panic level, presumably expecting to do battle with hordes of bloodthirsty Greeks and Turks, and found the island about as peaceful as Beccles [my home town] on a Sunday afternoon.

The island is now infested with Guards of all species: Irish, Scottish, Welsh and Grenadier. These characters wander around even on operations with brasses and webbing in a tradition of 'bull' that would render one liable to lynching in the Suffolks. Sometimes I feel quite thankful that the Suffolks, 'only a county regiment', have no pretensions to be superlatively smart.

We did not have much time for The Parachute Regiment either, who had earned themselves a fearsome reputation in the mountains on Operation Sparrowhawk in 1956, but that may have been out of professional and regimental jealousy. They did the high-profile operations that attracted the attention of the press. We did the unglamorous patrols and guard duties. But we were proud of our Regiment and would rather have worn our cap badge than theirs. We did not fancy jumping out of aeroplanes either.

Not for the simple Suffolks, of course, the glories of airborne invasion of Levantine principalities: all the fun to be had in this part of the world appears to be reserved exclusively for the Paras.

This was prescient. Not all regiments have equal status in the eyes of what was then the War Office and is now the Ministry of Defence. At the time of the Falklands War many years later the Royal Anglians (the Suffolks' linear successors) were the Standby Battalion and should have been part of the order of battle but were not. The Task Force was composed instead of the supposed *elite*, Scots and Welsh Guards, the Paras and Marines. The same thing happened with the early deployments to Afghanistan. The impulse again was to send in the Guards, Paras and Marines. This was the outcome of an unfortunate prejudice within the Ministry of Defence against the line infantry, that they would not be up to the rigours of the climate and terrain. The effect on morale was seriously damaging. In an over-stretched army the unfashionable battalions' time would come soon enough, and did so.

In Afghanistan the Royal Anglians proved the doubters comprehensively wrong. But it was still a costly and unwinnable war.

We had a special disdain for those regiments like the Paras which, unlike ours, had a reputation for being aggressive and warlike. We saw ourselves, relatively speaking, as gentle and civilised souls better suited to the task of counter-insurgency. Had we not proved it in Malaya? We thought it through and applied a lighter touch to it. The island needed fewer of them and more of us.

> Cyprus is coming to resemble a penal servitude camp. Even before, we had most of the tough regiments in the Army – Argyll and Sutherland Highlanders, Royal Welch Fusiliers, Ulster Rifles and Commandos [Royal Marines]. Soon the place will become a complete rough-house on the arrival of the Black Watch. The Suffolks, by comparison, seem very reserved and un-bellicose.

It seemed to us that we were punished for our long-suffering amenability. We were lucky enough to be serving on Aphrodite's island, one of the most beautiful in the world, yet we were camped in the wilderness of the Mesaoria, the barren plain which was its least attractive and most fly-blown corner, where only goats and lizards could feel at home.

> We stay put. A pity, because the mountains are lovely at this time of year, while Nicosia remains its old inhospitable self.

Yet the regiments still had to serve alongside each other. I even did time with the Household Cavalry because – then as now – the Horse Guards did not like to dismount, still less to march. So in August 1958 they asked for the PBI (poor bloody infantry) to do the foot-slogging for them. The Horse Guards had armoured vehicles but we did not. Our only protection was an angle-iron sticking out from the Land Rover at an angle of 45 degrees to prevent EOKA from killing us with a wire across the road. (It was crude but effective and saved the life of the Post Corporal.) With our rifle companies tied down on riot and guard duty, it fell to the 'odds and sods' of

Headquarters Company to do the foot-slogging, with Lance Corporal Bell commanding.

> The Royal Horse Guards, who patrol the countryside hereabout in their armoured cars, have lately taken to having a lorry load of infantry riding round with them to man road blocks and such like at various points. It is of this lorry load that I am at present in charge, and I find it a pleasant change from the customary pen-pushing.

Even the road blocks were done by the book. We handed out leaflets in Greek and Turkish to the people we were bothering to explain why we were bothering them: 'We regret the inconvenience which this search causes. With your cooperation, peace, prosperity and freedom from fear will be restored to the people of Cyprus.'

The gentleman soldiers of The Royal Horse Guards, true to their nature, managed to find a suitable ceremonial role for themselves at either end of Sir Hugh Foot's governorship. They provided the guard of honour at his swearing in in 1957 and escorted him to a waiting warship after Independence in 1960. Lady Foot called her autobiography *Emergency Exit*.

The Horse Guards, whose Commanding Officer was of course a Marquess, turned out in all their glory for guards of honour, but left the searches and the road blocks to the Suffolk Regiment. Their officers dismounted to give us our orders, but their well-polished boots were not on the ground for much longer than that. We saluted and got on with it. To be fair to them, their casualties during the emergency were substantially higher than ours. Nor were they able to escape foot-soldiering forever. It gave me some satisfaction, when I next came across them in my BBC days in the early 1970s, to find them dismounted as infantry in East Belfast.

We ORs (other ranks) were of course not consulted on tactics or strategy or anything else, but it became clear to us that the force in Cyprus was wrongly configured for the task. Armoured units withdrawn from Suez were posted directly to the island, which became the command centre of Middle East Land Forces. Their panzers roared through the villages, broke up the road surfaces, blew dust in our faces and were generally ill-suited to a mission of counter-insurgency. Or so it seemed to us foot-soldiers.

However unglamorous by contrast, the Suffolks had a reputation as a steady and reliable battalion. So while the Scots and Irish patrolled the mountains and wilder parts of the hinterland, and the Paras and Black Watch were spoken of in hushed tones, and the Horse Guards did whatever Horse Guards could do without horses, four regiments of the line were tasked with keeping the peace in and around the cauldron of the capital. Alongside us were such as The Beds and Herts, The Ox and Bucks and The Lancashire Fusiliers (all long gone since the end of National Service). It was no coincidence that the four battalions of 50 Brigade in Nicosia were mostly from the county regiments, supplemented sometimes by a regiment of Royal Artillery serving as infantry. The Gunners were some of the best soldiers on the island. Whether or not we could cope with a riot, we could be depended on not to start one. I took an extraordinarily nonchalant view of the duties we were assigned to. I noted at one point from my command post that there were reports of Turks rioting somewhere ineffectually. At another, I reported rather regimentally:

> Last week proved quite interesting, with EOKA letting off fireworks all over the place, though they have not ventured into the portion of the countryside allotted to the Suffolks – they obviously know what's good for them!
>
> You need not think of your son as manning the ramparts of Empire to great effect. We merely play our very small part in trying to keep the daily total of dead Greeks and Turks within reasonable limits – and even this comes hard on a number of regular officers who are only too delighted to see the 'Wogs' bump each other off.

It was to the credit of the Army that not all its soldiers were as unthinking and unfeeling as I was. A near contemporary, Major John Benjamin of The Royal Signals wrote, 'As part of my education I went out on a night patrol with 1 Para and a Toad [informer]. We lifted an EOKA suspect in a small village. We had a job to do and we did it. But to this day I still remember feeling sorry for the man's wife and children as he emptied his pockets of money and gave it to his wife.'

Chapter 9

The Thick of Things

The pace of operations quickened. In May 1958, in the mid-term of my statutory two years and on anti-riot duty in Nicosia, I had two nights' sleep in a week, one of them in a sleeping bag on the street as reinforcements rushed past. It was not an eye-closing experience.

It was really very eerie patrolling the quaint old streets. Also, for the first time in my life, I became a rough sleeper and slept in the streets, at intervals between patrols, and found them most comfortable. The only snag was the noise. I would just be dropping off to sleep when some patrol of the Military Police or the death-or-glory boys of an immediate standby company came rushing past to answer some alarm. Lorries full of troops in anti-riot kit kept tearing past our recumbent bodies at melodramatic speeds to quell disturbances in the suburbs. Then out again on Wednesday, this time hanging about a cemetery where one of the killed Turks was buried.

There actually was a cavalry regiment with *Death or Glory* as its motto. Even for a regiment with as many battle honours as ours, we thought that a bit odd.

This time it was an emergency within an emergency. It was EOKA's strategy – and an effective one too – to tie down as many British troops as possible on static guard duties in the towns, so that fewer would be available to go after them in the mountains. When it was our turn to be Guard Battalion, the rifle companies were deployed to protect such installations as the Central Police Station, the General's mansion, Government House and the internment camp at Kokkinotrimithia. Since they could not be withdrawn, and as hostilities between Greeks and Turks increased, the 'odd bods' of Headquarters Company found themselves increasingly in the front line. All hands were on deck and reinforcements were called for. The Royal Electrical and Mechanical Engineers who kept our vehicles on the road were deployed from their workshops as infantry. The Royal Signals manned road blocks. Even the Mobile Laundry and Bath Unit and the Pioneer Corps were enforcing the curfew in outlying parts of the city. Only the Band and Drums remained in camp, playing on regardless as if on the deck of the *Titanic*. Regrettably I did not seem at all eager for an outbreak of peace and inter-communal harmony.

> We have enjoyed every minute of the present crisis; such a change from the normal round of office routine and duties. I had the interesting job of leading patrols round part of the Turkish sector of the old city, with the object of catching curfew breakers, of whom my total bag for the evening amounted to one. Anyway, I have enjoyed myself as I would never have thought possible this time last year, surrounded by mountains of uncleaned kit. I only wish the present state of affairs will continue as long as possible. Certainly it makes the time flash by.

I would like to think this was irony, but I fear that it was not. It may have been a symptom of camp fever. Living behind the wire, we had little understanding of, or sympathy with, the islanders whom we were supposed to be protecting. Battalions were hierarchies. It may have been in the nature of them that we looked upwards to see where our next orders and harassments were coming from, rather than outwards to pay attention to what was going on around us. Whatever my condition was – quite severe, by the written record – it worsened. In June 1958, which saw the bloodiest inter-communal violence in all the years of British rule, I wrote the following:

> A fortnight ago, prospects looked quite good for a small-scale civil war between the Turks and Greeks. Such expectations have all been disappointed, however, and any chances of any action have diminished more or less in proportion to the arrival of vast numbers of Parachutists and Guards.

Again I would like to disown my younger self. Did I *really* wish the Greeks and Turks to go at each other 'hammer and tongs' (as I put in another letter) for the benefit of a bored British soldier? If that was the attitude, widely shared throughout the garrison, it was no wonder that the process of decolonisation was so difficult.

By this time, the summer of 1958, the days of coffee-shop patrols in distant villages were long over. My second home was the Nicosia Central Police Station.

> The whole outlook lately has become so one-sided that the abnormal is accepted as the normal, and the pattern of life before the present troubles has been lost. All the rural patrols and weekly routines have disappeared, and the life of the Battalion centres on its one remaining duty, the keeping of the peace in Nicosia.

The battalions rotated. When we were on immediate standby we had to be ready to rush into town at a moment's notice and pretend to have things in hand, which sometimes we did and sometimes we did not. When we were not on immediate standby and other battalions took our place, we were still available for cordons and searches outside it. Our principal mission was termed IS (internal security) and an integral part of it was cordon and search, which we claimed to have reduced to a fine art. We prided ourselves on being more expert at it than any of the battalions alongside us. But it was by its nature indiscriminate. We were fighting and patrolling blind, without any targeting except that contained in the arrest lists, which were notoriously inaccurate and based in some cases on disinformation by informers and guesswork by Special Branch. The Battalion Diary noted tersely on 15 October 1958 at the time of an EOKA offensive 'Battalion relieved 1 IG [1st Battalion Irish Guards] at Kythrea. Enforced curfew within village and maintained a cordon west, east and south of the village'. (I wondered, why not the north?) '6 observation posts from C Company placed on high ground overlooking Kythrea, north east of Nicosia. Sergeant Jones and vehicle patrol ambushed outside Akaki.' The operation lasted for three days and appears to have yielded nothing. The flow of useful intelligence went all one way, from informers in the Government to the EOKA insurgents. They were described by one of our generals as 'the enemy within'. Our methods were, to say the least, robust. Nothing in the training for internal security had prepared me for the reality of what we were doing. When I wrote home from the village police station, I euphemistically described it as a 'mind-broadening experience'.

In our convoy 30 vehicles strong, all of them bristling with weapons, we descended on the picturesque and heartily pro-EOKA village of Kythrea, cordoned off for about a week while Special Branch carry out their searches and interrogations of suspects. At least, 'interrogations' is one word for it: the most used, most noncommittal and most misleading. We turn a Nelson's eye to such proceedings (it is the police and not the Army at whom the barbed shafts of Mrs Castle [Barbara Castle MP] should be directed) and carry on with the unexceptionable task of helping with the cordon and the curfew. There are three other battalions in this caper, encircling the surrounding villages. Also there is a curfew to be enforced, which brings my chief headache, since in all such curfews passes have to be issued to such essential people as doctors, and somebody has to issue them, in this case me. There is a comic opera angle to the job. The police, who advise us generally, draw great distinctions between the amount of time allowed in the fields to drovers of sheep, pigs and goats. The sheep do quite well with a whole day in the fields. The pigs are allowed half a day, but the poor old goats are hardly given an hour in the open before the curfew descends on them again.

Barbara Castle was a prominent Labour MP even then. Cyprus was one of her causes. On a visit to the island, where she met Archbishop Makarios before his banishment, she accused its Government of permitting and even encouraging British soldiers to use unnecessarily tough measures against the Greeks. Governor Harding criticised her in his cables to Whitehall for playing politics with the emergency and making his task more difficult by encouraging the EOKA uprising. He wanted cross-party support but did not get it.

Late in 1958 Barbara Castle was travelling in the back of a taxi when she was stopped by one of D Company's road blocks in a restricted area near Kyrenia. The Sergeant of 11 Platoon, who did not care who she was, had the taxi slowly taken apart and then just as slowly put back together again. She threatened to protest to the Governor, which she did. The Platoon Commander, who was wondering whether he might be court-martialled, was congratulated both by the Commanding Officer and the Brigadier. That was how Opposition MPs were dealt with.

Many years later Barbara Castle asked to see me when she was in the Lords and I was in the Commons. She warned me to beware of 'those bastards', by which she meant New Labour. I had completely forgotten that she was the fiercest critic of the Army I served in at the time when I served in it. I was politically unaware to a degree which I find it hard to account for now. It was as if I would not dare to ask the questions to which I might not have liked the answers. I wrote:

> Of the rights and wrongs of these goings on nobody says very much, because nobody knows very much. But if there is going to be any sympathy for the Greeks for the maltreatment they received, I suppose it will have to come from Mrs Castle. The Army is understandably callous about the whole thing, but where we go from here I can't imagine. Certainly the British have never been more hostile to the Greeks, and the Greeks to the British, while the glee of the Turks mounts with every atrocity.

I seem to have shared the hostility without questioning it. I described the harassment of the Greek population, which is what this was, with a staggering lack of humanity.

> The screening itself was very simple – merely a matter of finding out whether the unfortunate Greek in our hands was or was not wanted, obtaining his particulars if he was, branding his best shirt with a chalked number, and packing him off to one of the detention camps. It would have been rather more congenial if we hadn't had to arrest people.

We shifted camp to one of the 'bad' villages. A cordon was flung round the village, and all the unfortunate men herded like cattle into barbed wire compounds in the playing field of the school. One by one the villagers filed through, with us checking their identity cards, asking any awkward questions that came to mind, and deporting the wanted men (of whose names Special Branch had provided us with some none-too-accurate lists) to the detention camp. The females of the village started weeping and wailing something 'orrible, and there was nearly a riot, but we just managed to get clear of the village before any major rumpus occurred.

By then it was midday, so we had plenty of time to 'do' another village, this time a picturesque and fairly harmless hamlet on a hillside, where there were only four men to be arrested anyway. These were duly nabbed.

The follow-up operations lasted for fourteen days and produced 300 more detainees.

Up again at 2am on Friday morning. We were armed with an interminable list of wanted identity cards and set up road blocks on the main roads out of Nicosia. So once more the chairs and tables were set up in the approved manner, and I spent most of the period from dawn to dusk pawing my way through mountains of tattered, grubby identity cards, looking for the 'wanted' numbers, forged stamps and false cards.

One day we had cordoned and searched to such effect, identifying and arresting all a village's 'wanted men' in short order, that we had time to spend the afternoon on the beach, for which we were duly punished.

We paid for it the next day with a drill parade, which was also an excuse for an address by the Commanding Officer, who pointed out that life would be more difficult now and the hours of sleep fewer (a point which in our view was hardly worth making, since we had already noticed it).

The road blocks and searches multiplied, as did the sorting out of sheep from goats. We were at the point of over-stretch. Over and over again, on the roads and in the villages, I found myself on an army chair (chairs/folding/flat) in front of an army table (tables/folding/flat) and checking the identities of the Greeks who passed through. It was hot work. We kept to the rules as best we could; but I cannot be sure that a truck which came to the road block with 200 water melons on it did not occasionally leave with only 199.

> I did not have the strength of will to decline. I'm afraid that all these searches, arrests and road blocks generated a great deal of ill-will; but the Governor has determined to be unpleasant and oppressive and we follow suit, much to the delight of the regular officers.

The night-time curfews closed down whole towns and villages. We prided ourselves on the thoroughness of our searches. We prodded every inch of ground and moved every movable object to find what might be hidden underneath it. Shanty towns were semi-dismantled and corrugated iron flew in all directions. It was standard procedure for the search parties then to be searched by their own officers as a precaution against allegations of theft. By the CO's own account, we expended much effort and sweat on operations which rarely proved rewarding. We counted ourselves lucky if we found so much as an improvised pipe bomb or a rusty old shotgun barrel. But we were not heartless; and I recorded that on one occasion, after the search of a shanty town, a soldier of the Regiment cleaned an old lady's floor for her.

> During the week I went on a couple of small foot patrols, one in the walled city itself and the other in a village about a mile outside. Here the whole place was dead, dark, deserted and dreary by as early as 8 o'clock in the evening, so utterly cowed has the civilian population become.

It was a typical misreading of the public mood. The summer of 1958 was the campaign's turning point. Our strategy was self-defeating. Our road blocks throttled the island's transport system. Our cordons and searches paralysed the villages. Our curfews benighted the towns. Our operations were like a poll tax: everyone suffered equally. It was not the intention, but it was the effect, to inflict collective punishment on whole communities. The result was a rising tide of quiet resentment. After years of being stopped and searched at gunpoint, even non-political Greek Cypriots who wished only for a quiet life responded by rallying to the cause of the so-called 'terrorists'. And then, in the deathward drift of affairs on the island, we made things wilfully worse. We did not have to do it, but we did. We went for the knockout blow. And in doing so we fell foul of the law of unintended consequences.

Chapter 10

Operation Matchbox

In June 1958 I calculated that there must have been 1,500 detainees behind the wire, hundreds of them put there by the Suffolks. The numbers were about to rise dramatically. The hand-written entry in the Regimental Diary for 22 and 23 July 1958 consists of just two words: Operation Matchbox. This was the most intensive security operation of all, an island-wide dragnet to round up as many as possible of the 3,000 suspected EOKA supporters on the Special Branch arrest list. Some were herded into barbed wire pens and identified by hooded Special Branch informers, known to us as 'Toads'. In a four-day swoop a further 1,800 suspects were arrested. Some of the detainees were schoolboys as young as 14. (Support for EOKA was strong in the high schools, or gymnasiums, where the children had sworn oaths of allegiance: 'I shall work with all my power for the liberation of Cyprus from the British yoke, sacrificing for this even my life.') On their release some detainees were subjected to a 're-education course' to try and persuade them to renounce the ways of violence. Most were just let go. For the period of their detention they were in effect no more than Government-held hostages.

Matchbox had been eighteen months in the planning. It took that long for Special Branch to refine its approximate arrest list. It was accompanied by an island-wide lock-down, curfew and censorship of telephones and telegrams for seventy-two hours, and even an 'administrative delay' on imported British newspapers for twenty-four hours. It was hailed as a success. An intelligence analysis dated 1 August 1958 estimated that Matchbox had seriously depleted EOKA's manpower. The Deputy Governor, George Sinclair, who had supported the operation, concluded that the island-wide pick-up had been more successful than expected: 'We succeeded in arresting about two thirds on the list instead of one third'. Even the Governor, who had opposed it, sent upbeat messages to London hailing its success. [FCO Archive 141/4216]

But the intelligence dividend was negligible. The majority of the young men we picked up were held not only without being charged but without being questioned. The major EOKA figures, who were already fugitives, remained at large. The only obvious effect of Operation Matchbox in July was to alienate the public still further and to provoke a backlash against those who had launched it. The Governor had predicted exactly this when he warned that an attempted knockout blow 'may well provoke serious EOKA counter-attack on security forces and the British community'. [FCO Archive 141/4216]

The backlash occurred ten weeks later, in what came to be known as Black October as the casualties rose. Forty-five British people died in that month: most were soldiers, but one was a sergeant's wife, Mrs Catherine Cutliffe, shot dead in broad daylight near Famagusta on 3 October. This provoked the most severe counter-measures against the whole Greek Cypriot community. The response amounted to a rampage by British troops which was widely reported. A soldier observed 'We have tried the "firmness with courtesy" routine, and look where it has got us'. A thousand Greek Cypriot men were rounded up, two were killed and 250 injured, of whom twenty-one were hospitalised. In Karaolos Camp the arrested Greeks had to run the gauntlet of angry off-duty soldiers as they were marched at the double for 70 yards to the cage where they were held. Three were seriously injured. The police report concluded 'It cannot be denied that cold fury took a very tangible form as they doubled to the holding centre'. [FCO Archive 141/4493] It was a disgraceful episode which did the Army's reputation much damage.

In the House of Commons an MP asked 'Can we be assured that the strict military discipline that we properly expect of British troops will be maintained in the future even in the face of strong provocation?' The Colonial Secretary, Alan Lennox-Boyd, told the House that many of the injured had been resisting arrest or trying to escape: 'Reports of ill-treatment on this and other occasions have been systematically fabricated or exaggerated ... The record of all security forces over the years of terrorism has been one of strict discipline and admirable restraint.' [*Hansard* 4 October 1958] The

Government denied that there had been a breakdown of discipline. The Governor knew that there had been.

All this happened not on Sir John Harding's watch, but Sir Hugh Foot's. 'Firmness with courtesy' was Sir Hugh's idea of winning hearts and minds. But he was at odds with some of his soldiers. On 4 October 1958, the day after the rampage, he wrote 'The very rough treatment of last night is inexcusable. I well realise how much harm it does.' And he reminded the Secretary of State 'I told you it would be difficult to hold the troops'. [FCO Archive 141/4493] Through the cable traffic there run two fault lines of disagreement – one between the Governor and his Secretary of State, and the other between the Governor and his Deputy.

Discipline held throughout in the Suffolk Regiment, as it always did; but the higher the numbers detained, the more troops were needed to guard them. That also fell to us. One of our rifle companies was frequently on guard duty at the détention centre in Camp K (Kokkinotrimithia), where on at least one occasion it had to put down a riot. Camp K, with a capacity of 1,600 prisoners, was not big enough. Nor was Camp C, wherever that was. Another 'concentration camp' (the term and inverted commas were mine) was built next door to Kykko Camp, the home of the Suffolk Regiment. I saw it as an intrusion into my space.

> The authorities had to look around for a spot suitably isolated, grim and escape-proof. Our camp hit the jackpot, so at the beginning of last week a vast camp was erected on the corner of it, within a few yards of my tennis court, and the unfortunate Greeks were shipped in. Maybe they'll find some more Greeks to 'put inside', and have to extend the concentration – sorry, detention – camp, thereby encompassing my tennis court on all sides.

Soldiers and prisoners had much in common besides such close proximity. We were neither of us free men, but camped on either side of the wire without means of escape. We both had identification numbers: ours were of eight figures and theirs were of three or four. The only difference was that they were more likely to get an early release than we were. And because they had not been charged with any offence, they had almost the status of political prisoners: they did no work and were paid up to £30 a month, which was more than twice what we were. This was duly noted by the disgruntled soldiery.

> The life led by the detainees is a cause of much envy among the ranks. True, they have to suffer to the extent of eating the same food that we do; but since they are not convicted criminals they are given no work to do at all and are in fact paid £30 a month for their enforced idleness. All this occasions much grumbling, as you can imagine, from those of us who consider ourselves over-worked.

At the height of the insurgency, when Camp K was becoming an issue, an independent British commission inspected it and concluded that the detainees in their huts were living in better conditions than the soldiers in their tents.

My understanding of Operation Matchbox was typically blind-sided and blinkered; and being merely a sleepless lance corporal was no excuse. I should have seen it more clearly for what it was, an ultimately futile exercise in preventive detention.

> On Wednesday morning we rose from our slumbers rather earlier than usual – 2 o'clock to be precise – and spent a most enjoyable day assisting in the round-up of some of the thousand-odd Greeks detained. By dawn we were in position in one of the suburbs of Nicosia, and the rifle companies began to drag in their suspects, looking most bedraggled, bleary-eyed and inoffensive. I was part of the screening team … Evidently the Governor's patience had run out, much to the delight of the Army, who have always regarded the 'firmness with courtesy' policy with deep suspicion.

I was of course quite wrong, not about the Army but about the Governor. The Governor's patience had not run out, but that of his military decision-makers and advisers had. Matchbox was a sensitive operation. The file on it was not declassified until 2013, fifty-five years after the event. One of the intelligence reports is so deeply buried that it will not be released *for*

120 years. The most remarkable document was a memorandum by the Governor, Sir Hugh Foot, drafted on 16 July 1958, six days before the operation, and arguing against the island-wide knockout blow: 'I record my considered and strong opinion', he wrote, 'that to undertake the immediate and mass arrest of EOKA supporters would be a grave error ... I do not believe it would prevent attacks by Greeks on Turks nor prevent EOKA attacking Government forces. Indeed I think it would increase rather than decrease the likelihood of all-out EOKA activity against both the Turks and Government ... We should also have to face all the difficulties (not to mention the expense) of guarding and maintaining a thousand detainees – and the arrest of the first thousand would surely be followed up by the arrest of very many more. I feel sure that we must find some other and better course ... I would be grateful if those concerned would reconsider the whole question of immediate action in the light of the comments which I have here recorded.' [FCO Archive 141/4216]

Those concerned did nothing of the kind. Despite the advice of the Commander-in-Chief, Operation Matchbox went ahead in three phases, starting on 22/23 July 1958. The case of the hard-liners who won the day was summed up in an unsigned paper, classified Top Secret and entitled *Arguments for a General Pick-up*: 'It is, literally, a matter of life and death that as few potential killers as possible should escape the initial pick-up. If we allow any killer to escape who could have been picked up, we shall have the terrible responsibility for any deaths he may subsequently cause ... As between picking up 500 or 1,100, the additional adverse effect on public opinion outside the island will be negligible. It will moreover be to some extent offset by the beneficial effect of showing that we really mean business.' [FCO Archive 141/4216]

Operation Matchbox was remarkably ill-timed in two ways. First, it was conducted barely a month after the announcement by the Governor of a new policy, a policy of maximum advantage for all: 'For myself, I believe that this policy of partnership is the just and right policy – indeed I believe it is the only policy which can prevent dreadful catastrophe and bring all Cyprus comfort.' [Broadcast, 19 June 1958] Second, it coincided with a concerted campaign by Greek Cypriots, through 'human rights committees' in every district, to accuse the security forces of indiscipline and misconduct.

The campaign had begun in April 1958 after the murder of two military policemen and was up and running at full force in July. The Commissioner in Paphos wrote to the Chief of Staff 'In my view allegations of unnecessary damage, theft and ill-treatment of persons will be made by the self-styled "human rights committees" following almost any operation'. Governor Foot's frustration showed clearly in a statement in September 1958: 'The campaign of abuse against the troops and police in Cyprus has been given a new twist by the suggestion that, if the security forces in carrying out their disagreeable task of suppressing violence, cause the death of terrorists and rioters, this is a "provocation" against which EOKA must retaliate by murdering more soldiers and police ... This wicked sophistry equates action duly taken by the security forces in the performance of their duty with brutal murder and terrorism directed to the overthrow of law and order.' [FCO Archive 141/4218]

I was not aware of it at the time – my non-awareness was a chronic affliction – but Governor Foot comes over now as a lonely figure, caught between the implacability of the EOKA leadership on one side and the hard-charging habits of his security chiefs on the other. He himself could do no more than advise on operations, and in the big set pieces like Operation Matchbox his advice was ignored. In his 'lessons learned' memorandum of April 1959 Governor Foot wrote 'In Cyprus there was often an attempt to make up for the lack of intelligence by using the sledge hammer – mass arrests, mass detentions, big cordons and searches and collective punishments. Such operations can do more harm than good and usually play into the hands of the terrorists by alienating general opinion from the forces of authority.' [FCO Archive 141/4233]

Chapter 11

Armed Repression

It was a relief to be despatched occasionally to the mountains for a restorative programme of patrols and ambushes, invariably unsuccessful.

I found myself trying to move noiselessly at dead of night down a precipitous pathless hillside of loose rock and shale, bearing a rifle in one hand and a fairly hefty battery (used for lighting up flares if anyone comes along) in the other. The requisite noiselessness was not achieved. The ambush of course was entirely fruitless. One nocturnal cat came within inches of being shot to pieces, but no EOKA.

Despite the negative outcomes, and the difficulties of pitching a tent on a slope of shale and pebbles, operations in the Troodos Mountains were a welcome change from the heat and dust and desolation of the central plain. Being close to Mount Olympus, they were also quite literally the high point of my two years in the Army.

Above our headquarters and dominating the countryside around was a mountain, and on top of this mountain there lived two forest rangers equipped with a telephone to the nearest village (for reporting forest fires, ostensibly). Thus it was impossible for us to carry out troop movements without being spotted and reported. Therefore I and two minions were despatched to keep the forest rangers out of harm's way and man the telephone. The rangers were most hospitable, giving us tea, coffee and water melons in return for the tinned rations and cigarettes we gave them. This mountain-top phone was, it seemed, the local exchange. We had a fine view from Morphou to Nicosia to Famagusta, and I had a delightful time disrupting the local communications.

The Cyprus Forestry Commission owned an island-wide telephone network of old-fashioned open-wire technology which Major John Benjamin of the Royal Signals called 'a terrorist's dream: a simple and reliable communications network operating in a terrorist-friendly environment and of course a first-rate early warning system'. Our job on operations was to get across it and stop it working.

We were in the former EOKA territory where Grigoris Afxentiou, Grivas's Deputy, had been killed near the Machairas Monastery, but with little chance of encountering the enemy. EOKA had moved elsewhere. The monastery was already becoming a place of pilgrimage by patriotic Greek Cypriots. It was a time of temporary truce and we lived in a world of our own, still confident of success. The intelligence chiefs assured us that that victory was within our grasp and that if only the top nine EOKA leaders could be eliminated the campaign would be over within weeks. Afxentiou was the only one who was. We thought mistakenly that we were in every sense on top of it all.

Such EOKA characters as there may be have withdrawn from the battlefield on learning (a) that the truce was still on and (b) that the Suffolks were there to bump them off if they thought otherwise.

It was a corporal's war. No doubt our estimable officers played their part, but patrols were usually conducted by sections of six to eight men led by a corporal or lance corporal, sometimes even by me. It was also a private soldier's war and even a batman's. The scrap-book which I kept records the following. 'On 25 May 1958 Private Cornish, batman to Second Lieutenant Catchpole of B Company, found concealed behind the shutters of a mineshaft at Mitsero Mine a parcel wrapped in newspaper. This led to the discovery of a cache of sticks of dynamite, most of it still wrapped up in bundles, and a lot of safety fuses. It had been known for a long time that Mitsero was a source of explosives for EOKA. Until this occasion the security of the site was left to a UK police sergeant.' This was the incident that led to the CO's mad-cap drive up the mountain the next day with me as his escort to thank B Company and the batman and to shout abuse at the 'Wogs' who got in his way.

From time to time we even did duty as firemen. The fires that we dealt with were not accidental. Turkish rioters regularly stormed across the Mason-Dixon line and set fire to Greek property. *The Times of Cyprus* reported on 11 July 1958 'An officer with a dozen men, equipped with gas masks, left the first fire as fire engines arrived and ran towards another nearby, climbing walls and roofs to get to it.' I was one of those dozen men – and was considerably excited by it.

> At one in the morning the Turks called an abrupt end to our slumbers by setting fire to a Greek-owned cigarette factory in the city. The cigarettes must have been highly inflammable, for the flames were easily visible from our camp, which is a good two miles away. There must have been one soldier in the city that night for every Cypriot.

A newspaper picture captioned 'Suffolks Turn Firemen' showed a soldier of the 'Royal Suffolk Regiment' throwing a bucket of water on one of the fires. This was a common mistake. Not that we didn't fight the fires, but we were never royal. The Norfolks were, but we were not. It had to do with some unfortunate incident in the regimental past. Instead we prided ourselves on being multi-skilled. We could turn our hands to anything. The report quoted an officer of the Nicosia Fire Brigade: 'The Suffolks did an excellent job'. I wrote:

> On Tuesday there was a most picturesque and spectacular fire started probably by arson in a shop along the dividing line between Turkish and Greek Quarters. I happened to be on patrol at the time. We rushed out and – lo and behold – there were magnificent flames leaping skyward from the shop.

I would like to think I helped extinguish them, but by my own account on this occasion the fire brigade arrived promptly and I seem to have been no more than a spectator. We were more at home with riots than with fires. A typical photograph in the local press in that high summer of 1958 shows a platoon in riot gear – helmets, shields and batons – pursuing demonstrators down the street. 'Troops go into action again: further baton charges took place in Nicosia yesterday morning when Turkish Cypriots demonstrated. The picture shows troops clearing a street east of Kyrenia Gate.' The troops were ours and the baton charging occurred almost daily within the Old City. Our relationship with the Turks was variable. Depending on the prevailing political weather, which blew hot and cold, sometimes we baton charged them and sometimes we fraternised with them. I noted that on some days the Turks waged war in the morning, cooled off in the afternoon, and offered us coffee and cakes in the evening. The Turks by this time were demanding partition rather than power-sharing. By a creeping process of empowerment they were acquiring the right of veto over the final settlement. Grivas professed to have fraternal feelings for the Turks. He wrote in his diaries 'I shall continue to avoid antagonising the Turkish Cypriot community'. It was too late.

> There seems to be plenty of Anglo-Turkish solidarity about these days. I had evidence of it when I turned out for the Battalion 2nd XI hockey team (great honour) to play a side from a local school. At least I think they were Turks, but after all these months I am still unable to distinguish Greeks from Turks: a habit caught from the Army, which classifies all foreigners as 'Wogs'.

I gave the Turks high marks for the ingenuity of their demonstrations. Early on, they too adopted the tactic of deploying their women against us. We were equipped not only with tear gas but with dye spray.

> The Turks have a flair for the spectacular that the Greeks haven't ... They have been in the procession and demonstration business such a long time they can put on a very spontaneous show.
> Dashing out on to the balcony of the police station, I saw some 300 frenzied females approaching up the street. They put on a most interesting demonstration/riot, tearing about in all directions. Screaming and yelling 'Taksim' (partition) in a most unladylike manner. The Army rose to the occasion well. It carried out one or two small baton charges – the normal method prescribed for male riots – but dispersed the women in the most effective way by spraying them

with orange dye. The street was clear in next to no time, which shows how clothes-conscious the Turks are.

Nicosia when we entered it was a most entertaining sight: curfew breakers, press photographers, and squads of efficient-looking police mingling around among Monday's debris: a burned out garage, an occasional police Land Rover in not very serviceable condition, and the streets thick with stones, bottles and any old iron; very interesting. Anyway, having arrived, I installed myself among swarms of noisy officers in the Operations Room, and there remained throughout the day. Whereas everyone else was quelling riots and storm-trooping above the streets, I was merely making marks on maps or running errands for irascible colonels.

There was not even an attempt to understand the enemy's thinking or wage any kind of an effective public information campaign. Instead it was a batons and bayonets and bullets campaign, all force and no finesse. Although I saw it as inefficient, I even defended the brutality of it.

Last week, when it fell to us to keep the peace in the suburbs of Nicosia, we requisitioned a club. The inhabitants of this club, on hearing the sad news of their expulsion, immediately smashed the place up, at which the Army, not to be outdone, gave them back their ruined clubhouse and took over a private house instead, which provided the most comfortable accommodation, all mod cons etc. Brutal, but necessary.

With similar severity the security forces took to blowing up cars in which weapons were found and buildings which might have had 'terrorist' connections. I seem to have had no qualms about this either.

One unfortunate Turk was found with a bomb in his car. On occasions such as this the police always decide that the bomb is far too dangerous to be moved and must therefore be blown up in situ. And thus Cyprus becomes one Bentley car the less. This practice has been employed to some effect on a number of Greek buildings where explosives have been found: there was one particular grand cinema which disappeared similarly, to the consternation of its owner – altogether a most ingenious way of staging reprisals without having committees of human rights on one's tail.

I wonder in retrospect whether I really meant that, and can only conclude that I must have done. I was a very small cog in the machine and never questioned its workings as much as I should have done. I knew little of human rights and nothing of the laws of armed conflict set out in the Geneva Conventions. Also, the Greeks retaliated.

Earlier in the week I did a bit of time at the police station, which was in a state of slight panic, because the Greeks were going about Nicosia burning English cars at a great rate and no one could stop them.

Then there was the night when I could have been a national hero but wasn't. I was one of the many in the Army who tried and failed to capture the EOKA leader, Colonel Grivas. A reward of £10,000 was offered for information leading to his arrest. Special Branch had a tip-off that a most wanted man was at a certain address in Nicosia. They needed some firepower in the event of a shoot-out, and I was one of the soldiers closest to hand. As usual Grivas was elsewhere and it was another of many false trails.

On Saturday the tedium was relieved by a most amusing and melodramatic character from Special Branch, who took us on a late night wild goose chase after an EOKA man was rumoured to be hiding in a house in the suburbs. Naturally enough he wasn't, but one felt most Special Branch-ish oneself during the search of the house and it was very interesting seeing how these people go about their business. I thought such activities were confined to Hollywood, but was obviously wrong.

I had never before heard a shot fired in anger, though I have heard many since. They are not at all as they are in the movies but sometimes barely audible, like the patter of rain on a windscreen. If you have heard them you have survived them. My baptism of fire came, unusually, not during one of our security operations but in the course of a humanitarian mission to ease the hardships of a village under curfew.

> I was put in charge of an escort party accompanying a bus from the curfewed area to carry supplies to and from Nicosia. We were just passing over the moat into the walled city, when shots were fired from the other end of the street. The firer had masses of time to escape in the general confusion, so he got away. By the time I had disentangled myself from the vegetables the entire crowd were flat on their bellies and quaking with fear. One poor old boy (a Greek) was hit, but not badly, so we bandaged him up and saw him off to the hospital, before climbing aboard our vegetables again and making off, quite pleased that something had happened.

By January 1958, a time of great inter-communal tension, I appeared to be enjoying the excitement of life at the sharp end to a quite dismaying degree. Other conscripts did the same. We had never known anything like it.

> I went in with the whole Battalion yesterday (Tuesday) when the Suffolks were about the only regiment coping with the riots – it is incredible how undermanned the place is, even with 30,000 troops on the island.

Actually it was 35,000. After all the reinforcements had arrived I calculated in one of my letters home that the ratio of soldiers to Cypriots on the island was one to sixteen. We had the strength of numbers behind us, and should have been able to do more with it than we did.

At the height of the disturbances the Battalion was on immediate standby for the riots one day in four, and in lower states of readiness, between two and four hours, on the other three. In both January and June 1958 we were on duty in the Old City and ordered to deal with massive demonstrations by Turkish Cypriots. The Battalion Diary recorded on 7 June, 'Riots in Nicosia. All companies called back from guards and patrols'. Sometimes it went beyond baton charging. On this occasion shots were fired and two of the Turks were killed.

The trouble was that for the first time in many months the riots got out of hand ... All the unwritten rules of riot drills appear to have been broken – not altogether surprising when cars start bursting through road blocks or when a platoon about 20 strong finds itself set upon by a mob of several hundred very fearless Turks, but nonetheless regrettable.

11 Platoon of D Company was cornered and outnumbered by rioters in the Turkish Quarter of the Old City. Turkish missiles were splintering British shields. The usual warnings were given and ignored. Then the Company Commander took a rifle from the soldier beside him, knelt down and killed one of the Turks with a single shot. He did it himself so that he, not the rifleman, should face the consequences. The Red Card that set out the soldiers' rules of engagement required them to assess what degree of force was required and to apply the minimum. 'If having done this carefully and honestly you decide that there is no alternative to opening fire, and then you do so, you will be doing your duty and acting lawfully.'

The two fatal incidents for which the Suffolks were at least partly responsible had to be relived endlessly the next day, as *The Times of Cyprus* demanded an eye for an eye and a tooth for a tooth, and the powers-that-be attempted to decide (a) whether we were blameworthy and (b) if we were blameworthy, how the blame should be apportioned ... I imagine that the doings of the past week will have more than ever strengthened the Governor's conviction that the troops are no earthly use to him. I suspect he is very keen to be rid of his trigger-happy soldiers.

Just for once I was right, but understated the depth of his disaffection. We now know, from the archives, that he felt that some of his soldiers (although not ours) were out of control and that the breakdown of discipline was not occasional but widespread. It was at this point that the mainly Turkish police force threatened to strike and the Battalion's two Turkish interpreters, Sami and Mustafa, prudently went AWOL for a while.

The recent troubles have so put up the backs of the Turks – latest slogan: 'we no longer want partition, we want the whole of the island' – that no solution other than the interim one of armed repression seems possible.

It may be that in 20 months of active service my clouds of prejudice were beginning to disperse. The 'Wogs' in my letters home were by now at least in inverted commas. I admired the Governor, a humane and decent man with the right instincts; but his motto of 'firmness with courtesy' fell on deaf ears. In the decision-making process in Government House he was surrounded by hard-liners. Some of the senior army officers seemed keener on the firmness than the courtesy. I stopped making excuses for the methods being used and recognised armed repression when I saw it. That is what we were engaged in, *armed repression* – and all we were engaged in. It dawned on me for the first time in my life – and I have become convinced of it since – that the application of armed force is always problematical and usually futile. Firepower intimidates, but it does not win people over or change their minds. I had the evidence of my eyes before me: it was tried and it did not work. It was an assault upon the people.

The Army came close to admitting this at the time. In 1958 its Internal Security Training Centre declared that cordon and search operations were normally mounted only under one or other of the following circumstances: (a) When there was insufficient information to enable a snatch party or search patrol to carry out the task, (b) where the village was located in an area where it was impossible to get the snatch party in without giving early warning to the target, or (c) as a punitive measure where information indicated a village was giving active support to terrorist operations.

Colonel Grivas wrote in his memoirs 'The weapon used by the British was force. But it was found that the harsher the measures used by the British, the more the population became estranged from them and inclined to our side.' He described the British as 'elephants chasing monkeys'. It was even reported by the Cyprus Prison Service that the hangmen's scaffold, which had been busy in Governor Harding's time, was in need of refurbishment.

Sir Hugh Foot signed no death warrants. He preferred persuasion to force. Among those he sought to persuade were his own soldiers. When he spoke to the Battalion on 1 August 1958 and we were standing at ease in

Corporal Martin Bell, 1959.

The author's letters from Cyprus and the chocolate box in which they were kept.

Regimental Scrapbook.

The author in the regimental archives.

Lieutenant Colonel Arthur
Campbell MC.

1st Battalion marching into Kykko Camp, Nicosia,
May 1957.

Soldiers of D
Company searching
a bus watched by the
Commander-in-Chief
Middle East Land
Forces.

Turkish Cypriot demonstration in Nicosia, July 1958.

Governor Sir Hugh Foot inspects the Battalion, August 1958.

Governor Sir John Harding with the Intelligence Section, 1957.

'The General laughs with RSM Gingell and CSM Evans.'

The Keep, all that remains of Gibraltar Barracks, Bury St Edmunds.

Regimental skiffle group.

The Commanding Officer, Lieutenant Colonel Silvanus 'Bertie' Bevan (left).

Band and Drums beating retreat, March 1959.

Governor Harding and soldiers of the Regiment in riot gear, 1957.

Soldiers of the Regiment escorting demonstrators in Nicosia, October 1958.

Drumhead service.

Soldiers of C Company searched by their own officers outside Kykko Monastery in the presence of a monk, September 1958.

TROOPS GO INTO ACTION AGAIN

Further baton charges took place in Nicosia yesterday morning when Turkish Cypriots picture above shows troops clearing a street east of Kyrenia gate.

SOLDIER TURNS FIRE FIGHTER

A man of the Royal Suffolk Regiment fights an arson outbreak in Nicosia yesterday. It was one of many such fires.

SUFFOLK TURN FIREMEN

Soldiers of the Suffolk Regiment fighting the fire which broke out in the Greek owned vulcanising works in the Turkish Sector of Nicosia yesterday morning.

Suffolks or parade

This picture was taken on Minden Day, the 199th Anniversary of the Battle of Minden. It shows the 1st Battalion of the Suffolk Regiment on parade.

Newspaper cuttings from the time of the Cyprus Emergency.

front of him in open order with rifles in hand, his message was sombre. 'The odds against us are great, but we must succeed here if we are to save the people of Cyprus from ruin and devastation.' When diplomacy failed, as it usually did, he spent more time with the soldiers. His standard message, which he encapsulated in a cable to the Colonial Office, was this: 'The cause on which we are engaged is no less than the cause of saving Cyprus. It is a cause that we can be proud of … There is no more exacting task than yours. You have to defeat terrorism which lurks around any corner at any moment. At the same time, by fairness and good sense and good humour, you have to win the trust and confidence of the ordinary people. I know that no troops in the world could do that better than you can – and I know that you will succeed.' [Colonial Office Archive 141/4451]

As a footnote to all this, or actually a Foot note, we are indebted to his son, the campaigning journalist Paul Foot, who died in 2004. As a son of the establishment he spent his life in a long campaign against it. We were almost contemporaries on the island in 1958. I was a corporal and he was the Governor's son on vacation from Oxford University. When he was 21, before he 'turned' – and maybe it was the Cyprus experience that turned him – he was staying with his parents in Government House on the day when Sir Hugh commuted a death sentence on two prisoners in the central jail. They then visited the jail. Paul Foot was deeply affected by it. He wrote: 'The prison was cold and noisy. Our dinner jackets compared grotesquely with the gloomy passages. The political prisoners howled their mournful chant to an apparently unheeding heaven … A few whispered instructions and I was standing outside the main office with a fat, English warder.

"Are they going to stop the execution?" He asked naively, as though we had come down in the middle of the night to wish them all a Merry Christmas.

"I don't know." (I did in fact, but in Cyprus everything is a secret.)

"Those are the politicals," he said. "The ladies join them when they get tired." And sure enough from the other side there came a thin wailing sound that first joined, then dominated the grim chorus.

"Most of them are operatic sopranos out of a job."

The rest remains in isolated pictures: a sudden light, the two hangmen standing straight and blue, their work for the evening cancelled; a hysterical priest; the two recently condemned killers receiving the news with a quiet

doubtful smile, cool and handsome in their simple clothes; the grateful authorities; the inevitable soldiers saluting; a final devastating roar from the "politicals" (news travels fast, apparently, in a prison). In the silence of the bullet-proof Humber, it occurred to me that a murderer can be patriotic.'
[*Oxford Opinion*, 31 January 1959]

Chapter 12

Routines

The Battalion's base was no holiday camp. The red dust continued to swirl around it until the autumn, when it turned to mud. The tents billowed and strained at their guy ropes. The washing facilities, known as ablutions, were primitive and not much more than stand-pipes over pig troughs. We shaved in cracked mirrors. Flies swarmed around the deep latrines. When the latrines became too much of a health hazard they were concreted over and new ones dug in their place. The roof of my tent leaked so much that I had to be careful where I left my kit. We learned to respect the seasons of Cyprus, because everything changed with the rains. I wrote:

> Any day now the first shower should be descending on us and we shall be longing again for the dry days of summer, when the water doesn't seep through the tent roof and fall in insolent pools on top of one's locker, and one's boots don't have to be dug out from the mire that clings on to them, and one's 'garden' doesn't have to be dug every day to make it look tidy, but only swept with a soft broom – or 'brooms/ sweeping' as the Army calls them. But that is half the fun of life here. There's always something to have a good moan about.

My wish list for Christmas 1958 included a leak-proof tent, self-polishing boots and a miraculously early demob. Then there were questions in Parliament about 'our boys in Cyprus' and everything changed, except for the boots and the demob. It was just after Black October. The streets had never been more violent nor the casualties higher. The Prime Minister Harold Macmillan promised flak jackets and better living conditions for British troops, and the details were announced by the Minister of State for the Colonial Office, a certain John Profumo MP, who led a committee to upgrade our kit. It was the high point of his colourful career. Suitably for the Macmillan era, we had never had it so good.

> Our tents have been re-roofed, we now have two lights not one, an arm-chair, an oil stove and lampshades! I planted nine chrysanthemums outside the tent (clumsy-hoofed tent-mates trample all over them), but when it was inspected I had to hide the coconut matting which was for officers only and not other ranks.

Since we were within two weeks of departure and six of freedom, it was late in the day for tented luxuries, but we appreciated them nonetheless. In my penultimate letter I wrote:

> Normally my weekend is taken up with loafing about, sunbathing or reading, or various permutations of the three. But this time my new arm-chair (we have just been given arm-chairs, rather at the 59th minute of the 11th hour) has not been sat in at all.

Our cup was running over even as our time was running out. Just as the accommodation was being upgraded, the hard-working and excellent cooks of the Army Catering Corps started offering us, for the first time ever, a *choice* of dishes in the cookhouse. This is standard in the new Army, but was revolutionary in the old one. It was another pioneering experience: I was there at the beginning of gourmet soldiering, especially when for once I was dressed in 'civvies' with jacket and tie.

> When I walked into the cookhouse in my new outfit last Saturday one of the cooks actually called me 'Sir' … most gratifying.

The Army Catering Corps, like The Suffolk Regiment itself, has passed into history. Mealtimes were announced by a bugle call. The food itself was mostly out of tins, and I warned those on the home front that when my soldiering was over they would have in their midst a barbarian who was capable of eating a meal of beetroot, kippers and gravy out of a single mess tin. The gravy was poured in first. Sometimes there was fresh fruit, especially grapes, but an occasional scarcity of oranges in an island of orange groves. That was because the orange storage sheds at Ayios Loukas near Famagusta were being used as an internment camp. The Duty Officer would regularly tour the cookhouse in Kykko Camp, as regulations required, to ask if there were any complaints. I never heard any – I mean, what was the point and where would one even *begin*? Instructions to the officers included the following: 'Facetious complaints should not be entertained and the offender should have disciplinary action taken against him.' The officers of course lived and ate separately. On operations my staple diet was army dog-biscuits and processed cheese out of Compo rations, which were delicious. And if our road blocks were close enough to the camp, the cooks would bring us beef stew in heated tureens. We carried no more important pieces of kit in our backpacks than the interlocking KFS (knife, fork and spoon) and the two all-purpose mess tins that folded into each other.

In fair weather and foul, and from start to finish, we held drill parades. It seemed to us that, although we were not as obsessively polished as the Guards, we held more drill parades than any other soldiers on the island. We needed no loudspeaker system. The RSM's voice was more piercing than a bugle call and resounded all over the camp. We also cleaned fire buckets, polished brasses, painted bed boxes and swept the so-called garden outside our tent.

Fortunately we can't paint the grass green for the very good reason that there isn't any.

The painting and polishing reached a climax during the run-up to the Battalion's annual inspection by the Brigadier, who like the CO had once served on the North West Frontier. So had Governor Harding, come to that. It seemed that as the colonial landscape shifted the Raj had been transplanted to the dustbowl between the Troodos and Kyrenia Mountains. Imperial history was all around us and a lot of parades went with it, attended by the whole Battalion and swarms of flies.

If H-bombs were falling all around us, I reckon the Suffolks would still have their drill parades.

I noted that the parades and rehearsals were the cause of 'much resentment in radical circles' – but the 'radical circles', to which I secretly belonged, were *sotto voce* and the discontent was not expressed in such a way as to reach the ears of the RSM. It was unwise for any soldier, especially a college boy, to be seen as a potential troublemaker. The RSM, who was not to be trifled with, came equipped with his own radar. He knew what we were thinking.

> Last week in particular seems to have been packed with haltings and marchings and salutings. We had drill parades on Monday, Wednesday, Thursday, Friday and Saturday with more to come next Monday and Tuesday ... There is no more to do now but wait and see what the Brigadier thinks of us on Thursday.

But it was not the marching but the inspection which gave rise to what I saw, being one of those inspected, as a military horror story. We were better at soldiering than store-keeping. Or it may be that, like many in the lower ranks, I was irrationally prejudiced against officers and senior NCOs.

> This inevitably causes chaos. When the Brigadier and his team of investigators, probers and purgers come along once a year they exert a considerable disruptive influence. A sergeant in charge of a store will move heaven and earth to prevent these experts from finding out that he is short of a 'pullover/woollen/heavy' or a 'mousetrap/wooden'. Everyone has a kit check. My office has to be spring-cleaned. Just as well, as I found a lizard in it, and I'm sure the Brigadier takes a dim view of lizards in intelligence offices: they might pry into the secret documents.
>
> This is the fatal time when the failings of the regular Army are exposed, and all sorts of officers and sergeants move with the desperation of caged tigers to pass the buck for their own inefficiency on to someone else.

Positions and promotions depended on passing the inspection. If significant amounts of kit went missing there would be an officer-led Board of Inquiry, like a court-martial in search of a culprit. No less alarming was a visit by the island's senior soldier, the General Officer Commanding (GOC), of whom I took a decidedly mutinous view. Actually he had every business to visit us. Because of the campaign's prominence, he was the highest-profile general not only on the island but in the Army. His battalions were of uneven quality – some were more suitable for riot duty than others, and one was notoriously difficult to control – and he was responsible for the success of our operations, which were attracting increasing attention from the outside world. He was also answerable for any acts of indiscipline that might occur. The Cyprus press was censored but the British press was not. Too many questions in Parliament and he would be out of a job. Nonetheless I did not enjoy having to smarten up for the GOC's parade.

> It seems unimaginable that with so many things to do out here we should go on spending our time straightening out the camp for the visit of the GOC. GOCs are a curse and ought to be abolished.

There was a long history in both the Army and the Regiment of obsessive attention to detail and appearance. Early in 1957 the Battalion had been visited by the previous Governor, Field Marshal Sir John Harding, in its base at Xeros before moving to Nicosia. He was a stickler for good order and military discipline, having once been Chief of the Imperial General Staff. The *Regimental Gazette* reported 'After going round the various departments he came to the Mess to have a few words with the members and congratulated those concerned on mopping up the remaining terrorists in our area'. He still thought he was winning. A regimental photograph showed him talking to men of the Intelligence Section before I joined it. The obligatory Int Sec map was pinned to the wall behind them. They looked somewhat ill-turned out even by my standards. In fact they were a total shambles. The caption explained why: 'The unpressed KD [khaki drill] was due to the failure of laundry arrangements at Xeros.' Just imagine the loss of face by the RSM!

There were no such failures on Minden Day, when we held the grandest parade of all to remember our victory over the French on 1 August 1759. It was a battle widely celebrated in the Army as having shown the fighting qualities of the British infantry in prevailing against the odds as well as the French: for the first time in European warfare, one line of infantry broke through three lines of cavalry. To be truthful, it wasn't actually our victory alone. There were five other British regiments of the line alongside us, including The Lancashire Fusiliers and The Royal Welch Fusiliers (also with us in Cyprus), as well as assorted Prussians and Hanoverians. But as far as we were concerned we had won it single-handedly. I wrote home:

> The finer points of military history carry very little weight with the Army.

Minden Day was the RSM's field day – literally a field day, because the parade ground doubled as the football pitch. It was his field of dreams. He had us rehearsing for this parade for *six months* before it happened. We were an impressive mass of khaki on the march with red and yellow embellishments. We wore khaki drill, with the Minden flashes on our sleeves and the Minden roses, red and yellow, behind our cap badges. The officers carried their swords. The old soldiers put up their medals. The parade took place on the sun-baked red earth in 101-degree heat and was attended by the Governor Sir Hugh Foot, who had serious doubts about his generals' emphasis on batons, bullets and bayonets. But he liked the Suffolks; and during the long hot summer of 1958, when the streets were seething with rioters, he appeared to acquiesce in the harder line at least for a while. We now know that he had no choice in the matter. It was just after Operation Matchbox, which he had opposed, and he probably had better things to be doing with his time than taking the salute as the whole Battalion marched past in columns of three to the tune of *Speed the Plough*. He addressed us also on the Forces Broadcasting Service: 'The cause on which we are engaged is no less than the cause of saving Cyprus. It is a cause that we can be proud of. It is a cause in which we must not fail ... Today we must resolve together to see it through to the end.'

Regimental rivalries were something else.

There had obviously been some very subtle dealings behind the scenes, since the Lancashire Fusiliers – another of the Nicosia battalions – also celebrated Minden Day, and we had managed to stage a brilliant military coup, whereby we had nabbed the Governor plus the General

Officer Commanding Middle East Land Forces to take our parade, and fobbed them off with the paltry Major General who commands the Army in Cyprus. Great victory!

So the Governor duly turned up, resplendent in his white uniform and ludicrous white policeman's hat with ostrich feathers on top, and we went through the motions of a ceremonial parade – quite well, too; as it should have been, after six months' practice. Then the Great Man gave us the expected address on the qualities of courage, service etcetera needed in Cyprus today, and we gave him three cheers in return (a very complicated drill movement, involving intricate manoeuvres in the removing and replacing of head-dress). After the parade, one or two 'bodies' were presented to him, including my friend Vic Jack from Rendham, the son of a prosperous farmer. On being told that he was going back soon to his pig-farming, Sir Hugh said he was VERY envious; as no doubt he was.

I'm not sure why I called them 'bodies' but we were after all just numbers in a roll call, and often selected at random. When one parade was over, another followed. The next one was for the five-day visit of the Colonel of the Regiment, who was actually a brigadier.

Naturally, all the Regiment's time is taken up in the terrific business of deceiving the Brigadier into thinking that it is faring wonderfully. To this end, two drill parades are held daily; stones are painted white in the classic army manner; and we have suddenly found that our living conditions have improved a hundred fold.

Because of this I was grateful for the impress-the-Brigadier campaign, especially because I avoided the parades by signing up for an aerial photography course in distant Episkopi, just in case I might be mobilised for a European war. From call-up to demob, the Army persisted in trying to turn us into all-purpose soldiers.

Chapter 13

Promotion

There were other duties too which came with rank. After a year in Cyprus I was promoted to the rank of substantive corporal, which meant that I couldn't be 'busted' without being found guilty of a serious offence by the CO or a court-martial. A small but significant pay rise went with it – from £2 a week to £3 – but more guard duties. The Army did not do financial incentives. I was made Secretary of the Corporals' Mess Committee and, because I was rumoured to be numerate, did the accounts. When it was my turn to be Orderly Corporal I had to advise the Regimental Police when it was time to throw out the drunks. It also fell to me to organise the Christmas party, for which £60 was contributed from regimental funds. It did not help that, with so many thirsty soldiers on the island, Cyprus was suffering from a beer shortage. We solved the problem by importing beer of indifferent quality from Malta. I was able to avoid the party itself by being on duty in the Central Police Station.

> By being in town I can escape the jolly bottle party which it is my unhappy lot to organise in the middle of the month. I have spent the normal unremarkable sort of week, devoting my time largely to computing the prices at which beer can be sold to the best advantage in the Corporals' Mess.

To become a substantive corporal I had to send home for my 'O'-level certificate; the Army wished its NCOs to be educated. Having never expected to be promoted, I was actually quite pleased to get the extra stripe ('two stripes look much more decorative than one'), although the record of corporals is mixed. A study of German history tells you that we can be a dangerous lot. I was 'made up' in November 1958, by which time I was seriously counting the days to do.

I have so far passed through the Valley of the Shadow without so much as being charged for having dirty brasses so reckon I should be able to keep out of harm's way for another seven months and one week.

Although the camp was bristling with armaments, it was for us the safest place on the island. We carried no valuables, since we had none. Occasionally a scrubbed piece of webbing might go missing from outside a tent, but there was no crime to speak of. The only exception was of course in the Officers' Mess, which was a law unto itself, and where one night a silver candlestick mysteriously disappeared. Despite the best efforts of the Regimental Police, it was never found. Even on active service, regiments still travelled with their silverware for the Mess Nights. It was unthinkable not to. As regiments amalgamated one of the problems they faced was what to do with their superfluous silverware.

The Battalion's ration strength, the names and numbers of the soldiers serving in it, was constantly in flux, as new drafts arrived and old ones departed. It was all held together by the senior NCOs, who in our time as in Kipling's were the beating heart of the Army. The Signal Platoon was typical. Its report red as follows: 'Many eminent and notorious signallers have left us, in fact the only "old" signallers left are Babe Hart and Rockey Lane, who after 18 months devoted service as Lance Corporal has at last been given his second [stripe]. Among those who have joined us is Stan Large, ex-Malaya, Hong Kong, and Korea. His signalling experience far exceeds that of anyone else in the Pl [platoon] with the possible exception of our beloved Staff Sgt.'

The soldier's loyalty was to the Regiment – and beyond and above that (in ascending order of importance) to his company, his platoon and most of all to his mates. This was what held us together. The worst offence among the rank and file was known as 'jacking', which meant looking after oneself and not one's mates.

It was still the world of *The Long and the Short and the Tall*. Private Clarke was Nobby, Private White was Chalky and Private Miller was Dusty. Private Short was Lofty. Sergeant Plaice was Kipper. I became Dinger. It was of course an all-male environment. We were issued with a something called a housewife, which turned out to be a small cloth pouch containing two needles, 50 yards of khaki thread and two cards of wool for darning socks. (It can now be found only in the Imperial War Museum.) I used a column in the regimental magazine to wonder subversively why the Orderly Room should have on its walls thirty-seven posters of military diagrams and staff instructions, but only one of Brigitte Bardot. It seemed an imbalance. Then in November 1958, on the order of the colonial Government, the Battalion had to dismiss its Greek Cypriot NAAFI staff. This was done, it was said, on security grounds. It was also intended as a political threat of some sort to the Greeks during the complex pre-Independence negotiations.

> The prophets predicted great catastrophe, neither beer nor cigarettes for weeks and weeks. But much to everyone's surprise the NAAFI was taken over by an efficient regimental staff. One of the officers' wives came and made such delicious cakes for sale to the troops that I became quite a regular customer ... Some time, I suppose, we shall be obtaining some samples of the new and much-vaunted NAAFI girls. The average soldier will have to tone down his language considerably. But neither girls nor rumours of girls have appeared yet.

There were two military hierarchies. One was the hierarchy of rank, from lieutenant colonel down to private soldier. The other was the hierarchy of service, from the chickos to the line-shooters. The chickos were the new draftees and the line-shooters were the veterans – even national servicemen could become line-shooters – who had done their time and got their knees brown. It was not necessary to be promoted, but just to 'serve on', to be a line-shooter.

Shooting discipline was variable, depending on where we were. Even on patrol, although our magazines were fully charged, we were not to load our rifles unless ordered to do so by the patrol commander. The same rule applied to sentries and guard commanders. I was shocked one day in a three-ton truck on the way to a cordon and search in the foothills of Troodos, when a soldier opened fire on a wild dog and killed it. Wild dogs were part of the landscape in Cyprus, and I noted that they were of a 'noisy and hostile disposition'. No disciplinary action was taken. Yet within the camp an accidental discharge automatically earned a spell of jankers or a period of more prolonged hardship in the Military Corrective Training Centre (MCTC), the Army's own prison. Officers of course did not do jankers, still less the MCTC. The worst that could happen to them (short of a court-martial) was a dressing-down by the Commanding Officer or extra duties. If a subaltern, like Lieutenant Alfred Waller, was Duty Officer for two days in a row, we knew he had fallen from favour. I visited the MCTC just once, as escort to a soldier who had served his sentence. It was the grimmest place on the island, and the very thought of it kept me obedient to the letter of Queen's Regulations: better a month of riots and drill parades than a day in the Army's prison.

From time to time we had a sort of theatrical show in the band hut and cinema, provided by Combined Services Entertainment (CSE). It was still the age of the music hall, and the singers and dancers did the rounds of the battalions. We had crooners, *chanteuses*, magicians, impressionists, comedians – one with what he accurately billed as 'A Cavalcade of Junk' – and even one day, at the top of the bill, the versatile and truly wonderful Peter Ustinov, already famous as Nero in the Hollywood epic *Quo Vadis*. He did not need to entertain us but chose to do so because he had once been one of us. He was neither a singer nor a dancer but a great raconteur, with a repertoire of wonderful sly jokes based on his own experiences as a soldier. (It was as common then to have been a soldier as it is uncommon now to be one.) His RSM used to call him *Utinov*. After his basic training he had served in the Army Film Unit in the Second World War, and had played the part of batman to Lieutenant Colonel David Niven. (Ustinov was never actually a batman but Niven was a real lieutenant colonel, having originally signed on as a regular in 1930.) I met Peter Ustinov again half a century later at a UNICEF dinner, when he was the guest of honour, in a wheelchair and hardly able to stand up for the Loyal Toast. I told him that there was at least one young soldier present in those days who had truly loved his act.

No one ever watched the clock or the calendar more than we did. Days to do became an obsession. So did length of service. We all knew who in the Battalion had spent more time on the island and who had spent less. True seniority was based not on rank but on the passage of time. Every few weeks, as the drafts came and went, the terms of trade changed in our favour. In the khaki-drill season, when the new recruits arrived, we pointed out to them how white their knees were. The slogan of the old soldiers was 'Get some in' (meaning some time) or 'Get your knees brown'. I was well on the way to becoming a line-shooter myself.

> We are due to receive our last batch of recruits before we go home. These drafts have been arriving at intervals of six weeks or so ever since I became one of them myself, and others have left for demobs at an equal rate, until I find myself now as a proud member of the second oldest National Service draft in the Battalion. That is to say, it only remains for the intake which preceded mine at the depot to go home, for me to be packing my own kitbags. Not much more than 100 days in the Army. Cheers!

The Army had a vocabulary all of its own. An easy duty was 'peachy'. What was useless was 'bush', what was good was 'pukka' and what was surplus to requirements was 'buckshee'. To be on guard duty was to 'stag on'. Spit and polish was 'bull'. To go on parade was to 'get fell in'. To be early on parade was to 'get fell in previous'. An issue of new equipment was an 'ish'. To be promoted was to be 'made up'. To be demoted was to be 'busted'. A charge of misconduct was a 'fizzer'. A regimental field punishment was 'jankers'. If you were fed up with something, it was 'played out'. Time did not just pass but 'rolled on'. The UK was 'Blighty'. The world beyond military service was 'civvy street' or sometimes 'civilian street'. Expletives of course were not deleted. We swore like the troopers we were. It was expected of us.

And the Army loved its acronyms (as it still does), especially when its command structure changed half-way through the emergency and COSHEG, Chief of Staff to His Excellency the Governor, was replaced by COSDO, Chief of Staff to the Director of Operations. The acronyms proliferated like bindweed. Nothing was encrypted, but only a soldier could have decoded Company Orders: 'I SUFFOLK will be Bde res in Nicosia with Bn HQ and two Coys. B, D Coys will take batons and shields and GAS GRENs'. Bde rear link will move with Bn HQ.'

There were two 'f' words. The other one was fatigue or fatigues, which could mean anything from the exhaustion that we felt at the end of the day, to the clothes that we wore, or to the scrubbing and cleaning that we were ordered to do. The Army of today, with so much of the basics contracted out, is surely more soldier-friendly, although I wonder if that helps to boost morale. Many years after my own service, in an operational brigade headquarters in Bosnia, I saw a notice that said 'It would make the RSM very happy if you got your hair cut!' I can testify from personal experience that RSMs had no interest whatever in making us happy, or we them, in the late 1950s. They saw their role as rather the reverse.

Guard duty, or 'stag', was always unpopular. We did it armed and in pairs on the beaten path inside the coils of perimeter wire, two hours on and four hours off, with a hard bunk in the guard room for the four hours off, where we were kept going by bacon sandwiches and urns of hot sweet tea. Between his drinks in the Officers' Mess, the Duty Officer would graciously drop by from time to time to check up on us. It was of course a most punishable offence to fall asleep on guard duty.

> There are three debatable courses to choose from, to patrol the outside
> of the camp in an anti-clockwise direction, to do likewise in a clockwise
> direction or to stand at the gate and open and close it for people coming
> in and out. I have chosen the latter as there is a gargantuan carouse
> going on in the Sergeants' Mess tonight, and there ought to be some
> amusing scenes as we witness the last revellers tottering homeward.

Heavy drinking was more for the regulars, though a departing draft would celebrate in style. One of them earned the wrath of the RSM by hoisting up the regimental flag-pole something other the regimental flag. Late one night a drunken soldier from one of the rifle companies accidentally threw a brick through the window of the Officers' Mess (he was aiming at the latrines, but missed), then offered the Duty Officer a beer if he would only hush it up. The Duty Officer, Second Lieutenant Mayes, who had taken cover behind a sofa fearing an attack by EOKA, did not oblige.

It was the scarce little luxuries of life that meant more to the conscripts. Kykko Camp boasted few amenities except a library containing 100 paperbacks (mostly thrillers), the barber's tent, the bathhouse and the NAAFI. It was a home from home and the only civilised corner of the camp.

We had nowhere else to retreat to, no private space except the chapel, and took the good things of life where we could find them.

> This, by any standards (and after all you can't judge these things by civilian standards or you'd be miserable) is quite pleasant. It is only a very small portion of a Nissen hut, but in it are housed all sorts of luxuries – before I joined the Army I would have called them necessities – such as gramophone records, books and newspapers.

The NAAFI's sound system was a juke box on which soldiers could play their favourites. It was the dawn of rock and roll. Bill Haley and the Comets were challenging the crooners in the charts. The crooners were still in the ascendant. Top of the Pops was *April Love* by Pat Boone. I wrote home for such luxuries as bulls-eyes, Penguin paperbacks, copies of *Punch* and a proper jumbo-sized calendar on which I could count down the days to do in style. In times of high alert (which I always called 'panic'), the shops in Nicosia were inaccessible to a soldier looking for a birthday present for his twin sister. Sylvia had just become a secretary at the BBC (checking the foreign correspondents' expenses, as it happened), and I told her I was jealous of the 'gay' social life that went with it. 'Gay' had a different meaning in those days.

> The only time when I get within a mile of a Greek shop is when I'm on patrol, and it would look rather bad to stop the patrol to go present shopping.

Chapter 14

From Sports to Char Wallahs

Sports were an obsession, except for cricket. The Battalion actually had a Cricket Officer, Lieutenant N. J. Lewis, and an impressive 1958 fixture list, suitably embossed in red and yellow, from the Cyprus District Signal Regiment on 2 June to the 1st Battalion The Argyll and Sutherland Highlanders on 20 August. But I cannot remember that any of these matches were actually played. That was because in high summer the cricket season coincided with the riot season, in which we needed batons rather than bats and shields rather than pads. So the cricket season was over before it began, which was a pity in view of Lieutenant Colonel Campbell's proven prowess at the crease. The Battalion had a parade ground but no cricket pitch worthy of the name. Its mission was to hit EOKA for six.

The football team, which played at the inter-battalion level, was very strong. It included two professionals, Dave Pygall of Watford and Eddie Gray of Ipswich Town. We were known to our rivals as Swedes (meaning 'swede-bashers'). We didn't mind. We stood on the touch-line chanting 'Come on you Swedes!' I shared a tent with Dave, was regularly beaten at tennis by him in the off-season and noted that he did not seem to have his name down for as many fatigues and guard duties as I did. I should have been a footballer. During a lull in the disturbances he was chosen to captain a Combined Services team which beat the Turks in the Moat (their stadium outside the city wall) before going on to a two-week tour of Malta and then Persia.

The Commanding Officer, however, with his acute awareness of rank, was incensed that a private soldier, however gifted a player and even from his own regiment, should be appointed captain of the football team. (Captains were officers, were they not?) So he ordered his Adjutant, Captain Pat Hopper, to get on the phone to the senior officer at Army HQ who was chairman of the selectors. After the CO had made his case, and been interrupted several times, he ended the conversation with the words 'I am glad you agree with me, sir, that you cannot have a private soldier as the team captain'. Then, having lost the argument, he turned to the Adjutant with a look of resignation: 'Pat, make Private Pygall a lance corporal!'

One day towards the end of our tour of duty, our sergeants (not normally known for their sporting achievements) challenged the sergeants of The Royal Horse Guards to a game of football. In the fine traditions of the Sergeants' Mess, the prize money was payable in beer, at the rate of a gallon a goal. Let it be recorded for posterity that The Suffolk Regiment triumphed over The Royal Horse Guards by three gallons to one.

I followed from afar the fortunes of Norwich City, who were on one of their rare winning streaks. (Those of us from the north east of Suffolk supported Norwich rather than the other place: it was a matter of propinquity.)

> PS. I've just heard the football results and am delighted beyond words. Please could you try to get hold of Monday's EDP [*Eastern Daily Press*] commemorating the great occasion.

Football was exclusively for the other ranks. The hockey team, who looked like harlequins in chequered red and yellow shirts, was led by the Adjutant (a proper captain in both senses) and recruited mainly from the Officers' Mess. And rugby was officer-led. Rugby was the infantry's religion and its trophies were the Holy Grail. Our CO had captained the 2nd Battalion when it won the Army All-India Cup in Bombay in 1938. Our General in 1957, Douglas Kendrew (also known as Joe), had played ten times for England in the 1930s. The surest way for a young infantry officer to be promoted was to dominate scrum and lineout. The cavalry did polo but the infantry did rugby. Even an intelligence clerk was occasionally allowed to make up the numbers at wing forward. The season began in November, when the dust on the plain turned to mud, and ended in the spring with an excruciating seven-a-side tournament between the battalions. We always did well until we met the Welsh, especially The Royal Welch Fusiliers (the regiment of Siegfried Sassoon and Robert Graves); in our time its ranks seemed to be teeming not with poets but with gifted refugees from Cardiff Arms Park. Our first game against them was more like mud polo, after a week of heavy rain. Their score was so high that we actually lost count of it. What I liked about the rugby, even when losing to the Welsh, was that for eighty minutes the officers and other ranks mixed together on terms of equality.

> They [the Royal Welch Fusiliers] are depressing to play against, although superb to watch. We have another game against them on the 12th – this time it is 15 a side and they have promised to turn out a weakened team (i.e. leave out their galaxy of internationals) to give us a chance of stopping the score from running into three figures.

I learned later that the superiority of The Royal Welch Fusiliers was so overwhelming that the Adjutant had offered them a walkover, but this was over-ruled by the Brigadier, perhaps rightly. It would have been the first time since Singapore that the Suffolks had run up the white flag.

The dress codes, like the sports, were seasonal. For half the year we wore the stifling and hideous battledress in which we had trained. 'BD for long periods,' I wrote, 'can be very irksome'. Even the Grenadier Guards, for all their spit and polish, were hard put to look smart in it. It gave our Commanding Officer a remarkable resemblance to Captain Mainwaring in *Dad's Army*. For the warmer half of the year we wore the more popular KD, khaki drill, which was cooler and smarter and easier to press. It came in two versions, with long trousers or short. The short ones, starched like boards, were worn during the day with long khaki socks held up by elastics with flashes on the outside, inevitably in the regimental colours of red and yellow. We even wound on Indian-style puttees to keep out the dust. We wore the short trousers for most parades and the long trousers in the evenings and for riot duty – we wouldn't want to shock the natives, I suppose. It was in shorts like ours that General Percival surrendered Singapore, including the 18th East Anglian Division, to the Japanese in 1942. It was not the right sort of kit for winning wars. I was hardly fashion-conscious at the time, but noted that nothing looked more ludicrous than shorts below the knees. Yet I was lucky to wear the lighter kit for three seasons; and when I changed back into it for the last time in April 1959, I felt that I had finally joined the ranks of the old soldiers. I had also learned the importance of blending in. The secret of wearing army uniform, whether BD or KD, was to do it in such a way as not to catch the eye of the RSM.

In the winter we were saved from trench foot by the marvellous invention of boots/whiskey/whiskey (cold wet weather boots). The only problem with them was that they wore out the regulation grey woollen socks very rapidly; so I sent home for civilian socks, undetectable even by the gimlet eye of the RSM. They were colourful too, and reminded me that beneath the uniform there still lurked a civilian who could hardly wait to get out. They were discreetly hung out to dry inside the tent where the senior NCOs could not see them.

No one volunteered for anything, and dealing with our officious superiors became an art form in itself. For the regimental magazine, which I edited and used as a platform for mildly subversive comments, I composed a handy guide entitled *The Ready Answer, or How to Answer Awkward Questions from Superior Officers*. One of the options was the 'baffle them with science' method: 'Well, sir, one shouldn't oil this particular type of equipment, as it just collects dust which forms into an abrasive paste and results in excessive wear'. Then there was the 'deny all knowledge' alibi: 'I'm afraid I wasn't there when the order was issued, sir, so I haven't seen it'. My favourite, which never failed, was the all-purpose 'army bumf' defence: 'An 1133 was submitted, sir, to the Coy [Company], but no action was taken to complete the 1955 and 1957. The result was a further 983 had to be rendered. The 419 was therefore incorrectly completed, thus making my own 1457 incorrect. My staff have to do a great deal of re-writing 2006s and 1298s'. At this point the investigators' eyes glazed over and they went away to bother someone else.

There were, however, limits to what dodging the column or 'skiving' could achieve. We learned early on that avoiding guard duty by reporting sick was not such a great idea. The Medical Officer Captain Chris Pettit was a delightful man, mainstay of the hockey team and a good doctor, but I avoided him where possible except on the hockey field. His orderlies were not so sympathetic after I contracted pneumonia during cold winter weather in the Central Police Station. The temperature in the police station, which had neither heating nor air-conditioning, ranged from extremely cold in the winter to unbearably hot in the summer. Spring and autumn seemed to pass it by.

I emerged from the sick bay after two days' hibernation, feeling if anything rather seedier than when I went in and firmly resolved never to set foot inside the place again except in a case of extreme emergency. Next time I shall know better than to put my faith in the Army's medical services.

Besides, I had work to get back to. The Intelligence Section by this time was virtually a one-man band. I had forms to fill in and filing to do. There were maps to be marked and pins to be stuck into them. There were profiles of villages to be completed and pictures of EOKA suspects to be pasted on to posters. There were posters to be painted. There were intelligence summaries to be circulated. There were forms for Government of Cyprus work permits to be filled in. There were logs for letters in and letters out and reference numbers for everything. The files expanded to fill the space available. It was made clear to me, while I was sick, that the Intelligence Officer did not enjoy doing his own typing: it was not on the Sandhurst curriculum. Looking out of the window on standby days, I could see the rifle companies with batons and shields waiting to be deployed come rain or come shine, for riots or worse, and blessed my good fortune that I was becalmed in the backwater of Intelligence.

Our lives were made easier and literally sweeter by the services of the char wallahs. These were Indian camp followers, inherited from the days when the Indian Army was led by British officers and included British battalions. I knew them all personally, since one of the odds-and-ends duties of the Intelligence Section was to ensure that they had valid work permits. They were mostly Khans of one sort or another – that is, they had Khan in their names. The char wallahs accompanied us on exercises but not on operations. On Exercise Mountain Goat, held near Dhavlos in the Panhandle of Cyprus in December 1957, the following exchange was reported by D Company.

'Where am I going to sleep, sah?' asked the char wallah.

'You will be sharing the 160 pounder [tent] with the Alsatian tracker dog.'

The char wallah retired mumbling to himself to get out his prayer mat and indent for another. He emerged the next morning.

'All right, Char Wallah?'

'No, sah … last night I only sleep five or ten minutes.'

'Why was that?'

'Oh, that ***** dog, sah. All night long he snore, snore, snore. That ***** dog no like me, sah. Tomorrow I sleep in open.'

The char wallahs lived inside the wire and also offered laundry and sewing services. But their chief business was brewing tea – hot, strong and heavily sugared. The char wallah would carry it around the camp in two urns slung on a bamboo pole over his shoulders, hawking his wares with a cry that sounded like '*char wallah char wallah ka-hai*' (it was known as 'the char wallahs' howl'). At night he would wrap himself in an army blanket and hang an oil lamp on the bamboo pole. The charges were modest, just a few pence for a mugful, and we were as indebted to them as they were loyal to us. When eventually we left for home, they saw us off at the quayside. For all my life I have tried to emulate them and brew tea of their quality. Forget the fancy scented stuff: we drank real soldiers' tea. It was part of our education. The Army of today, less fortunate than the Army I served in, has somehow to get by without them. I have even written a memorial ode in their honour.

> The char wallahs and the dhobi wallahs,
> These were the Regiment's camp followers,
> They did the laundry, made the tea,
> Served private soldiers such as me,
> And they were better men than we.
> But so much change has happened since
> And now a newer India thrives,
> Touching and changing many lives,
> And even multitudes of dollars
> Won't bring us back those long lost wallahs
> Who were our Gunga Dins.

Chapter 15

Excursions

Christmas 1957 was the first I had ever spent away from home. I was 19 and the omens were not good. The week before, I had a falling-out with the RSM – or, more accurately, he had a falling-out with me. He had an unerring eye for the awkward squad and decided that I was a potential source of trouble and therefore needed to be 'gripped'. 'Gripping' is an army term which means singling out a soldier of a lower rank and requiring him to change his behaviour or face the most unpleasant consequences. The RSM had been 'gripping' people over many years from Palestine to Malaya to Cyprus. Even the officers were in awe of him. He was the most gifted 'gripper' the Regiment had ever known.

I cannot remember what his grievance was and certainly did not write home about it. It may have been a technicality, like brasses unpolished, webbing unscrubbed or an officer unsaluted. The officers were lurking all over the place. The Battalion had twenty-five of them and 700 of us, and as there was only one road through the camp, they were difficult to avoid. When passing them in or out of camp, if one was wearing a beret, one saluted; if not, one jerked one's head towards them ('eyes right'!) and they would respond with a nonchalant and casual wave of the hand, a sort of virtual or semi-salute which totally lacked conviction. From 1956 newly-commissioned officers had actually been issued with a booklet called *Customs of the Army*: 'It is an officer's duty to return a salute smartly, with the correct hand and without a cigarette or pipe in the mouth. When returning a salute, an officer should look towards the person whose salute he is returning. An officer must remember to "return" a salute and not merely acknowledge it.' I also knew that the RSM would love to have had me for the peculiarly military offence of insubordination, which was lack of respect for those like himself who were set in authority over me; but he could never quite find the evidence to support his suspicions. In public I was extremely deferential. For whatever reason, I feared being threatened with a charge and even a regimental field punishment. I could have faced the grim ordeal of Commanding Officer's Orders. Those who came before the CO were marched in by the RSM under escort and had their belts taken from them, lest they should use the belt to attack him.

I was saved from the RSM's 'gripping' by the Chaplain the Reverend Tom Metcalfe, who had received a request from one of the established colonial families, the Ballards. He was the chief legal counsel to the Attorney General. She had generously suggested that they and their three children – girls aged two, four and six – who had their family together should invite an ordinary soldier, who did not, to share their Christmas. The Padre volunteered me for the privilege. I had no civilian clothes, so I rushed on the back of a mate's motorbike to a shop in Ledra Street and blew my savings on a pair of grey trousers, a shirt, a pale green tie and an officer-style tweed jacket. It was a time of relative truce in the hostilities (except those between the RSM and myself), when a soldier on the spree was allowed out in civvies and without a weapon. It would not be like that again for most of my time on the island.

I spent Christmas Eve and Christmas Day with my kind adopted family. We went to church on Christmas morning in St Paul's, the Anglican church, among the great and good of the colony including the Governor Sir Hugh Foot. I met the Government's Head of Information and successor to Lawrence Durrell, whose book on Cyprus, *Bitter Lemons*, I revered; but the Ballards, as colonial servants, thought it disloyal. Thanks to my 'civvies', I could look the colonial world in the eye and pretend to be at home in its high society. Both Lady Foot and the Deputy Governor gave young Anna Ballard a benevolent pat on the head and I pretended to be part of the family. I helped the two older girls with their new bicycles. The day ended in typically British fashion with a grand party and a game of charades in the mansion of the Attorney General, Sir James Henry. It was as far from the spirit of Kykko Camp and the strictures of the RSM as I could possibly imagine. I was, and remain to this day, extraordinarily grateful to the Ballards, although I have no idea what became of them. Mrs Ballard wrote to my mother 'We loved having him and he is a great help about the house. He looks very well, Mrs Bell, but doesn't really like army life'. How right she was about that.

She added that when her daughters grew up she hoped they would marry someone like Martin!

My friendship with the Ballards also gave me an insight into the working of the island's legal system under the emergency powers regime. This became critical in August 1958 after a notorious period of inter-communal violence.

> My friend Mr Ballard is now acting as Crown Counsel in the case of nine Turks accused of mass murder in one of the earliest and certainly most notorious incidents of the crisis. He is involved in a heated wrangle with the Defence Counsel over whether the nine Turks can be tried together, or whether each one has to be tried individually. He will certainly have to excel himself to obtain any convictions, since there are no witnesses at all and the Turkish lawyers are extremely clever.

Actually there were eight Turks, accused of the brutal murder of eight Greeks in what became known as the Geunyeli massacre. They were acquitted on the grounds of a lack of evidence, provoking a great outcry among the Greeks who accused the British of being complicit in the killings and the judicial system of being corrupt.

The judges, to their credit, were even-handed and more independent of the Government than the Government wished them to be. An interesting case was that of Nikos Sampson, a *Times of Cyprus* journalist who was also an EOKA assassin: he would kill his victims, then photograph them. He was a calculating and cold-blooded murderer even by the standards of the time. When he was on the scene of the crime once too often, he was arrested by the security forces but acquitted of murder because it could not be proved that his confession was voluntary. (He was President of Cyprus after an ill-advised *coup* for just eight days before the Turks from the mainland invaded and partitioned the island in 1974.) Mr Justice Shaw, the judge who disallowed the confession (and had himself once been wounded by EOKA) said that Mr Sampson had been subjected to 'unconscionable treatment' during his arrest. 'The handling of the accused was something that he had not seen in 47 years of [judicial] experience.' [*Observer*, 24 May 1957] Sampson later boasted of having killed fifteen British soldiers and civilians, including one of his colleagues on the *Times of Cyprus*. The independence of the judiciary was one of the saving graces of the colonial set-up, even at the height of the emergency.

In another case, the murder of a British sergeant, the suspect was freed after the judge ruled that the prosecution had not established that the body was that of the sergeant. The Crown Counsel resigned his well-paid job, as there was no other way of registering his disagreement with the verdict. One of the Governor's advisers wrote 'The legal system is used by clever and unscrupulous lawyers to bring about miscarriages of justice and leave murderers unpunished'. General Sir Kenneth Darling, our General from 1958–9, added 'It is very important that the wheels of justice should turn as quickly as possible, otherwise there is a danger that the security forces will lose faith in the judicial system and attempt to mete out rough justice themselves'. [Colonial Office Archive 926/1077] Which was in some cases exactly what happened; but at the time I was on the side of the prosecution (and of my hosts).

> The law out here is falling into disrepute, and the poor Crown Counsel are having a stiff time of it. Better to be a soldier.

We soldiers, of course, were in the streets, not the courts and often needed a break. Again, the Padre saved me. I used to attend Evensong in the Nissen hut which was the regimental church. I was home-sick and the evening service reminded me of Redisham church in Suffolk. There were few other worshippers. On one occasion I was half the congregation. As a private soldier, I even read the first lesson in the Service of Nine Lessons and Carols. (The CO in all his grandeur read the last one.) When the Army's Chaplain-General visited from the UK, Evensong was cancelled for miles around and we just managed to fill St Paul's church in his honour. I wish I could remember his sermon. I am sure it was not about turning the other cheek. I remained a regular church-goer throughout my time in uniform. It was, like the NAAFI, a private space and a refuge from being ordered about and shouted at. The Army calls its soldiers privates but gives them zero privacy. A further advantage of army churches was that at the end of the service they did not have a collection. Ours was a free church.

I objected, however, on behalf of 'peace-loving-soldiers like myself' – meaning those who liked to lie in on Sunday mornings – to the Remembrance Sunday ceremonies. This was not because they were the Padre's, but because they were the CO's – God and the gun joined together in what seemed an unholy alliance. I changed my mind about them later – not only soldiers, but soldiers especially, have a duty to honour the fallen – but my views at the time were highly dissident. I wisely kept them to myself, except in letters home.

> Drumhead services are invariably ridiculous, as they try to find a compromise between Army and Church, by holding a display which is half a church service and half a drill parade. One moment we are marching on to the strains of *Colonel Bogey*, and the next we are singing to the strains of *Crimond*. As might be expected, the Army proves the more powerful of the two. In the end the Padre retires from the dais for some visiting brass-hat to take the salute at the march past ... However hard they tried, they couldn't make the whole affair any more ludicrous – not even by having the Padre taking the parade or the RSM preaching the sermon.

Salvation was again at hand. Once more through the grace of God (at one remove, through the Padre's intervention) I left the drill parades and the guard duties behind me for a totally unearned rest cure.

> The Army maintains a beautiful old house in Kyrenia, the main summer resort of the island, where the Church Department plays host to various Christians from all over Middle East Land Forces. These lucky beings, at the price of joining in a few discussions, are housed in conditions of the utmost luxury. Well, it appears that the Padres have exhausted their supply of Christians – so for the next five days they have invited me to the house party.

The week in Kyrenia was a tonic – good food, civilised living conditions, daily trips to such lovely places as the thirteenth-century abbey at Bellapais, to which I later returned as a literary pilgrim, and a library which even held a well-thumbed copy of *The Cherry Tree*, one of my father's books, with a town plan of Alexandria pasted into the fly-leaf. From time to time, since this was the point of it, there was a spot of religious discussion thrown in and in the chapel a religious service, Compline, which I had never even heard of before: it turned out to be a sort of liturgical Last Post, a nightcap without the hangover. Even the discussion groups were preferable to long hours in the Central Police Station, which is where I would have been otherwise, for it was a week of high 'panic'. But theologically I had led a sheltered life, well away from the rifts and divisions of the churches in Ulster. Kyrenia opened my eyes to them.

> One of those assembled on the course turned out to be an argumentative Calvinistic Irishman whose firm belief it was that the Pope was the Anti-Christ.

We were also fortunate that the Army had its own beach, guarded and patrolled, some six miles east of Kyrenia. On quiet weekends – those without 'flaps' and 'panics' – we would pile into three-ton trucks and spend the day there. (Except for the day when a departing draft ran riot in the camp and we were all confined to it as a collective punishment.) In high summer, if the alert state was low, the beach would look like Blackpool with armed guards. I took advantage of being a strong swimmer – I had been the second-string backstroke swimmer for the county, until beaten by an eleven-year-old in its championships.

> I have been included in the life-saving party that the Suffolks are providing for the Army's official beach. If anyone were actually to get into difficulties I am sure he would drown; but from the point of view of enjoyment the scheme couldn't be better, for it means spending whole weekends floating about in the balmy Mediterranean. Furthermore we have a boat – the official property of the life-saving party – to muck about in. So all is well.

The Army took its soldiers' welfare seriously. It even considered establishing its own holiday camp near Kormakitis in the north west of the island. This had the advantage that it was populated by neither Greeks nor Turks but Maronites, Christians of Arab origin. The reconnaissance was conducted by the second-in-command, at that time Major Dewar, with me as escort.

They speak and write Arabic, though they use Greek among themselves. Also, they are the only racial group in Cyprus unreservedly friendly to the British, though as they live in an island where there are 400,000 Greeks to a mere 2,000 Maronites, there is a certain amount of self-interest involved in their allegiance. The idea was that men should be sent up for a week of recreation-cum-training in the summer. In this weather – the temperature on Monday was 102 degrees – it is no great game to be virtually confined to camp for weeks on end.

Nothing came of it. It is in the nature of army plans they tend not to survive their first contact with reality, which in this case was the violent summer of 1958. After that, the nearest we got to a holiday camp was an operational deployment, otherwise known as a wild goose chase, pursuing an elusive enemy in the cooler air of the mountains.

A night out in Nicosia depended on the state of alert. If it was high, because of a specific EOKA threat or the prospect of riots, we were confined to barracks. A notice outside the Guard Room told us that Nicosia was out of bounds. If it was the next stage down, we could go out provided we were armed, uniformed and in groups of at least four. Sometimes I would make up the numbers as a favour to a mate. One of these was an Orderly Room clerk, Phil Levy, who in his other life was a gifted violinist. Nicosia was not such a cultural desert after all.

One hardly ever finds four people who want to go to the same place at the same time. Some of my friends were much perplexed by this problem on Tuesday night, as they wanted to go to a concert in which one of them was playing; gallantly, I made up the four for personal and cultural reasons, and was rewarded not only by an extremely good concert (so far as I can judge, which isn't very far), but also by the unique sight of our budding violinist, exquisitely garbed in evening dress (for which he received a special exemption from uniform) with his violin in his left hand and a Sterling sub-machine gun in his right. No, he did not play his violin like that, but at all other times he and the weapon were inseparable. The military police out here are very watchful ... with squads of them hovering about in dark corners.

In quieter times, when the state of alert was lower, we were allowed into town in civilian clothes, but still in groups of four and armed with handguns, normally for the use of officers only. I cannot remember having been trained on them but we carried them anyway in bulging pockets. On my birthday, we even ventured into the grand surroundings of the Ledra Palace Hotel, also a favourite haunt of the young subalterns, 'to enjoy the most luxurious and civilised surroundings in the whole country'. It may well have been reserved for officers only, so the other ranks could not observe their misbehaviour, but we managed to slip in somehow. Clearly we were getting ideas above our station.

We clerks and other ranks had something else in common: a great admiration for Lawrence Durrell, whose *Bitter Lemons* had been published at about the time of our arrival on the island. It was an instant best-seller. With the notable exception of Field Marshal Harding, whom it praised to the skies, the officers and colonial officials didn't like it, but we did. It spoke to our sense of romance and mystery about the recent past and parts of Cyprus which we seldom glimpsed. There was neither romance nor mystery to be found in Kykko Camp. We were looking for something more from our two years of soldiering than cordons and searches, inspections and drill parades and whatever was proclaimed in Battalion Orders. Durrell provided it.

So, on one of the rare weekends when the alert state was low, we rented cheap bicycles with only one gear and rode the 16 miles to Kyrenia, back-breaking going up the pass and breath-taking coming down it. We did not linger in the town, because this was a literary pilgrimage and Durrell had condemned it as too Anglicised and 'subtopian'. Instead we turned right on the coast road and pushed our bikes up the hill to his village of Bellapais: its coffee drinkers, its Tree of Idleness and its abbey just as he had described them. He had also described its cordon and search by the

Parachute Regiment. Again we felt conspired against: how was it that the
Suffolk Regiment had no such beautiful villages in its area of responsibility?

> In the magnificent Gothic abbey ... we found a window ledge in the
> vast and cool refectory which commands a wonderful view over the
> coastal strip. There we sat for a long, long time, very much envying
> people such as Durrell who could settle here rather than in an army
> camp.

But just two years previously, having worked for the Government of Cyprus,
he had been forced to leave Bellapais because of the threat of assassination.
Being ourselves still in mid-emergency in 1958, we remembered the dramatic
ending of *Bitter Lemons*: "'You see,' said the driver of the taxi which took
me up by night to the heavily guarded airport, "you see, the trouble with the
Greeks is that we are really so pro-British ... Yes, even Dighenis [Grivas].
Although he fights the British, really he loves them. But he will have to go
on killing them – with regret, even with affection'".

For the next excursion I had both the Army and the Royal Navy to thank. It
appeared that someone in the War Office (we still had one then) had decided
to 'grip' the old bugbear of inter-service rivalry. So, from 27 February to
18 March 1958 a period of *détente* set in.

> HMS *Alamein* [a destroyer] was sailing to Beirut to give the overworked
> crew a day or two's holiday, and evidently being brim full of goodwill
> asked the Suffolks to see what the Navy has to put up with, and the
> Navy sends men to patrol with the Suffolks and generally sample the
> horrors of the Army.

I was among the lucky eighteen whose names were drawn from the tin hat.
The *Alamein* had been patrolling the coast on a mission to intercept EOKA
gun-runners. Now she was sailing to Beirut on the Royal Navy's equivalent
of a leisure cruise.

> Only the day before we joined, the ship lost three men overboard in an
> accident at sea. However, this didn't appear to deter them in the least;

we were duly invited on board and made to feel thoroughly at home, given cups of tea at all hours and offered countless cigarettes. Space in any sort of ship is difficult to come by and things were certainly very cramped in the *Alamein*, particularly at night, when there are hammocks slung all over the place and you can't move an inch without banging your head into the underside of someone's prostrate body.

We sailed to Beirut overnight and spent three days sightseeing. It was a politically interesting time to be there, just 18 months after the Suez misadventure, when President Nasser of Egypt was at the height of his power and prestige. His image was plastered everywhere in the streets and on the back windows of cars and buses. 'It is only surprising,' I wrote in my usual naïve way, 'that the country isn't convulsed in revolutions perpetually.' There were in fact serious disturbances shortly afterwards, for which we might have been mobilised but were not. Since the Suez operation had been a predominantly British affair, it seems in retrospect to have been a risky time for a port call by British forces on the tinderbox of Beirut. At least we went ashore in civvies. And my impressions of Lebanon were as politically mindless as they had been of Cyprus. It was then that I wrote of Beirut as being more Oriental and 'Woggish' than Nicosia. So far from Suffolk, amid the magnificent ruins of Baalbek, I was as unimpressed by the Romans as by the Arabs.

> Why they should have built temples to Jupiter, Bacchus and Venus in the middle of a vast oriental plain is more than I can imagine. Nero started it, of course … That was more or less the last I saw of the Lebanon, as the next morning at 8 we were Cyprus-bound again.

I revisited Beirut (and was in due course expelled from it) as a TV reporter fifteen years later, at the start of the long ordeal of its civil war. I hope that, under gunfire on some rooftop, I understood it better by then. But at the time, and as a soldier on leave, the experience was completely wasted on me. It was merely a holiday from cordons, searches and parades. I had to hope that the naval ratings, on their reciprocal visit to the Regiment, had been as hospitably treated, had not had to conduct any cordons and searches *and that they had not under any circumstances encountered the RSM.*

All the same, the naval experience made me appreciate the Army rather more. At least there were no hammocks. The tent had some space in it, was relatively comfortable and – except when the rains descended on it – stood more or less on dry land. Soldiers and sailors had something else in common. It was the end of Empire too for the Royal Navy. HMS *Alamein* was about to be decommissioned and broken up, as was the Suffolk Regiment. But unlike the Regiment, the ship could not be amalgamated. It seemed a more dignified retirement.

We could hardly depend on the Senior Service for any more free rides. We had a leave entitlement of twenty-one days in our first year and twenty-eight days in our second, but where could we take it? Nowhere was safe on the island outside the wire for an off-duty soldier. One of my wealthier friends flew home in mid-tour and then, when his service was over, got himself demobbed in Cyprus itself before riding a motorcycle home to Suffolk. The officers envied the gleaming motorcycle and the other ranks envied the demob.

> Travelling 3,000 unknown miles on a motorcycle seems a very hazardous affair; but I suppose a chap feels the need for adventure when the rest of his life is likely to be spent in the companionship of pigs.

I was anti-pig but pro-sunshine. With a friend, also a corporal and clerk and more worldly-wise and 'clued in' than I was, we decided to spend three months' pay on a holiday in Israel in our last summer as soldiers. The cost was £20 a day for a week, of which £30 came out of my very modest savings and £5 as a subsidy from home. In an entire year of soldiering I had saved the grand total of £100: not much to save but not much to spend it on either. It would have been a pity to have lived in the Middle East for so long and to have seen so little of it. It would have been even better if I could have had some understanding of what I was seeing, but I did not. I knew nothing about Israel except that it was close to Cyprus, that the sun shone there and that we could wander about it unarmed and in civilian clothes, without any risk of being ambushed by EOKA or lifted by the Military Police. Fortune smiled on us. On the very day we left, we missed a drill parade.

We flew out of the island, just as we had arrived on it, in an elderly propeller-driven aircraft. We stayed in Tel Aviv at the Bristol Hotel, not very grand, but it seemed to us whose home was a tent to be the last thing in five star luxury. For the first time in a year *we were free*. Israel should have enlightened me about the Middle East and its history but sadly did not. My first impressions, insular to an extreme degree, were those of a farm boy from Suffolk whose horizons ended at Lowestoft and Felixstowe. I clearly had no future as a travel writer.

> Tel Aviv's sea front excels Yarmouth's as Yarmouth does Lowestoft's.

We visited Haifa, Galilee, Nazareth, and the Dead Sea – but not Jerusalem, which at the time was still a divided city. In 1948, at the end of the British Mandate, the 1st Battalion of the Suffolk Regiment had actually been based there, with its anti-tank guns mounted on rooftops. It was typically the last of the garrison to leave. Even then it was playing a part in the retreat from Empire; and when the retreat was over it would disappear. As with Cyprus and Lebanon I had no idea of the politics of the place and not much of the history. But the Israelis, who were attentive to their visitors, impressed me.

> The Israelis are a marvellous people. Like all Jews [our driver] was immensely proud of his country and throughout the journey to the Dead Sea was pointing out various development projects, war memorials to 'our boys' and other items of national pride.

The driver, an immigrant during the time of the British Mandate, was vociferously anti-Arab. Israel at the time (excluding the Suez fiasco) was half-way between its previous war, the 1948 War of Independence, and its next one, the 1967 Six Day War, which I was later to report, as well as the one following, the 1973 Yom Kippur War. It was a time of immigration and irrigation. I wrote of the Negev:

The Jews, who can't afford to let a desert remain a desert, are trying to cultivate even this arid waste, rather like the Russians in Siberia. All the new refugees are more or less plonked down in the desert and told to grow wheat on it. To help them, the most hare-brained irrigation schemes are actually made to work. The one currently under construction consists of an 8 foot concrete pipeline through the mountains all the way from the Sea of Galilee.

If I had asked more questions I might have been better prepared for future assignments, including the wars which I reported, and the infinite complexities of Israel/Palestine. Instead, I went to the opera – *Nabucco*, of course.

It was sung in Hebrew except for one guest artiste, who sang her part in English until the final aria, when she launched into Hebrew to the obvious delight of everybody, including myself, who cannot bear opera sung in an understandable tongue, because the whole thing sounds completely ridiculous.

The end of the visit coincided with the Jewish New Year. The streets of Tel Aviv were as empty, I noted, as those of Nicosia under curfew, except for the window-shoppers. The return flight was 12 hours late – and we stumbled back into camp, which I called the slaughterhouse, at three in the morning, the most depressing home-coming of my life. All good things come to an end. The next night I was back on guard duty, with drill parades to follow.

The resulting Israeli travelogue was so superficial that you could have waded in its depths without getting your feet wet. Written in the Guard Room, it was the longest of all the letters that I sent home, more than 2,000 words over eight pages. However, there was one episode that I left out. On the final afternoon, when all the sightseeing was over, I took myself to the beach in Tel Aviv for one last swim as a civilian in the sunshine. I came across a friendly young man of about my age and asked him about life in Israel, especially what it was like to be conscripted into the Israeli Defence Force. I felt we had much in common. He invited me for a drink in his flat nearby, and it was only when he put his hand on my knee I realised I had made a mistake. I was much more innocent than most 20-year-olds are today, or indeed were then, and needed an exit strategy. Having no idea what to do, I panicked and played the part of the proper Englishman. 'I'm very sorry,' I said, 'but where I come from we don't do that kind of thing!' (Which of course was quite untrue.) I made my excuses and left.

Chapter 16

Media Matters

In the early months of 1959, during the battledress season, my home-town newspaper, the *Beccles and Bungay Journal*, carried a picture of me on an inside page under the headline 'Dictionary as Prize for Beccles Corporal'. The story was as follows: 'There is news from Cyprus that Martin Bell, of 19 Northgate Beccles, and his two team mates put up a good show in the army Spelling Bee organised by the Broadcasting Corporation Television Service on the island. They spelt their way to the final, only to be beaten by a doughty trio from Headquarters, Cyprus. This was the first appearance of Corporal Bell on television.'

But not, as it turned out, the last one, and a foretaste of things to come. The island's TV service was still in its infancy, but having had no TV set at home, still less in the camp, I was mightily impressed by it.

A fascinating experience it was too – seeing at first hand the terrific complications of a television studio, its blinding lights, frantic producers, and so on.

In the first round we prevailed without difficulty over some rather gamesmanship-minded characters from the Royal Army Service Corps. We looked down on the Royal Army Service Corps much as the Grenadier Guards looked down on us. As a soldier I was average at spit and polish, but I was good at spelling. The words that came my way were 'occasionally', 'panegyric', 'obstreperousness' 'antirrhinum' and 'brassiere'. In the next round we were soundly beaten by a team of whizz-kids and apprentice Oxbridge professors from Army Headquarters. But it was also an early lesson in life's injustices.

We were, as anticipated, no match for our opponents who were quite repulsively brilliant. I managed to spell most of my words, but on one of the words I spelt right, 'viscous', I was counted out by the compere, who had looked it up wrongly in the dictionary, and was flooded with phone calls from indignant viewers.

The *Concise Oxford English Dictionary* was a consolation prize. The photograph of the smiling corporal was taken by the Army's public information service, as part of a programme, which still exists, to provide local newspapers with stories about cheerful squaddies doing their duty in the far-flung corners of the world. The picture was posed and taken in the Intelligence Office, against a background of 50 Brigade's antique radio set and the indispensable portable map case. Was there ever a happier soldier than Corporal Bell with microphone in hand and earphones so attuned to the incoming signal? I wrote home:

> It's all a gigantic fraud, anyway, because in actual fact no one ever wears earphones to listen to the wireless, but lays them down some distance away in order to interpret whatever message happens to be coming through amid all the crackling and whistling noises.

Only to this very limited extent could the security forces manage their relationship with the media. In the national and international press, and in the swirl of events around them, they were fighting a public information campaign against a resourceful enemy.

Unlike the British Army, EOKA had a media strategy. According to the diaries of Colonel Grivas, the main target of attack was public opinion. The intention was 'to stifle the dissentient voices of the traitors [Communists] and to give the impression that the Greek Cypriots are a united, determined and militant people whole-heartedly devoted to the prosecution of *Enosis*, if necessary by force'. The Greek press was of course anti-British and Radio Athens was vitriolic. To them EOKA were the heroes and we were the villains. They did not do understatement. There was nothing in the catalogue of Nazi crimes that they did not accuse us of. For instance the detention camp at Kokkinotrimithia, which we guarded, was described as a British Belsen. The state of the latrines in Kyrenia Castle was a human rights issue ... and so on.

By contrast most of the British papers were strongly supportive, regularly referring to Makarios as 'Black Mak'. They were also gung-ho, in a *Boy's Own Paper* kind of way, in their day-to-day reporting of the conflict. This was the *Daily Express* of 21 January 1957 on the Suffolks' big success story: 'They stood alone, face to face, near a moon-lit mountain track, the private from Ipswich and the tough veteran killer of the Cyprus terrorists. The time: near midnight. Both were surprised. For moments they stood stock still, ten yards apart. Then the spell broke – and their guns blazed – ALMOST together. But the 19 year old private, who had never killed a man in his life, was just that split second quicker. That was how Sidney Woods, of Goldsmith Road Ipswich, ended the dangerous life of 24 year old Markos Drakos, "Field Commander" for the terrorist leader, Colonel Grivas.'

The death of Drakos was the high point of our campaign against EOKA. Other fighters met the same fate. Some were convicted of murder and executed. Grivas himself had narrowly escaped from a patrol of the Parachute Regiment. Considerable caches of arms were being found. The Greek Cypriot leader Archbishop Makarios and the outspoken Bishop of Kyrenia were in exile in the Seychelles. The Governor, Field Marshal Sir John Harding, was pursuing a hard-line policy and looking to the Special Branch and Army to produce a decisive result. By the time Harding handed over the governorship to Sir Hugh Foot, in December 1957, he was under pressure because of the harshness of his regime and the ill-will it attracted, but he believed that the destruction of EOKA had been largely achieved.

The press, as always a mixed bunch, were not convinced. Some went along with the official optimism of the Government's spokesman and its news releases. Others did not. Among the sceptics was James Cameron of the *News Chronicle* whom I admired even then, though the other ranks' access to the newspapers was somewhat restricted in the operations room of Nicosia Central Police Station.

Two papers are received: the lone major takes one, swarms of subalterns gather round the other, and the poor intelligence clerk doesn't even rank among the 'also rans'.

James Cameron was the leading Fleet Street journalist of his day. He was not so much a news reporter as a roving columnist, the Robert Fisk of his time. He wrote of what he found in Cyprus, 'More and more is the situation dominated by personal factors in the Governor's mind – his personal feud with Archbishop Makarios, his personal stake in the capture of Grivas, his personal necessity to prove the unprovable, that Cyprus can be held by force'. [*News Chronicle*, 13 June 1957] The Army of the time advised each of its officers 'To keep himself up to date an officer should read a good newspaper daily and as many periodicals as possible.'

The Governor at the time was still Field Marshal Harding, a soldier who appeared to his critics to be seeking a military solution to a political problem. In December 1956 the Labour MP Kenneth Robinson called for his replacement. He accused the Government of being far too fond of appointing military figures to senior positions: 'It is not a suitable background ... indeed I can think of no career more unfitting'. [*Hansard*, 21 December 1956] Harding was not only Governor but also Director of Military Operations. On his departure in 1957 the Prime Minister Harold Macmillan wrote kindly even of his divisiveness, 'I have no doubt your governorship will be remembered with pride even by those who have not agreed with you'. It was remembered with gratitude by the EOKA leader. When the emergency was over and Cyprus was independent, Colonel Grivas mischievously suggested that they should erect a statue to Governor Harding, since he 'had done more than anyone else to keep alive the spirit of Hellenic resistance'. In a note from the Governor's office in 1957, a senior official described the conflict as 'a hard and bitter struggle between the forces of law and order and an utterly ruthless terrorist movement run by a church that is prepared to use any means to secure its political ends'. [*The Guardian*, 27 July 2012]

By the time the soldier Harding was replaced by the diplomat Sir Hugh Foot, EOKA was by no means defeated; tensions between Greeks and Turks were rising; and the Cyprus emergency was becoming a big story back home. 'Our boys' (I was one of them) were patrolling the streets, putting down riots, searching and suppressing, seeking out suspects and trying to keep the peace. We were like a gigantic fire blanket cast over the island, but with the fire still smouldering and the embers still burning beneath it. There were papers which 'backed our boys' and papers which didn't – it was the

heyday of the old Fleet Street, reporters and photographers everywhere –
and charges of brutality were sometimes made against us, which had to be
dealt with. The press hotel was the Ledra Palace just outside the walled
city. It rivalled Meikle's in Salisbury (now Harare), the Continental Palace
in Saigon (now Ho Chi Minh City) and later the Holiday Inn in Sarajevo as
one of the trouble-shooting journalists' great watering holes. It was there
that they quenched their thirsts and filed their stories, often by telephone.
(It was still more than thirty years before the internet.) The cry of 'get me
copy' would ring down the corridors.

The press were the island's resident prophets of doom. Iris Russell, then
with the *Sunday Dispatch*, wrote a front-page splash on 24 November 1957,
in the interregnum between one Governor and the next, which had such an
impact that it is the only press report included in the official archive: 'It is
my firm belief that, short of a miracle, within one month from today Cyprus
will be hurled into horrors of murder, intimidation and counter-repression
even worse than the incidents which gave this Mediterranean colony the
nickname of "terror isle" two years ago.' [FCO Archive 141/4422] Then as
now the press excelled in alarmist reporting.

We knew what the journalists were writing, because all the British papers
were available in the camp by the next day at the latest, and we tended to
dislike it on regimental grounds. They were either giving us the blame for
something we had not done, or not giving us the credit for something that
we had. We were reasonably well-informed by dint of our own experiences
and dismayed by the sheer scale of the misreporting. We also had a radio in
our tent, 'hired from the Wogs' as I put it, so we could hear the less hectic
coverage of the BBC Overseas Service (and in much better quality than the
50 Brigade radio link). I was not at all in favour of my future profession.

The Cyprus correspondents are usually so infuriatingly wrong. They
get particularly peeving when they start gassing about various battalions
and give credit to the wrong ones.

I read a paper the other day, and was quite surprised to learn that a
minor war is raging in Cyprus. The British papers produce the most
distorted accounts of what goes on. The disturbances of the past few
days have in fact been so inconsiderable that the crack regiment on the

island – 1 Suffolk – was not even alerted. So please don't believe a word of what the papers say.

The detainees burned down all the doors to their compound in one of their camps. According to the *Daily Mail* they also burned down 19 huts and had tear gas thrown at them, but the *Daily Mail* is apt to let its imagination play havoc with its facts.

Actually I was there, which the *Daily Mail* was not.

I heard the CO roaring for me afar off, so I dashed round to grab a weapon and accompanied him as personal escort to the detention camp; not that being the CO's escort is the most thrilling of jobs, but at least on the first day I was able to witness such destruction as had been done, and on the second day I saw the ringleaders being packed off to the Central Prison, which is much less of a holiday camp.

I seemed to have had it in for the officers' newspaper, *The Daily Telegraph*, too.

One of the greatest differences between Me before army treatment and Me after it, is that papers of the *Daily Telegraph* slant – army officerish, true blue and cunningly biased – irritate me beyond words ... 20 months in the ranks wipes any tinge of blue from one's political slate.

I did not like the Labour-supporting *Daily Mirror* either. It was definitely not 'onside'. It ran headlines like 'Caning on Terror Island', when the previous Governor authorised the beating of schoolboys as a punishment for rioting. The Secretary of State, challenged in the House of Commons, said that in such cases caning the child was more appropriate than fining his parents. The *Mirror* was on the same wavelength as our arch-critic Barbara Castle, although she actually wrote for another left-wing newspaper, the *Herald*. In June 1957 the *Mirror* editorialised 'The policy of the British Government in Cyprus is now inhuman. There is no other word for it: a stupid plan of repression that has not succeeded and cannot succeed in the second half of the 20th century'. [*Daily Mirror*, 17 June 1957] The *Mirror* was also sharply critical of the GOC General Darling and (as we were) of our own Commanding Officer.

> Although not mentioned by name, he was the president of the court-martial which sentenced a corporal to nine months detention for printing anti-EOKA leaflets … Much weeping and wailing in the national press.

Actually the press had a point. If the corporal had been printing *pro*-EOKA leaflets it might have been treasonable, but he wasn't. Instead he was caught in the blackthorn thickets of Queen's Regulations. The unfortunate corporal was Brian Ford of the Royal Signals and his defence was that he had done it 'as a joke'. This cut no ice with Lieutenant Colonel Bevan's court-martial. After his conviction, the outcry against it reached the House of Commons. MPs asked why a soldier was given a nine-month sentence for distributing anti-EOKA leaflets, when Cypriots merely had to pay a fine for possessing pro-EOKA leaflets. The Commander-in-Chief of Middle East Land Forces bowed to the pressure. The corporal was released and returned to his family in England.

To say that we did not mind our CO being criticised in the press would be understatement. Ordinary soldiers take a certain satisfaction when those in authority over them attract their share of the 'incoming'. There is a long tradition of this. The regimental history of the Great War, in which the Suffolks lost nearly 7,000 men, records the following: 'The shelling of superior headquarters was often greeted with hearty laughter.'

The left-of-centre *Observer* also fell out of favour, when it ran a story about British soldiers armed to the teeth forming into gangs and roaming the streets at night to terrorise the people.

> What the correspondent actually ran into was a patrol belonging to a very highly organised set-up designed to protect the married families in the suburbs. I happen to KNOW it is highly organised, as I have been doing quite a lot of its paperwork myself.

Yet the story may have had something to it. Towards the end of our tour of duty, after the Zurich and London agreements, the problem became one of keeping the peace between the civilian population and some of the off-duty soldiers themselves. It was the Scottish regiments which made the greatest impact. The Battalion Diary recorded between 19 and 27 March 1959: 'Town patrols in support of the Royal Military Police. Task to prevent clashes between Cypriot population and Security Forces.'

> These became such a menace to public safety that eventually a force of about 100 NCOs was set up to help the military police control the town o'nights – and the control of these keepers of the peace reposes at present in the hands of the Suffolks.

Veterans of the Black Watch may find this hard to believe, but we had a particular problem with their regiment, the 42nd of Foot, who were piped in as reinforcements late in the emergency. It was one of my last patrols in the Old City. I had dealt with riotous Greeks and Turks, but the Black Watch on the spree were something else.

> My own 'beat' is enlivened by the presence of multitudes of Black Watch, in Nicosia for the night. The Scots certainly seem to have a mysterious capacity for getting drunk far more quickly than anyone else, and in no time at all the streets were full of roaring drunk Glaswegians staggering along under the support of such of their comrades as were relatively sober, and one Scot in particular who sat down in the middle of the road and conducted an intimate private conversation with a stray dog.

In the summer of 1958, following clashes between Turks and Greeks, we mounted a cordon and search operation in a Turkish suburb of Nicosia.

> We moved down at about eight, and then caused havoc by searching with considerable thoroughness every house in the neighbourhood for offensive weapons. We got quite a haul, too: sticks and crowbars, cudgels, knives, ammunition, a bomb or two, and one particularly endearing little weapon consisting of a cudgel-shaped instrument

with a plaster-of-Paris knob covered with razor blades sticking out on unpleasant angles.

I instructed a police sergeant to force open the locked cupboards of a school where we found nothing at all. What was remarkable – and it happened over and over again – was the response, or lack of it, of the people whose properties were being ransacked and searched.

The Turks really took this intrusion very well: in most of the houses we visited we were offered lemonade or some such refreshment; nor did we refuse, for the temperature must have been drifting somewhere near the hundred mark, and rummaging in cupboards is hot work.

The weapons we found were laid out on three army trestle tables (tables/folding/flat) for the benefit of the cameras. The press were invited. It was the first time I had seen foreign journalists in action. I was unimpressed, except by their suede shoes.

There were long gaunt-looking men with artistic beards, short dapper little men with ingratiating manners and suede shoes, and Iris Russell, a female (of sorts), who stands in a class entirely by herself. For further enlightenment read the *Daily Mail*. The men who were brandishing the cameras were of course delighted with our museum collection of primitive weapons, and a good time was had by all.

I can neither explain nor excuse my prejudice against Iris Russell, who was writing by that time for the *Daily Mail*, and was no doubt a perfectly competent journalist without any animus against us. She could certainly have done us some damage on 28 January 1958, when we were on riot duty as the lead battalion alongside other units in the Turkish Quarter of Nicosia. Five Turkish Cypriots died that day, three in Nicosia and two in Famagusta. Her report was low key and factual. 'Today's trouble in Nicosia began when Turks defied the curfew imposed last night and attacked troops patrolling the streets. Men of the Suffolks, Gloucesters, Royal Artillery, Royal Horse Guards and Grenadiers fought off rioters who shouted "Britain get out!"

When the stone-throwing rioters got out of hand, troops fired, killing one Turk. A few minutes later a car which broke the cordon and failed to answer a challenge was fired on. Another Turk was killed and a third, who died tonight, injured.'

Like most of the British press, she did not question the use of lethal force: 'Violence will come from the Greeks if Britain backs Turkish demands, and from Turks if Britain tries to introduce self-government in a single community. The casualties bring the total of deaths in the last two days' rioting to seven – the heaviest in the history of the troubles.'

I shared the prejudices of soldiers against journalists which would haunt me later in life, although we probably understand each other better now than we did then.

Today's doings have been repercussing all over the place. The newspapermen are flocking around like vultures. The *Express* reporter looks the complete blueprint of the fictional newshound, long and hawk-nosed, and very much in need of a regimental haircut; and two film cameramen hung about with great patience for a long time merely to take a sequence of two perfectly innocent armoured cars leaving the city. (I think they were trying to compare our habits with the Russians'.)

Chapter 17

Hearts and Minds

In the war of words, which as in all conflicts ran alongside the war of arms, the Greek Cypriots were initially at a disadvantage. Their press was censored from the outbreak of the campaign, to the point where much of its reporting made no sense. Leafleteers were fined. Leaflets were seized by soldiers such as me. Government was by decree. The local political leadership had no access to the airwaves. *The Times of Cyprus*, suspected of EOKA sympathies, was banned from army camps. Its British owner and editor Charles Foley was prosecuted under the Emergency Powers Act in 1956 and fined £50 for publishing an article under the title 'Hatred, Despair and Anger' on the alleged ill-treatment of Cypriots which was judged 'likely to be prejudicial to the maintenance of public order'. His editorials complained about 'the angry tones of Harding, justifying his troops in all circumstances'. Mr Foley, formerly of the *Daily Express*, had settled in Cyprus for a quiet life, which turned out to be a miscalculation on his part. He had the courage to write against the grain; but the end of Empire was not a good time for liberal journalism. Charles Foley's *Times of Cyprus* and James Cameron's *News Chronicle* both folded in 1960.

The British controlled the streets and the skies, and pro-government leaflets were air-dropped on towns and villages in industrial quantities. The average print run of these was 120,000. Some took the form of crude cartoons depicting Grivas as a Hellenic Hitler. Others were surrender leaflets, offering safe conduct to EOKA fighters who gave themselves up. So far as I know none did unless they were surrounded – and even then some, like Grigoris Afxentiou, would fight to the death. An intelligence summary in mid-campaign, classified Secret, conceded grudgingly that most of the hard core in the mountains would do the same.

Leaflets were intended to influence public opinion. One showed a mother cradling a dead child in her arms over the caption 'Making a Deplorable

Sacrifice for the Bloody Fury of EOKA'. Notices were displayed offering rewards for surrendered weapons: £100 for Bren guns, £40 for rifles and £10 for sporting guns. Anyone defacing such a poster or tearing it down was liable to imprisonment or a fine. Very few weapons were handed in. The leaflets were ineffective.

The one public relations *coup* on the Government side was the discovery of the Grivas diaries. Some of these were found in his leather satchel when he narrowly escaped capture in the Troodos Mountains in June 1956. Other papers were found in glass jars outside Famagusta two months later. Extracts from the diaries were published by the Stationery Office (price two shillings) in September 1956 under the title *Terrorism in Cyprus*. But their impact was blunted. Being type-written, they were hard to authenticate absolutely beyond all doubt, and only 10,000 of 250,000 words were put into the public domain. The rest remained unpublished on security grounds, on the orders of Governor Harding: 'We must keep the enemy guessing by not revealing the exact extent of the captured documents ... It is still imperative to hide our blind spots'. The Government did, however, make the most of a message from Grivas to Makarios: 'I will not lay down my arms unless you yourself ask me to do so.' Harding observed that the whole thesis of Makarios as a moderate and reasonable man was 'blown sky-high as soon as we published the Grivas diaries'. [FCO Archive 141/4353]

A Government leaflet *Corruption of Youth in Support of Terrorism in Cyprus*, published in August 1957, lamented the indoctrination of students in schools and churches: 'It is a disquieting thought that not only has their education been curtailed and confused and their outlook warped, but in place of the self-discipline which normally springs from the controlling influences of home and school the only discipline they know is the shadow of the gunman.'

Yet the British were also at a disadvantage, which grew over time, simply by virtue of being the colonial power. As early as October 1955, the Cyprus Intelligence Committee conceded that the EOKA propaganda campaign 'backed by threats, murders and attempted murders has had a large measure of success'. We soldiers were properly expected to be courteous to the civilian population. This was hard to achieve in the course of a thorough cordon and search operation, with a rifle in one hand and a list of suspects in the other. There was also no identifiable *policy*. Lawrence Durrell noted that when he joined the Government's service in 1955 'there was nothing vaguely resembling a policy line which one could study and interpret ... For the first time I realised that we had no real policy, save that of offering constitutions whose terms made them unsuitable for acceptance, and of stonewalling on the central issue of sovereignty'. The most thoughtful and articulate of our Regiment's officers, Lieutenant Colonel Arthur Campbell, observed 'The machinery on the island for waging the campaign for people's minds was inadequate, and indeed the problem was never solved. It proved impossible to conjure out of the air a propaganda organisation that had any chance of countering successfully the long-term brain-washing of Makarios and his henchmen and the fear which EOKA had imposed on the Cypriot people'. [*Flaming Cassock*, p. 104] And when it was all over he concluded 'Makarios and Grivas have won their victory in the sense of successfully poisoning the minds of most Greek Cypriots against the British connection'. [*Flaming Cassock*, p. 319] His conclusion was surely justified although challenged at the time. The Cyprus Local Intelligence Committee (renamed and reconstituted in June 1958) wrote 'It is perhaps not wise to suggest that Makarios and Grivas have won their victory'. Nonetheless they did.

The Government knew that it was on the back foot in the war of words. In June 1957 it produced a booklet 'Allegations of Brutality by British Forces Refuted'. Yet the longer the emergency lasted the more these allegations multiplied. After his release from the Seychelles Archbishop Makarios flew to Athens, where he held a press conference providing details of 317 cases of alleged abuse by the British against Greek Cypriot civilians. EOKA supporters under arrest were encouraged to compile their own 'black books' of evidence of ill-treatment.

Such policies as there were lacked clarity and were left largely unexplained and unpromoted. Recently declassified documents show that the Governor in 1958, Sir Hugh Foot, found it deeply frustrating that when diplomacy failed he was muzzled by the Colonial Office in London and not free to promote the 'new policy, the policy of the advantages', or whatever the policy of the moment might be, as he wished. He wrote 'In the end we must convince the Greeks. In the meantime it is surely more important to convince public opinion generally and in England and elsewhere that our policy generally is sound and fair'.

On 18 September 1958 the Secretary of State instructed him: 'I think it would be better to avoid ... any general statement at this juncture'. He replied: 'I am very much disturbed by your telegram 1479. I thought it was understood that I can talk openly here in explanation of what we are doing. We are now going into a phase probably more difficult and dangerous than anything we have had to face before. Even our friends don't understand what we are up to. We shall be playing into the hands of our enemies if we don't try to convince everyone of the justice of our policy. We have always said that if we have to fight we need a line to fight on. We now have a good line. We must surely go flat out in telling the world that we believe in it and why ... It is an impossible position to have to carry out a policy without being able to explain and justify it.' [FCO Archive 141/4451] He sounded as if he was close to resignation.

In a column in *Oxford Opinion* in January 1959, the young Paul Foot, son of the Governor, observed: 'Politicians, journalists, soldiers, they've all got a lot to say. But does anyone ever think about the Cypriot people?'

Three hundred and twenty-seven foreign correspondents passed through Cyprus in 1956. The Army Chief of Staff, Brigadier George Baker, felt that he could deal with them more easily than with the local press: 'A hard core of some 20 local representatives were of a quite different category, being unscrupulous, unintelligent and a general nuisance; they had an undesirable influence on visiting correspondents.' Governor Foot wrote that one of the lessons of the conflict was that 'The press always wins in the end. The press is a necessary evil and my experience is that attempts to suppress it or pursue it with restrictive action nearly always recoil to the disadvantage of the Administration.' [FCO Archive 141/4233]

The conduct of regiments such as ours could have international ramifications. Britain, assuming that its own affairs were unaffected, had signed up to a European Human Rights Convention in 1953. Now the Greek Government was making moves, under the terms of the Convention, to arraign it before the European Court in Strasbourg, causing dismay in Nicosia and Whitehall. When European commissioners were about to be sent on a fact-finding mission to Cyprus, the Foreign Secretary Selwyn

Lloyd expressed 'dismay and incredulity that the Convention could have got us into this fix, and even more incredulity that it applies to so many colonies'. Every effort was made to block international visits to the internment camps, except by the International Red Cross. Brigadier Baker concluded 'Her Majesty's Government should never enter into international obligations, such as the European Human Rights Convention, without being fully aware in advance of their implications'. [FCO Archive 141/4459]

The rampage that followed the murder of Mrs Catherine Cutliffe, the wife of a Royal Artillery sergeant, near Famagusta in October 1958 was a turning-point in relations between the military and the media. The disquiet at home was profound and affected the public will to continue the campaign against EOKA. A senior Army officer was quoted in the press, as if in extenuation, 'Nothing that has happened during the emergency has outraged troops more than the shooting of service wives in Famagusta'. *The Times* wrote 'The aim of EOKA's leaders must have been to provoke the troops who would be presented in the island, In Greece and in the United Nations as evidence of a reign of terror'. The breakdown of discipline, though denied, was a matter of record. The line had not held.

The Governor, Sir Hugh Foot, flew to Famagusta two hours after the murder of Mrs Cutliffe and was appalled by what he called the soldiers' 'extensive indiscipline and ill-treatment'. He did not see their reaction as an isolated incident. Unlike Governor Harding, he was in theory the Commander-in-Chief but in practice not the Director of Military Operations. The Deputy Governor, who chaired the Intelligence Committee, had more operational power than he did. Foot wrote to the Colonial Secretary Alan Lennox-Boyd 'For a number of reasons I am afraid that some troops and some police too are inclined to deal very hardly with the Greek Cypriots when they get the chance.' [FCO Archive 141/4493]

The word went out that there must be no repetition of the military rampage. We, the soldiers of the Army of anti-terrorism (or of occupation, depending on how it was seen), were duly lectured by our Commanding Officers and from that point on under special scrutiny in the conduct of operations. Some of us, including notably the unfashionable county regiments, heeded the orders more than others. The steady Suffolks did not rampage. We believed that the Governor, who had no control over the

Army's deployments and operations, wanted more of us and fewer of the others, Scots and Irish especially.

Britain's hold on the island was loosening, and the more thoughtful journalists were aware of it. James Cameron was one of them. 'One has the conviction that the British Government has now manoeuvred itself into a position from which it would give quite a lot to extricate itself. The sudden uncharacteristic anger of this sunny little island grows daily; for once they feel that the British with whom they had such sympathetic ties have seriously let them down.'

So did the outcome depend on the Suffolk Regiment in general and Corporal Bell's conduct of its operations in particular? Obviously not, though we were gentler than most; but we were aware of the hosts of journalists out there, some of them perhaps ill-intentioned, and of the damage that they could do to our reputation. Officers had no idea of how to deal with them. They had expected the press to be supportive, whatever they did. Neither Sandhurst nor the Army Staff College had trained them in media management, or the Rules of War or any of the outward-facing courses which are now routine before deployments on active service. A brigade commander in today's Army has two right-hand men. One is his brigade major. The other is a lawyer from the Army Legal Service. We had courts-martial aplenty in the late 1950s, but no such thing as an Army Legal Service.

The Army not only enforced the law: in Cyprus it *was* the law; and the journalists, if considered at all, were kept at arm's length and dealt with rather brusquely. In theory each major unit should have had a public information officer (PIO) attached to it; but from my perch in the Intelligence Section I never saw anyone in the Battalion, not even the most junior subaltern, who was designated to manage relations with the press. General Darling complained that throughout his time in command (October 1958 to July 1959) there continued to be indiscreet disclosures to the press: 'Equally harmful were those who distrusted all pressmen and never hesitated to say so in public places.' Most of us viewed them with deep suspicion, whether we said so in public or not. It was my first experience, of many, of the difficult interface between the media and the military.

The behaviour of soldiers before the press men is a comic thing to behold. On the one hand the officers deplore the effete ways and shaggy hair of the journalists, but on the other hand they love publicity, being simple souls.

TV news was in its infancy, having only just superseded the cinema newsreels – many of the cameramen were the same – and we knew that the cameras of the BBC and ITN with their black and white film were roaming out there somewhere in the streets unsupervised and uncensored. Then came a day of maximum panics and flaps. The Battalion itself was due to appear on television.

> The BBC intend to produce a Cyprus film … On Tuesday they are scheduled to take shots of the Suffolks in the walled city: which at once sends the CO into a turmoil of activity, arranging scenes like a born film director, and commissioning regimental signs to be painted and placed in the camera's eye, less the regimental significance of it all be lost to the millions of viewers.

Nothing came of the TV programme; but we practised our own journalism of a sort, the regimental magazine, which was called (of course) *Castle and Key*. Its pale green mimeographed cover showed two soldiers of the Regiment, one ancient and the other modern, standing on guard outside a drawbridge with a castle beyond it, above the regimental motto *Montis Insignia Calpe*. This came from the coat of arms of Gibraltar, Calpe being the original name for the Rock. The Regiment saw itself, because of its history, as owning the Rock of Gibraltar.

After fifty years in my attic, along with the letters, I unearthed a copy of the magazine's edition No. 7, which I edited in December 1957 under the benign supervision of the Adjutant. He ordered me to get on with it and I did. It was a platform for opinions which, expressed elsewhere, might have had me marched under close escort to the Guard Room. It provided an insight into the life of my comrades in arms and included much banter between the platoons of the rifle companies, all of whom regarded themselves as the cream of the cream (unlike the other lot) and gave themselves nicknames.

There was no spell check in those days, and the reports from the platoons needed a fair amount of editing.

It is a bit of a literary shambles, but you should have seen some of the contributions before we corrected the spelling mistakes.

'7 Pl (GRAVEDIGGERS) distinguished itself by winning practically every inter-platoon contest from marching to firing and section attacks. But of course, with only 8 Pl and 9 Pl to compete against, what do you expect?' This from 9 Pl (GREEN DEVILS): 'Our brief stay at Dhavlos proved pretty eventful, what with leaving a rocket-launcher on the beach … What we don't like are weapons inspections. The barrels are never just right for our Platoon Commander'. 10 Pl (PEASANTS) complained about their sergeant's war stories: 'I once stormed a hill held by … ' and observed that the new draftees were causing concern: 'The only thing that divides us is Ipswich Town versus Leyton Orient … We can't see why 11 Pl lap themselves up so much, as they are second only to the Heap alias 12 Pl'. And from 11 Pl (WRECKERS): 'We would like to point out to anyone in doubt that we are not "the Heap" as we have been termed by ignorant PEASANTS'.

The report by 12 Pl itself (STAGS) was doubly intriguing: 'Our comedian Don Cobb tried to do the Indian rope trick from a chopper and found himself suspended 15 feet from the ground (he has since recovered). Our Platoon Sergeant can also be proud of himself, he must be the only Sergeant to have hit an officer in the mouth and got away with it'. Since *Castle and Key* did not do investigative journalism, we would never know how the Sergeant got away with it

As editor, I relegated the Band Notes to the final page. That was because the Band enjoyed special privileges. They were 'base wallahs' and usually excused guard duty. They rehearsed every day in the Nissen hut which doubled as the cinema. The Bandmaster wished the rest of us to know that while we were away on Exercise Mountain Goat they had been filling in for us like real soldiers. 'We ushered in the Christmas season by playing carols to the married families. We have even (dare I say it) done a couple of guards while the Battalion was training at Dhavlos.' (Despite the emergency,

Nicosia was actually a family posting for some of the officers and senior NCOs; and we used to patrol the suburbs where they lived.)

Thanks to its editor, the much smaller Intelligence Section achieved an undeserved and more prominent billing in the magazine: 'Our well-bred diffidence will not allow us to brag of our success in the planning and execution of operations, nor of the way in which we left all competition panting behind us in the recent route march. We merely mention such things in passing, and wish all our readers a merry Christmas.' I sketched a sprig of holly for the magazine's cover.

I also appointed myself the Battalion's resident bard. A couple of my poems, or rather verses, appeared anonymously in *Castle and Key*, under the by-line 'Nemo' (no one). It was obvious that rank still rankled. The first was called *Chain Reaction*.

> The Major General cut himself while shaving
> And cursed the Brigadier who, madly raving,
> Then cast the most chastising and infernal
> Aspersions on the morals of the Colonel
> Who passed them to the Major; and he, rapt in
> The darkest thoughts, relayed them to the Captain,
> Who rocketed the subalterns, who rose
> To loose all hell among the NCOs,
> Who in their wrath and mad acerbity
> Picked on one last poor buckshee Private – me.

The other poem was about promotion, and how it changed the nature of the soldier promoted. It was entitled *Per Ardua Ad Nauseam – a Cautionary Tale*.

> Young Egbert Snooks, when in his eighteenth year,
> Embarked unthinking on his life's career,
> Inscribed his name upon the dotted line,
> And very soon began to peek and pine,
> Lamented, as he scrubbed the cook-house floor,
> The heartlessness of Destiny, and swore
> On every oath he knew (a fearful lot)

To make no effort physical or mental
Or ever be the least bit regimental.
But twenty years have smothered that brave vow
In the obscurity of time; for now
Old Snooks displays three stripes upon his arm,
His presence is a source of great alarm
To all recruits, who oscillate and pall
To hear his vast parade ground caterwaul.
In short, he has become as old a sweat
As ever relished a dog-biscuit yet
Or wore that hale well-lubricated air
That sergeants and their like are wont to wear.
And you, my friend, with just three years to do,
What if the same fate should encompass you?

Chapter 18

Reluctant Soldiers

A conscript army is inherently difficult to manage. Its soldiers would prefer to be anywhere other than where they are. Ours was no exception. We watched the clock and counted the time on our days-to-do charts on our walls or in our lockers. Every day gone was a day gained. We muttered and malingered and did all we could to avoid the attentions of the Regimental Sergeant Major, the Company Sergeant Major, the Provost Sergeant or anyone else with the mark of authority embroidered on his sleeve. Sometimes we complained about doing too much and sometimes about doing too little. Complaining quietly among ourselves was what we were exceptionally good at. We were the wizards of whingeing. What was surprising, looking back on it, was that our morale was as high as it was. It may have been the sunshine, or the Keo beer in the NAAFI (the quantity not the quality), or the little luxuries available in the shop outside the wire, or the weekend outings to the Army's beach, or maybe the shared hardships and discomforts, or the excitements of active service, or even a grudging affection for the Regiment (as opposed to others), but in a strange kind of way we sometimes actually enjoyed ourselves. And even when we didn't, there was nothing like army humour to get us through it. One of our comedians in Headquarters Company asked a mate of his which was the heavier, a ton of coal or a ton of feathers. 'You can't catch me out on that one,' said the soldier, 'It's the ton of feathers of course!'

It also helped that none of us had ever done anything like it before. We were in the prime of life and had more future than past. We were physically fit and in better shape than Lieutenant Colonel Campbell thought we were. We were in it together and tried to make the most of it. We did not have much alternative. And we had each other for company. By the time of my second Christmas in uniform the old RSM had been replaced by a new one, RSM Hazelwood, and we were left rather more to our own devices.

I intend to shut myself inside the tent with a few particular cronies and celebrate as best we can – quite well, I imagine, for they are all cheerful coves; even the professional footballer, who has about 18 months to do and every prospect of staying in Cyprus when the Battalion goes home, isn't the least bit depressed.

My friends, or cronies, ranged from the footballer from Watford to a tailor from Sudbury, a pig farmer from Rendham, a bricklayer from Cambridge, and an extremely well educated guitar player from parts unknown with no job at all. In the tent next to us were two maestros of the skiffle group and one Old Wykehamist bound for Cambridge. Because we could read and write, most of us were clerks of one sort or another and had ink-stained fingers to prove it, because the Orderly Room duplicators leaked like sieves through their waxed stencils. I started National Service with few real friends and ended it with many.

> You get all sorts of queer fish brought together in this clerkish business
> ... At least the Army has been of some value in this respect.

The only problem was the occasional arguments which were hard to avoid in the space of a shared tent. One of the cronies was a Greek scholar with a passionate interest in nuclear power stations, about which I knew nothing. Another was a Plymouth Brother who was for ever trying to convert me with tracts and pamphlets printed in Australia and assuring me that it was time to repent my sins because The End Was Nigh. Actually, I knew exactly when The End was, because I kept a chart in my locker which told me. It was 117 days away and called demob. We were an oddly assorted bunch but got on well. We shared the same adversities and could bear them more easily by complaining about them to each other. And we were well aware that, since military service had to be done, we were better off doing it abroad than at home.

> For such time as I have to be a soldier of the Queen, I should rather
> be well clear of the frustrations of soldiering in England, about which
> fearful tales are told.

Because our camp was on the airport road, we watched the other regiments in transit and were sometimes as sorry for those leaving as for those arriving.

I'm on guard tonight always a god-send from the letter-writing angle. Have just seen the Paratroopers roaring off to the airport from their transit camp, presumably home-bound. I envy them that, but I pity them for having to undergo the horrors of a soldier's life in England.

Active service had a further advantage over the passive service of peacetime soldiering, in that for most of the time we supposed that there was actually some point to it – indeed we were led to believe that we were winning, which we were not. At the same time we were obsessive about demob. Our thoughts were constantly drifting homeward. Whatever the Army had done or failed to do, it had certainly cured me of my wanderlust for a while. Suffolk would suit me nicely,

As operations scaled down we speculated endlessly about a quick withdrawal as a gesture of goodwill by the Governor. Only two other battalions had been on the island longer than we had and their return was imminent. When the CO came back from an amalgamation conference at the War Office he held a parade (what else would he have done?) at which he told us we would be serving the full term. An audible groan went up from the assembled Battalion. It was as near to mutiny as we ever got. (There was a history to it. Our 2nd Battalion had been caught up in the Curragh Mutiny in August 1914, just before leaving to be slaughtered in Flanders. The officers had not actually mutinied but had threatened to disobey if ordered to march on Ulster. The other ranks, as usual, were not consulted. Some things never changed.)

I was no longer a teenager, and whatever my apprehensions about National Service, I had not expected to find it for much of the time a positive experience. I wrote:

Looking back on my history as one of HM forces, I was surprised the other day to realise how very un-miserable my service has been.

What did surprise us was that many of the regulars beside us, who had chosen soldiering as their career, were having second thoughts about it. We were made aware of this, towards the end of the tour of duty, when the Regiment ran a recruiting campaign, not in the towns and villages of Suffolk, but in its own back yard in Cyprus. It was trying to persuade its own soldiers to sign on for longer. Alarm bells must have been ringing in the War Office about retention rates. Maybe careers depended on it. Either heads would roll, or drums. It was time to bring on the Band. We had proper bands in those days. There may have been as many as nineteen of them on the island. We could have staged a tattoo if we had not been busy trying to put down a rebellion. Each battalion had its own band and ours was rather a good one. The regimental quick march, *Speed the Plough*, was an adapted Irish folk tune and (as any piccolo player will tell you) the most demanding in the entire military repertoire.

> The Commanding Officer is staging a grand recruiting drive. He is obviously disturbed because the men who signed on for 22 years three years ago are claiming their right to be demobilised now. To this end the Band and Drums turned out in their brassiest uniforms on Friday to beat the retreat. This, as a matter of fact, was unusually well done for our Band and most impressive. But it will take more than brass bands to get me to sign on.

The grand finale, by our Band and Drums no fewer than fifty men strong in all their glory, occurred on 14 March 1959, when the political *denouement* had already begun. The Beating Retreat was attended by the Governor and performed in front of an ingenious replica of a castle built by the Pioneer Sergeant out of wood and hessian sack-cloth. It was a virtual castle before the age of electronic wizardry and with the most practical special effects. The Band marched in through the castle gates, playing 'Swanee River' as a quick march, and the gates then slid impressively shut behind it, being pushed unseen by two of the Pioneer Sergeant's soldiers. There was no evidence, however, that anyone signed on for a day longer as a result, certainly not the national servicemen.

> The Regiment has taken to inserting incredible little notices in our pay
> books, saying that you, X, are receiving two and a half pence per week;
> if you were fool enough to sign on your allotment would be increased
> to three and three quarters pence.

The Band then left for home, the Royal Tournament and a series of concerts
in the county culminating in the Suffolk Show. ('Oh to be a bandsman!' I
wrote mournfully when I still had 200 days to do.) There was even talk, on
our own return to 'Blighty', of the Regiment being given the freedom of
Lowestoft. I liked the idea of parading through my home town (almost) with
bayonet fixed, but nothing ever came of it. I could have worn my solitary
medal, the General Service Medal (Cyprus). It did, however, parade through
Sudbury.

Next to go was the Commanding Officer, Lieutenant Colonel Silvanus
'Bertie' Bevan. Time just ran out on him. In retirement he wrote a book,
Topees and Red Berets, in which he described rather defensively how it all
ended. His bluster masked a deep insecurity. He was 44, which was quite
old for a battalion commander. He had not been to Sandhurst but had
entered the Army through a side door, a Supplementary Commission, and
had impressed his superiors with his marksmanship. He had also excelled
in war games and TEWTS (tactical exercises without troops), but in our
experience he was not quite so gifted at tactical exercises *with* troops. By the
time he reached Cyprus the years had taken their toll. When I escorted him
on a gentle route march from St Hilarion Castle downhill to Kyrenia, being
less than half his age, I noted unkindly 'He is chronically unfit and moves
at a snail's pace'. His further promotion was blocked because the Army
was down-sizing and he had never held a senior staff job, so his prospects
were not good. On his final confidential report in Germany, written by an
unsympathetic brigadier, he was rated 'average', which was a professional
death sentence. 'It was just my luck,' he wrote, 'to come up for promotion
when the Empire was being run down with consequent reductions in the
armed forces.'

To his credit and behind the scenes he worked hard to secure good
postings for his senior NCOs when the Norfolks and Suffolks amalgamated.
The difficulty was that the Norfolks were historically the senior regiment,

although we were of course in every way the better one: they were the 9th of Foot and we were the 12th. (We did it in Roman numerals, IX and XII.) Together we were a complex fraction, like the Tenth and a halfth of Foot.

On the CO's last day in command, 31 March 1959, we held a farewell parade for him, after which he was carried shoulder-high and towed out of the camp as if after a wedding party (which was how such things were done in those days). He would have wished for a neater end to it all by bringing the Battalion home with him.

> The CO, who is a very determined and aggressive man when it comes to arguing a point, is known to be pressing for an early return during his present discussions in the War Office.

But it was not to be. Major Malcolm Dewar was promoted to lieutenant colonel and took command. Lieutenant Colonel Bevan left the Army in 1961, not of his own volition and (he noted) still with three children to support. It was typical of him that after his retirement and when he was job-hunting in 'civilian street' he prepared a CV which included his panther-shooting as one of his qualifications. For any employer in the UK in need of an experienced panther-shooter his credentials were quite outstanding. It was a long farewell. He died forty years later.

Chapter 19

End Game

The Suffolk Regiment was winding down. It would be gone from Cyprus in six weeks and from history in six months. It was to be merged with the Royal Norfolks and become The First East Anglian Regiment and then, in short order, the 1st Battalion of The Royal Anglian Regiment. Suffolk and Norfolk were neighbours, but that was about as far as our sense of comradeship went. In my home town of Beccles, on the River Waveney which is the border between them, the church clock has only three faces: it will not even give the time of day to Norfolk. The merger between the 'keen and polished Norfolks and the scruffy but embattled Suffolks' (the words were mine) seemed a military mismatch. Being by far the more accomplished soldiers in our view, we felt that they feared being 'Suffolkated'. Even before we left the island we had to exchange the old cap badge for the new. We did it on the parade ground. Where else would we do it? And we were not impressed.

The Band looked resplendent (bands always do, even if the remainder of the Army has to be dressed in sack cloth), the only slight calamity being that during the counter-march one of the bandsmen had his hat swept from his head by another's trombone … The occasion for all this was the coming to pass of the first step of our amalgamation with the Royal Norfolks: the substitution of the new cap badge for the old one. Of course, it is quite out of the question that such a minor alteration to our appearances could be managed off the parade ground. Oh no: we all assemble on parade to be addressed in turn by the CO and the Padre (the Padre always pops up in the most unlikely places) and finally receive the new cap badge, which is a really hideous object, consisting of what appears to be a golden bauble set in a silver star-fish. But at least it has the advantage that it doesn't need to be cleaned, being made of some untarnishable substance.

The senior officers were obliged to see the amalgamation otherwise. One of them, Major General Sir Douglas Kendrew (I called him 'The Big Brass Hat out here') had told the Regiment at the previous year's Minden Day: 'Some of us older ones know that the Regimental System has cracked and creaked in action, and something had to be done. With this reorganisation of the strength of the Army it is now being done.' What he meant was that amalgamations were inevitable. National Service was about to end, and with it the Army's supply of abundant and cheap manpower. The Empire was shrinking and conscription was politically unpopular and no longer affordable. There would be no more soldiers available for service at 28 shillings a week. The Defence White Paper published at the time of my call-up had announced the disappearance or amalgamation of fifty-one major units, the Suffolk Regiment among them. The Army would be reduced in numbers to 168,000. My only contribution to military history was that I was there when it happened and part of the down-sizing. It has since been halved again. I joined a large army and left a small one. The cuts to the Regular Army were followed by cuts to the Territorials, overseen by two generals whose names were Hackett and Carver.

So The Suffolk Regiment, the 12th of Foot, or 'Old Dozen' as it was called, marched off parade after 274 continuous years' history, serving sometimes in victory (Minden and Normandy), sometimes in defeat (Singapore) and sometimes in sheer futility (Cyprus). The Regiment's historical distinction, it seemed to me, was not to have been in the vanguard of an advance but in the rearguard of a retreat: from Mons to India to Palestine, Malaya and Cyprus, the Suffolks seemed to be universally the last to leave. We turned out the lights and withdrew, still facing the enemy. It was a no less honourable position in the order of battle and one that required discipline, courage, restraint and steadiness under fire. In this twilight zone, with two months to go before demob, I had a further promotion to announce:

From what obscure motive I do not know, but the unpredictable powers-that-be have just made me a sergeant. Very odd!

I had no idea why the CO did it, except that he was the new CO not the old one. I had no choice in the matter. The RSM, who was in charge of sergeants, informed me of the promotion 'whether you like it or not'. And I suspect that he did not. It was most unusual, outside the Education Corps, for a national serviceman to be made up to sergeant. Actually I was only an acting sergeant and never got to be substantive (meaning permanent); but I wore three stripes and a red sash, carried a swagger stick, or hinged silver-topped pace stick, as a symbol of my brief authority and occasionally mounted the guard, which I did more quietly than most. The stripes were sewn on by the dhobi wallah. My pay increased by another few shillings a week. I kept the company of some seriously heavy drinkers in the Sergeants' Mess and failed lamentably to match them pint for pint. My attempt to do so earned me such a dreadful hangover that I did not try it again. Reluctantly I abandoned my mates the clerks and orderlies and the professional footballer in Headquarters Company, and moved my kit to the sergeants' lines, where I shared a tent with only one other rather than five. He was a kindred spirit, a National Service sergeant from the Education Corps.

> I must assure you that I am not turning into a parade ground martinet and my job does not involve any of the animal behaviour traditionally expected of a sergeant. Even on such parades as we do have, of which I hope to have attended my last anyway, I stand well behind and out of the way of everyone else, gratefully leaving the shouting to such as are more adept at it. The only shouting I have to do is when I occasionally have to mount the guard, which fortunately happens about once every three weeks.
>
> This business of being a sergeant is having more and more advantages. The food is really wonderful and there are even waiters on hand to serve it out. I am woken up every morning by the arrival of someone with a hot cup of tea.

The sergeants lived in a world of their own, run by the RSM who 'gripped' them too, and in which the strangest things could happen and sometimes did. One morning towards the end of the tour the Provost Sergeant, who had once survived an EOKA ambush unscathed, emerged from his tent with burns all over his face. He had somehow managed to set fire to himself the night before in the bar of the Sergeants' Mess. It may have been an experiment in fire-eating. And this was the man responsible, through the Regimental Police, for the good order and military discipline of the entire camp. These were the same Regimental Police who had failed to find the silver candlestick which disappeared from the Officers' Mess.

It was another age then and I am privileged to have lived in it. The Army's *Advice to Young Officers*, prepared under the Direction of the Chief of the Imperial General Staff in 1956, includes a section on etiquette when visiting the Sergeants' Mess: 'When attending Sergeants' Mess dances it is customary and good manners to ask the RSM's wife and the wives of the senior warrant officers and sergeants to dance. Officers should avoid spending their whole time at the bar or monopolising the attention of the prettiest girls in the room.'

This being the Army, we did not just pick up our kitbags, sling them over our shoulders and head for home. Things had to be done by the book. There were standard operating procedures to be followed. We packed our kit into wooden boxes with addresses stencilled in distinctive colours and lists of contents in quadruplicate attached to them. It was a time to reflect on what, if anything, we had achieved.

As after most military campaigns – Iraq, Afghanistan and yes, even Cyprus – we who had borne the brunt of it were left at the last parade wondering what it had all been for: such great expectations, and yet at the end so little to show for them … *And bugles calling for them from sad shires* … The Last Post still makes me shiver. Usually there is more to be learned from failure than from success – but not, it seemed, in Cyprus. Even as the settlement was being negotiated, great plans were being laid for an all-out and decisive drive by the security forces to defeat EOKA once and for all. The death or glory boys never gave up. Had it happened, it would have been what is described in the military academies as 'reinforcing failure'. And it was not the foot-soldiers' fault, nor even the generals', that such fantasies were entertained. The politicians then as now seemed to have no idea how much, and how little, armed force could achieve. Instead of burning my cherished files in perforated oil drums, I wished that I had smuggled some of them home in my kitbag, at the risk of being in breach of Queen's Regulations. I would then have had a better idea of where it all went wrong. It seemed even at the time like a bonfire of the policies.

> The business of packing up and going home is reaching a very advanced state of chaos. My own preoccupation over the past week has been consigning to the flames all the documents which I spent hours filing earlier on. As our departure from Cyprus coincides more or less with the end of the emergency, there is a vast amount of material to be disposed of: internal security instructions with impressive 'Secret' and 'Top Secret' markings splashed all over them, the maps I spent ages gluing together and marking, mountains of photographs of formerly wanted men, and all sorts of paraphernalia which we seem to have gathered over the months and lacked the initiative to throw away. It does all seem that the fruits of our labour have gone rotten on us.

The handwritten Battalion Diary noted on 19 February 1959 'Final agreement in London conference. All ops withdrawn'. [Actually it was in Zurich first, bilaterally between Greece and Turkey, then London.] On 1 March, 'Archbishop Makarios, the Greek Ethnarch, returned to Cyprus'.

> As I write, Archbishop Makarios is being feted in the town, the Greek population of almost the whole island having gathered in the narrow streets to give him a hero's welcome, which he will doubtless enjoy. For the occasion the police are doing all the security work and the Army has been completely hidden up. No one is allowed to enter or leave the camps, which are thus virtually in a state of siege; and even inside our camp (which lies on the road between Nicosia Airport and the town) we were not allowed to show our inquisitive faces as the bearded wonder swept past.

In my defence I must explain that a 'bearded wonder' was part of the Suffolks' folklore. They had used the same term about their principal adversary in Malaya. But this campaign was ending differently. The colonial government worried that the BBC would address the Archbishop as 'Your Beatitude'.

The following week he urged EOKA fighters to lay down their arms. Most of them did, for a while at least. It was the overdue end of *Enosis*.

The Turkish Cypriot leader, Dr Fazil Kuchuk, also returned from exile. I was clearly unimpressed with them both.

> He is a ridiculous looking man, with a sparse growth of hair that stands poor comparison with the Archbish's flowing mane; but nonetheless was cheered wildly by the Turks and carried shoulder high to his house. With a bit of luck it may prove to be the last time we are on standby at all. I reverted to my old job of hanging round the Central Police Station, not very exciting in normal times but quite interesting with fire-breathing nationalist orators arriving from various corners of the world.

For the return of the Archbishop the camp was in lockdown. D Company's orders stated 'Guard commanders should ensure that great care is taken by all personnel to keep out of sight of Cypriots as much as possible and not to provoke any trouble with the locals. All personnel are confined to their immediate area and guard commanders must ensure that personnel do not line any perimeter fence to watch any demonstrations etc.' We held parades but no exercises, because the Greek press would not have seen the difference between an exercise and an operation. And finally and by way of bathos, because all operations had been withdrawn, the official Diary entry for the day noted 'Battalion defeated 43 Regiment RA by 3 goals to 1 in the 50 Brigade hockey cup final' – as if it mattered: some things never changed from start to finish. A soldier in 7 Platoon A Company wrote 'One thing we are all certain of is that Cyprus is "played out". What we all long for is a whiff of home. The other day one member of the platoon got just that. In a food parcel from home, in among the cakes and bags of sweets, was one bag, very carefully sealed and apparently quite empty, bearing a label marked "Leicester air"'.

> So it looks as if all my pin-sticking will have been in vain! The Army's well laid plans have been thrown into utter confusion … and it will have to find the wherewithal to occupy its idle hours somewhere else

... I foresee great training programmes, vast drill parades and so on – enough to make one wish for 'the troubles' to start again, almost.

It was the bored young soldier syndrome again. The saving grace note by this time was the 'almost'.

And that was really the end of it. The remaining political prisoners were released. The detention camps closed. Press censorship was eased. The campaign was turned on its head. Before our withdrawal from Cyprus and after the Archbishop's return to it, EOKA fighters were also being feted in the streets of Nicosia and Colonel Grivas (whom among others I had personally failed to capture) was letting his exploits be known in outwitting the British. By the time of the final agreements the British believed they knew his hiding place, but to have lifted him then, or more probably killed him in the course of it, would have wrecked the London Conference. By chance it seemed that I served in Cyprus at a pivotal time. If Intelligence was to blame, then I was part of the failure. When I arrived in the island in 1957 the Army was convinced that it was winning. When I left in 1959 there could be no such illusions. The game was up when the Mayor of Nicosia declared 'We are all EOKA now!' We had done what we could and made the most of it but were not going home in triumph. I wrote:

> The Army is having to swallow an awful lot of pride over these Greek festivities. Not only has Colonel Grivas started to disclose the unpalatable facts about his various escapades, but all the EOKA gentlemen have emerged from their rat-holes in the hills to ride in triumph through Nicosia. Why, we are not even allowed to take away from them the pistols that they display quite openly. Much gnashing of teeth in military circles!

Why 'rat-holes'? The only explanation I can offer is that after their setbacks in 1957 the hard-core EOKA fighters survived by living in well-concealed mineshafts and tunnels in the Troodos Mountains. Soldiers would set fire to the undergrowth in vain attempts to burn them out of their hiding places.

As part of the agreement, Colonel Grivas returned to Athens on 17 March 1959, still packing a pistol. He too was a national hero. He was promoted to General by the Greek Government and awarded the 'Order of Valour' by King Paul. (Greece then was still a monarchy.) His departure from the island was diplomatically sensitive and carefully managed, for the British still controlled the airports and seaports. After so much spilt blood on both sides, there were courtesies to be observed or ignored. The Greek Government wished to send not just one aircraft but two to pick up Grivas. On 13 March the Colonial Office instructed the Embassy in Athens 'Governor must know as soon as possible full names and status of crews and passengers on both aircraft and whether any Greek officer or other representative of the Greek Government will intend to disembark and greet Grivas on the airfield in Cyprus'. [FCO Archive 141/4493] Legend had it that his departure was supervised by a disabled former British officer who, lacking a right arm, was unable to salute him.

Nikos Sampson, the EOKA assassin twice reprieved by the British, was accorded a hero's welcome in the village of Tymbou. The newspaper *Phileftheros* reported 'The streets of the village were decorated with Greek flags, and as soon as he arrived he was showered with flowers'.

The colonial authorities did not shower anyone with flowers, not even a departing and long-serving infantry battalion. But at about the same time and three days before the troopship sailed, we received a sort of bouquet, a farewell message from the Governor Sir Hugh Foot: 'Congratulations on all that the Suffolks have done in Cyprus. The Battalion has answered every call made on it splendidly and we have all greatly admired the spirit in which you have carried out your duties. You go home with the satisfaction of having done a fine job and the knowledge that your resolute and persistent effort has contributed to the settlement which has now been reached.'

The settlement – a complex constitutional compromise between British, Greeks and Turks – was probably doomed to failure from the outset and did not last. Makarios himself wrote later 'I am the one who signed those agreements on behalf of the people of Cyprus ... But not for a moment did I believe that the agreements would be a permanent state of affairs'. And in his speech on the inauguration of the new Republic: 'New bastions have been conquered and from these bastions the Greek Cypriots will march on to complete the final victory.' There was no *Enosis* for the Greeks and (at that time) no partition for the Turks. If Archbishop Makarios and Dr

Kuchuk had appeared jointly before their supporters and proclaimed the advantages of a shared independence to their people, the peaceful option might have prevailed. But after the inter-communal violence of 1958 there was too much bad blood between them. Instead, the Turkish leader said that Makarios held the steering wheel but he had his foot on the brake. It was all downhill from there. At the Battalion level we had no idea of the politics of it. We lowered the flag, turned to the right and dismissed. It was the twilight of Empire and a time of farewell calls by the Top Brass.

> One of the signs of our departure has been the visits by local generals, who tour the camp, passing remarks here and there to the odd soldier, and paying calls on the Officers' and Sergeants' Messes. In this way I had quite a long hob-nob with the Commander of Middle East Land Forces, who professed to be envious of my prospects: he said that he too had once tried for King's Cambridge (and presumably failed). Very good for morale.

I liked the symmetry of frustrated ambition, for had I not once aspired to be an officer – or a 'Rupert', as the other ranks now call them? We had each wished to be the other and failed. Better still, liberation (in the form of demob) was almost at hand. I had never looked forward to anything so much in my life.

> All who first joined up on June 13th 1957 are now the great envy of everyone else and much prestige attaches to our happy position.

There were two further signs of the approaching demob. One was the notification that I would still be liable for reserve duty with the Regiment's 4th (TA) Battalion in Ipswich; the Cold War was at its height and the Army, having trained us to the point of adequacy, was reluctant to let us go. The other was that my uniform had seen so much service that, like an old soldier's, it was beginning to wear out. It had got some time in and seen some service.

> I find it very encouraging that my clothes are with one accord coming through in holes. Trousers are going through at the seat, shirts at the

collar, and I am at the moment wearing out my seventh pair of gym shoes. (Tennis courts are very hard on them.) My conclusion is that most of the Army's clothing must have been designed for the time when National Service was 18 months. A soldier who has done 22 months is very much a thing of shreds and patches.

On the eve of departure, we discovered to our surprise that we had been underspending.

The Regiment now finds itself in the enviable position of having far more money to spend than things to spend it on. This came about largely from the time it took to take over the NAAFI from the Greeks (who were all sacked over the wave of sabotage in December and whom we suspected of having over-charged us). The Greeks, as part of the general amnesty, are back in control, but in the meantime the Battalion made a profit of over £700, largely as a result of having so few overhead costs in the way of wages etc. Now frantic searches are made to find something to spend it on.

Being soldiers rather than academics we didn't do the Roman ruins or historical monuments for which Cyprus was famous, but blew some of the windfall on a free bus trip to watch the Army, captained of course by the Suffolk Regiment's Dave Pygall, defeat the RAF at football. We kept our sense of proportion to the end. If we could not beat EOKA, we could at least prevail over the 'crabs'. (This was from inter-service rivalry: we soldiers called the airmen crabs because we believed that they marched sideways.)

The officers who were returning with us to regular soldiering, and not as happy as we were, included my Intelligence Officer Charles Barnes. The new amalgamated Regiment would be based at Iserlohn in Germany.

The IO has expressed great misgivings about his prospects on amalgamation. Never much of one for the social life, he won't be able to plead the call of duty as an excuse for avoiding Mess functions in Germany as he has done in Cyprus.

His misgivings were unfounded. He did very well in a career that took him regularly, as mine did, to Belfast. There he commanded the 2nd Battalion of The Royal Anglian Regiment in 1975 on internal security duties not totally dissimilar to those of the Suffolks in Cyprus. It was my pleasure after so many years to offer him dinner in the Europa Hotel during one of the quieter interludes when it was not being blown up. He was eventually promoted to brigadier, which was much harder to achieve in the new Army than the old one. In the old one he would have become at least a major general. As the Army shrank, its ranks deflated accordingly.

On the eve of our departure, the camp was hit by a great thunderstorm, which flooded the ground and was especially ill-timed because my groundsheet (or poncho) was in the kit-bag that had been sent to Limassol docks ahead of me. One of the useful lessons of soldiering, which I never forgot, is that a fool and his equipment are easily separated. Reveille was at 3am, the first time it had been that early since we cordoned and searched our last village. We left Kykko Camp at dawn. We were sublimely happy to see the last of it.

Our troopship was the *Dilwara*, built on the Clyde in 1936. The same ship had brought the Battalion, along with the Ox and Bucks, to the island in August 1956. The return journey was one of her last voyages, for she was too was on her way out and about to be sold to a cut-price shipping line in Kuala Lumpur. Troopships belonged to the end of Empire too. We did not expect a cruise ship and we did not get one.

> We were inoculated against tetanus or some such contagion which, presumably, finds breeding grounds on troopships … It takes these dilapidated old troopships about ten days to labour their way from Cyprus to England.

On the voyage home I became a teacher, giving lessons to the officers' children in a makeshift classroom. Being total unqualified, of course, I read to them from *Wind in the Willows*. It seemed right to immerse them in its Englishness, especially since our former Commanding Officer had appeared to me to be Mr Toad in uniform.

The *Dilwara* docked in Southampton on 16 May 1959. The Band of the 4th Battalion was on the quayside to greet us with *Speed the Plough*. The families disembarked first and the soldiers afterwards. They entrained to Shorncliffe in Kent, the Battalion's new home for most of its remaining few weeks. I was due three weeks' leave, took them in Beccles and had the best homecoming of my life. I tried not to bore my family with old soldiers' stories, but began to prepare myself for Cambridge with the help of a copious reading list. I started to paint the boat-house battleship grey. I mowed the lawn with the greatest pleasure, not having seen any grass worth the name in nearly two years. Cyprus was already a dream.

On the appointed day I returned to Gibraltar Barracks where it had all begun. Being a sergeant at the time, I hoped for an amicable separation from the Army. On the eve of my demob, not wishing to be shouted at for one last time, I took the precaution of getting a haircut. This was a mistake, because the barber in Bury St Edmunds, supposing I was an officer, gave me an officer's haircut, which is not the same as a private soldier's or even a sergeant's. When I presented myself to the Regimental Office the next morning I had such a bawling out from the RSM – yes, the same RSM, my old nemesis – as I had never been given before even in basic training and have never been given since. The RSM had views about haircuts. I suppose it was the Army's way of saying goodbye. Then I was marched before the Adjutant, Captain North, who tried to persuade me to sign on. I politely declined. After such a detonation I was not in the mood to soldier for one day longer.

And with that I reclaimed my freedom. I changed out of battledress for the last time. I kept the red sash as a souvenir, but gave my pace stick to Sergeant Jones (the Provost Sergeant of the burned face) because he asked for it and needed it more than I did. My marching days were over and I was back in 'civilian street'. With a rail warrant in my pocket, I strolled past the Guard Room, through the gate and into a new life.

Chapter 20

The Other Side of the Wire

But for an accident of birth, he could have been the one doing the cordons, searches and internment and I could have been the one being cordoned, searched and interned. We were about the same age. Neither spoke the other's language. We came from where we came from. We had no choice but to be where we were and doing what we were doing. Each could so easily have been the other. We called them Wogs. They called us Johnnies.

In the course of Operation Matchbox in July 1958 the British cordoned the village of Kologrea 22 miles east of Kyrenia. They were armed not only with guns but with lists of names supplied by Special Branch. They took away fifty men and boys in army trucks. One of the fifty was Panayiotis Michael, who was just 17 years old. Their first destination was a British Army camp in nearby Ayios Amvrosios. Panayiotis recalled 'Funnily enough, I helped to build that bloody camp!' Every detainee had a number. His was 3197. The total of detainees held by the British under the emergency powers, mostly in 1958, was 3,363.

In the course of Operation Matchbox, 1,800 men were picked up. Most were not even questioned about possible EOKA activities or sympathies. Not enough was known about them. The lists of names were supplied by informers in the villages, who would be paid the same whether the information was true or false. They could use the lists to settle old scores against neighbours, which in some cases had nothing to do with politics at all. Right wing against left wing also came into it. So did debtor against creditor. The suspects were locked up as a deterrent to others and to get them out of the way. Internment may actually have saved some lives, in keeping men of military age out of the line of fire. My personal account of Operation Matchbox, typically insouciant, showed the Greeks, its victims, to have been remarkably co-operative.

This was done in Nicosia by an unholy alliance of Special Branch (smooth gangsterish types with fast cars and concealed automatics), the Irish Guards and the dear old Suffolks. On the first two days of the operation we surrounded the local villages and extracted our victims from a sort of human heap gathered from all corners, nooks and crannies. Then we set up vast road blocks causing, I regret to say, maximum inconvenience to everybody and hunted for yet more wanted men …

Considering the indignities to which the Greeks were subjected in the way of herding together and searching, they behaved extremely well and were most amicable – much more than the occupants of an English village would have been in similar circumstances.

The same theme recurred repeatedly. Greek Cypriots were not, unlike the British, historically warlike people. They preferred their vineyards, coffee shops and trees of idleness. Both Grivas and his deputy Grigoris Afxentiou were both former Greek army officers from the mainland. Over the centuries, the people of Cyprus had a history of adjusting to foreign rulers, among whom the British were relatively benign. Only in 1960 did they finally achieve self-government.

For more than a month Panayiotis Michael, like many others, was held in an army camp near Kyrenia before being transferred to Ayios Loukas near Famagusta and put into storage – quite literally – in one of two vast warehouses built for the orange trade. Like all the camps it was surrounded by barbed wire and watch towers manned by British soldiers. Lawrence Durrell described them as looking like turkey farms. There was no contact whatever between captors and captives. The British spoke no Greek, and those Greeks who spoke English were careful not to be seen talking to the British, as if the wire and watchtowers were not enough of a barrier. One of the prisoners, an English-speaking schoolmaster, was suspected of collaboration and roughly treated by his fellow internees. The special relationship between British and Greeks was under considerable strain.

Conditions for the prisoners were similar to those for the soldiers – except that the soldiers were still mostly housed in tents. Inside the wire, the Greeks had beds and hot water and better amenities than those who guarded them. They also had three meals a day provided by Greek cooks. They were paid between £5 and £30 a month, depending on whether they were single or had families to support. They were not required to work and passed the time in sports, football and tennis, or in making handicrafts such as intricately-carved wooden tables, or ornate decorations for which the raw material was two plastic combs melted together. Internment was the mother of invention. Few of the prisoners tried to escape – there seemed no point to it. They just waited for their release, which was bound to happen in the pre-Independence negotiations as a gesture of goodwill.

The detention system was over-stretched and understaffed. By November 1958 it needed 127 more warders inside the wire than it had. If the Governor had had his way, hundreds of the young men picked up in Operation Matchbox, which he had strongly opposed, would have been released within days of arrest and before formal detention orders were issued against them. But he did not have his way. Yet again he was overruled by the military, the Colonial Office and even his own advisers, including the hard-line Deputy Governor who wrote: 'Such a step might destroy the renewed sense of purpose and confidence given to the security forces by Y.E.'s [Your Excellency's] decision to deal vigorously with terrorism from any quarter'. [FCO Archive 141/4216] Throughout these exchanges there was an undercurrent of tension and disagreement between the Governor and the Deputy Governor, always politely expressed. The misfortune was that in matters of internal security it was the Deputy Governor who carried the day. If wiser counsels had prevailed, especially on the big decisions and major operations like Matchbox, a great deal of subsequent grief could have been avoided.

So the months of internment dragged on. Panayiotis Michael, with many others, was finally released the following December. The strange thing about it was that like many others he was offered not just his freedom but a safe passage to the country that had locked him up. It did not matter either that he was suspected of EOKA sympathies or that he spoke no English. 'On my release they gave me a letter to say I am allowed to come to this country. They were encouraging us to come. When they were releasing us from a camp, they gave us a certificate to say that we were free to come to England if we wanted to. What they were doing was they were trying to make the youngsters leave Cyprus. On the day of our release they were telling us that we were British citizens and we were free to come here.'

This was extraordinary. On information supplied by Special Branch the detainees were thought to be a threat to public order in their own country, yet not just allowed but encouraged to settle in ours. Many of them did, learned the language and made new lives here. That was how they came by their British passports. They were among our most successful immigrants. They still remain so. After all that had happened, the Anglo-Greek relationship survived and prospered. It was to the credit of both sides that it did so.

Among other incomers to Britain at the time were the Special Branch informers (or 'Toads') – those who survived, for some were exposed and murdered – who had identified the likes of Panayiotis Michael and his brother. Since 1956 the British had been using the Colonial Prisoners Removal Act of 1884 to deport so-called 'ringleaders' of the rebellion. Panayiotis Michael was no ringleader.

Neither was his future father-in-law, Photios Grivas, who was detainee number 634. Long before his internment his name had given him endless trouble at road blocks. He was not anti-British but a '100 per cent patriotic' Greek Cypriot. He was of another generation and had served in the British Army in Palestine during the Mandate. A photograph from that time shows him in a khaki drill uniform remarkably like mine twenty years later. He was (unlike me) quite free of prejudice. When a British Army patrol passed through his village while his wife was baking the week's bread he told her to give them a loaf. When she demurred, he insisted. 'Feed the British', he said, 'They're just kids' (which is indeed what we were). But if he had not been respected for his status in the village and for his pro-EOKA patriotic sympathies he might not have got away with it.

The internees were abducted not only from the towns and villages but also from the monasteries. I discovered this on a rare deployment to the Troodos Mountains and the area where the EOKA commander, Grigoris Afxentiou, had been killed in 1957. In my typically mindless way I described it as 'infested with EOKA'. In fact we met no one in open countryside but two mountain rangers, who were typically hospitable.

I paid a visit to the monastery yesterday and found that apart from a couple of novice monks all the younger inmates, including the Abbott, have been moved to detention camps, leaving a quorum of dotards with venerable beards.

Internment camps were not new to Cyprus. The island had been notorious for them before and on a larger scale. At the time when young Photios Grivas was serving in Palestine, the British had established twelve camps for would-be Jewish immigrants intercepted at sea while trying to land there – more than 50,000 of them. The British were the world's leaders in the operation of internment camps. The first had been built in South Africa and St Helena in 1900 for prisoners of the Boer War.

The year of Operation Matchbox, 1958, was the turning-point of the Cyprus campaign. It could have gone either way until then. It is now clear that we actually helped EOKA by our heavy-handedness. Its support ran wider and deeper than we knew in the towns and villages. Children as young as 11 acted as couriers and some as young as 14 were interned. At great risk to themselves, communities sheltered and fed the EOKA fighters or 'terrorists' as we called them. The security forces' Intelligence failures began at the grass-roots level, in streets patrolled so fruitlessly by the Suffolk Regiment among many others over the four years of the emergency. Two weeks after Operation Matchbox I was still getting it spectacularly wrong.

Everything is in a high state of preparation for the next crisis, which we reckon will not be far off; it is not commonly expected to last long either, for EOKA is already disrupted and one more intensive operation could see it finished off altogether.

When it was over we all got our gongs. Ours was the General Service Medal (Cyprus). Theirs was a medal struck by the Government of Cyprus after independence for heroes of the EOKA struggle (the actual fighters) and later on for the former detainees, though they were required to pay £22 for it.

It was many years later, after Operation Attila, the Turkish invasion of July 1974, that the doubts and recriminations set in. When the independence settlement fell apart, many Greek Cypriots were left wondering whether the sacrifices and hardships had been worth it. More than 140,000 of them in the north of the island lost their land, their homes and everything they had in the course of a parachute drop. This was exactly what Governor Foot had predicted when the two communities started separating. They remembered other and better times, when Greeks and Turks lived in relative peace together; when the Turks in the Paphos and Famagusta areas especially also spoke Greek; and when Turkish shepherds, having herded their sheep to the sea near Kyrenia to wash them, would spend the evening in Greek coffee shops on their way home and at ease with their neighbours.

Some Greeks blame their politicians of the time – especially those in mainland Greece – for the dead end of *Enosis* and the empty rhetoric that went with it. Other options were available. Union with Greece was never going to be viable in an island where nearly one in five of the people were Turkish. The British were retreating from Empire anyway, including Cyprus, and it did not have to be done as it was done. There had to have been another and better way. The decolonisation of Cyprus was a catalogue of failed initiatives and missed opportunities. Paradoxically, the British managed to be both too stubborn in holding on to the colony and too hasty in letting go of it. It is not a defence of colonialism, but the view of many dispossessed Greek Cypriots, to this day, is that they were better off then than they are now. Among a once peaceable people the habits of violence became too deeply ingrained.

One of the villages seized by the Turks was Kythrea, north east of Nicosia, which I had described as 'heartily pro-EOKA' when we cordoned and searched it for three days in the hectic October of 1958. Now all its Greeks are gone – fled, dead or disappeared. *Cui bono*: to whose advantage but the Turks'? And the Greeks in Kyrenia and Famagusta lost everything.

Sir Hugh Foot, the last governor of Cyprus, was prescient about partition sixteen years before it was imposed by force of arms. Drawing on the experience of the intercommunal violence in June 1958, in which 600 Greek and Turkish families abandoned their homes, he broadcast to the people a month later and predicted a disaster if partition came to pass: 'We all have a pretty good idea how much suffering that has caused. Ask yourself what the total of hardship and unhappiness would have been if the number of families on the move had been not 600 but 30,000.' Which was just about what happened. He should have been listened to because he was right. All three parties to the final agreement miscalculated – perhaps the British most culpably of all, in guaranteeing the settlement.

The United Kingdom's failure to intervene was on the face of it a scandalous breach of its undertakings. A House of Commons Select Committee was baffled by it: 'Britain had a legal right to intervene. She had a moral obligation to intervene. She had the military capacity to intervene. She did not intervene for reasons which the Government refuses to give.' [Report from the Select Committee on Cyprus 1975–1976] The Prime Minister in 1976, Jim Callaghan, later explained that Britain was no longer a superpower and could not afford to deal with 'another Suez'.

After all that we did to antagonise the Greek Cypriots from 1955 to 1959, and then not to help them by honouring our guarantees in 1974, many of them remain remarkably pro-British. Panayiotis Michael, the former detainee now 74 years old and living in Southgate, holds no grievance against his adopted country or the conscripts such as myself who cordoned his village and took him away. He says 'The soldiers were there because they had to be there. *I have a feeling that the British are the best people in the world.*' And yes, he really said that. On Christmas Day, he stands to attention to listen to the Queen's broadcast.

Chapter 21

Lieutenant Colonel Arthur Campbell MC

The most remarkable soldier I served under was Lieutenant Colonel Arthur Campbell MC, who should have commanded the Battalion but did not. He was not only charismatic and a natural leader, paying particular attention to the men under his command who might otherwise have cracked – or, as the Army now puts it, 'wobbled' – he was also a linguist, literate and even literary, which was as rare then as now, when the memoirs of Chiefs of the General Staff are almost invariably ghost-written. He was an accomplished cricketer too.

His MC was won as a company commander with the Suffolks during their successful tour of duty in Malaya. He gave his recruits, fresh out of basic training, a crash course in jungle-bashing. 'I pushed them hard,' he said, 'there was so much to learn and so little time.' His book about the Malayan emergency, the lightly fictionalised *Jungle Green*, celebrated the courage and dedication of the national servicemen who followed his leadership and whose campaign it was. He dedicated his book to the British soldier, 'the bravest, most patient and most stoical of men'. His account of the campaign was published in 1953 and ran through thirteen editions until 1968. It was also outspoken and by today's standards 100 per cent politically incorrect. He was vehemently and offensively anti-Chinese. He wrote 'I did not like that man. To begin with, he was a Chinaman. They are all two-faced beggars, waiting to see who will get the upper hand'. He quoted one of his soldiers 'I'll admit it is not our country, but all the niggers who live here look to us to see the place is decently run'.

It was not only Arthur Campbell's misfortune, but ours, that in length of service he was slightly junior to our CO and therefore not in line for the command. So he moved from Malaya to Cyprus, with postings to the War Office and Staff College between the two, still as a company commander, but unusually with the rank of lieutenant colonel to go with it. He was Officer

Commanding D Company, running the operation in the mountains which accounted for Grivas's deputy Markos Drakos. His qualities of leadership were immediately apparent and we were all aware of them. One of the younger members of the officer corps described him as 'head and shoulders' above all the others. As in Malaya, he led from the front and his company carried no passengers. A platoon commander fresh out of Sandhurst was greeted as follows: 'Great to see you. Super job for you tonight. You're out on ambush patrol. The second in command will fix you up with the right kit.' The subaltern never unpacked for the next three days. Arthur Campbell was known to us all as 'the Colonel': Bertie Bevan was just 'the CO'. 'The Colonel' gave free rein to his platoon commanders, but was less accommodating to portly and superfluous majors.

In 1958, and after the Battalion's move from the mountains to the plains, the long-serving company commander became the Battalion's second-in-command. It was then that I met him and, like others, fell under his spell. On one occasion during the riotous summer of that year we represented the Battalion, just the two of us, in the operations room at Nicosia Central Police Station. I marked the maps and he gave the orders. I was impressed by his authorship as well as his leadership. Even the other ranks knew about *Jungle Green*. I described him in a letter home as:

> An extremely nice man, and most unmilitary, which makes him all the nicer: most surprising to find an officer capable of applying pen to paper.

The CO was often away on consultations, presiding over courts-martial, or on one occasion, before the Saddam Hussein regime, even observing Iraqi military manoeuvres. Iraq's monarchy fell shortly afterwards: there seemed to us other ranks to be something ill-omened about whatever the CO did. When the rioting in Nicosia was at its height the burden would fall on the broad shoulders of Arthur Campbell. On the eve of Operation Matchbox the Commanding Officer with his typical sense of timing went on leave in Kyrenia and Arthur Campbell took over. He paraded all of us in front of him and gave us one of his inspirational addresses: we were physically unfit, he said, and we had to shape up *immediately* to meet the operational challenge and to honour the Regiment's traditions. It was under him that the Suffolks enhanced their reputation for steadiness under the direst circumstances. And it was there that we lived up to the old motto of the 12th of Foot, *Stabilis*. We became the Governor's favourite battalion. He knew he could depend on us.

Arthur Campbell was as demanding of his soldiers in Cyprus as he had been in Malaya, believing that when we arrived on the island we were in many cases just not up to it. It would take another three months as least to turn us into proper soldiers fit for the purpose we were there for. He was by nature a gentleman but he was also a perfectionist and hard task-master. He had thought it through. He wrote 'The lesson of Cyprus is that too little time is spent in our Army on the efficient training of the individual soldiers, while officers are not insistent enough during training on proper behaviour and obedience to rules. The strict discipline of the thug, imposed as it is by ruthless leaders and by daily risk of arrest or death, can be countered only by battlefield discipline'. [*Flaming Cassock*]

One of the mind games soldiers play is working out which of their contemporaries will rise to high command. Arthur Campbell was clearly fast-tracked, to the dismay of some of his less gifted contemporaries. We were convinced that he would make it to lieutenant general at least. When Bertie Bevan left, it should have fallen to Arthur Campbell to take over command, whether or not on an acting basis, and bring the Battalion home for amalgamation. Fate decided otherwise. In the summer of 1957 when the insurgency was faltering, the outgoing Governor Sir John Harding was aware that he had an established author commanding a rifle company in the mountains. Perhaps with an eye to his place in history as the architect of the defeat of EOKA, which he thought to be almost a *fait accompli*, Harding decided that Arthur Campbell would be more usefully employed in Government House going through the files and writing the official history of the campaign. Harding had been Commander-in-Chief Far East Land Forces when the 1st Battalion served in Malaya, where the young Major Campbell first caught his eye. He was the perfect choice for the task.

So Arthur Campbell moved into Government House and went to work. He combed through the records and spoke to soldiers, policemen and officials in Cyprus and London. They were under Harding's orders to help him. His manuscript, when almost finished, was called *Flaming Cassock: History of the Cyprus Emergency 1955-1957*. The title was an unflattering reference to Archbishop Makarios, who was banished to the Seychelles by Governor Harding. *Flaming Cassock* was also the original title of an anti-Makarios pamphlet put out by the colonial Government at about the same time and re-titled *The Church and Terrorism*. Its source material included files that were seized from the Ethnarchy when the Archbishop was banished. The pamphlet was published but the book was not. When Sir Hugh Foot succeeded Field Marshal Harding as Governor in December 1957, he decided that the soldierly historian in Government House was surplus to requirements. He used the bureaucracy to require all copies of the book to be destroyed, on the grounds that its publication would impede a settlement. It thus became a non-book and was never spoken of again, except in whispers in the regimental family.

In 1960 Arthur Campbell became Commanding Officer of The 1st East Anglian Regiment, the fusion of Norfolks and Suffolks, in Berlin. He was then deployed with the Battalion to British Honduras (now Belize), at one day's notice and on active service because of a territorial claim by neighbouring Guatemala. He was a meteor of a man who fell to earth following an episode which had nothing to do with his soldiering, but rather more to do with the Army's high command in one of its sporadic fits of morality. He had acquired too many envious detractors along his career path, including a stiff-necked guardsman and a field marshal. If the lady in question had been British rather than Belizean he would surely have got away with it. The customary OBE was denied to him. Now as then, it is a characteristic of the British Army that, except in wars of national survival, it distrusts the *unusual* officers, the outliers and mavericks and risk-takers. It prefers the political soldiers, the ticks-in-boxes types who would never dream of resigning on principle, and turns them into four star generals rewarded with knighthoods and peerages.

In 1961 Anglia Television produced a documentary about the Battalion in Berlin while Campbell still commanded it. It was clearly shot before his fall from grace because, although his voice remained on the soundtrack, his face and name appear to have been edited out. He was written out of the record. He faded from view but not from memory. He died in 1993.

As a professional underling and other rank, I was not easily impressed by officers, but I was by Arthur Campbell. It was his misfortune that he was caught between two governors and two views of the campaign, the illusion of victory and the reality of stalemate. It was an assessment widely shared in the regimental family, that he was the finest soldier we ever knew and the best general we never had.

Chapter 22

Buried Treasure

Although *Flaming Cassock* was suppressed by Governor Foot, at least three copies have survived. Two are held in the National Archives at Kew. One is an edited text under a sixty-year gagging order which requires it to remain unopened until 2022. An earlier draft is even more deeply buried under an eighty-year restriction. The decisions to suppress were confirmed as recently as 2012, the year before the release of the highly revealing file on Operation Matchbox. Why one and not the other? The inconsistency of judgement was all the more striking because *Flaming Cassock* was not a sensitive government communication – like a cable from a colonial governor to a secretary of state – but a book that was actually commissioned by a governor for publication in the first place.

Campbell's brief, according to Harding, was 'to write an account of the campaign in Cyprus between 1 April 1955 and 14 March 1957 that was factually correct, readable by the general public and of value to the professional student of internal security. In my opinion he has carried out his instructions admirably'. [Colonial Office Archive 926/1106] March 14th 1957 was chosen as the cut-off point because it was the date of an EOKA ceasefire which held for several months. Campbell added that his instructions were to refer to the politics of the conflict 'only in sufficient detail to explain the actions of the security forces'. One of the grounds on which he was later criticised was for not providing enough political context. Another was for providing too much. *Flaming Cassock* was surely the most authoritative official history ever not to be published.

By the early months of 1958 it was ready for publication. The *Sunday Dispatch* offered serialisation. Campbell had worked overtime. The royalties would be split: 50 per cent for the author and 50 per cent for military and police charities in Cyprus. Some clearances were still needed, but were thought to be routine. Campbell had already checked the whole book with the Deputy Governor in February 1958 and the chapters relating to intelligence with the island's senior Special Branch officer, L. W. Whymark.

But the book had enemies who, with its take-off so close, were determined to crater the runway. On 21 August 1958, six days before leaving the island for his next posting in Germany, Arthur Campbell wrote to Harding from Kykko Camp on Suffolk Regiment notepaper 'The I [Intelligence] people have put a very large spoke in the wheel.' This was a note to Whymark from a Major Stibbard, on the intelligence staff at Army HQ Cyprus, urging the suppression of the book on security grounds. Campbell was indignant: 'I find it bitter that he should make these comments at this late stage and that a year's hard work should virtually be brought to nothing by a note scribbled on one sheet of a memo pad.'

Events were also conspiring against him. The EOKA offensive in 'Black October' 1958 supplied his critics with further ammunition. On 11 December 1958 a Colonial Office official, J. D. Higham, wrote to Field Marshal Harding 'The book is out of phase with current events in Cyprus. It was conceived at a time when EOKA was on its knees and publication now might lay Her Majesty's Government open to criticism for having allowed EOKA to reorganise successfully after 1957'.

Sir Hugh Foot, Harding's successor as Governor, wrote on 29 November 1958 'It would be better if the book were not published at all; it is, of course, for him to say, but it would be a pity if the book were published with a foreword by the Field Marshal'. He left the task of killing it off to the Cyprus Local Intelligence Committee, chaired by the Deputy Governor. All of its members but one had also served under Harding. Both Whymark and Stibbard were on the eight-man Committee.

Its loyalty was now to Governor Foot and it did his bidding. In November 1958 it drafted a 'killer memorandum' which ran to six Top Secret pages and objected to the book on grounds that ranged from operational security to military protocol. On security, the book 'discloses the names and motivations of Greek Cypriots, who have served, or are still serving, loyally and well in the campaign against the terrorists'. [Colonial Office Archive 926/1106] On protocol, it suggested that it was inappropriate for a serving lieutenant colonel to assess the effectiveness of operations planned and executed by his superior officers, generals and brigadiers. Sir Edward Playfair, the senior civil servant in the War Office, agreed: 'A serving officer should not appear in print to judge his seniors by praise or criticism, no matter how discreet he may be'. Playfair, who had originally supported the book – 'The sooner it is published the better' – now joined the chorus against it: 'No one who knows the military scene could fail to recognise the people responsible for the actions criticised.'

The Committee, composed of soldiers, policemen and colonial officials, even felt qualified to venture into the field of literary criticism. It would be sorry, it said, to see the Field Marshal's name 'associated with a book of such poor quality'. One of its members added, astonishingly, 'On the grounds of style and good taste no comments are required as both are entirely absent from this book. The book has fallen, and fallen very low, between two stools. It would bore the unintelligent reader and both bore and offend the intelligent reader, and therefore it is an inept, if not disastrous, propaganda effort.' [FCO Archive 141/4456]

The Administrative Secretary, John Reddaway, dismissed *Flaming Cassock* as 'badly written, naïve and crude'. And the egregious J. D. Higham chimed in peevishly from the Colonial Office 'It is a kind of child's guide to dealing with terrorism: (National Service officers, for the use of)'.

On 27 December 1958 Governor Foot sent a further and definitive message to the Colonial Office: 'The Committee now reports to me their advice that the book should not, repeat not, be published'. Foot's intervention was decisive. On 12 March 1959, just before our Band and Drums serenaded him, he noted 'I agree that we need take no further action here'.

The fact of the matter was that colonial officials did not like being written about. They lived in a world of their own, were sensitive to criticism and preferred as little scrutiny as possible. They were no better disposed to Arthur Campbell's book than to Lawrence Durrell's, who had been one of them. Both men drew attention to their original unpreparedness. The Administrative Secretary was unimpressed: 'It would be a pity if this book were to be dismissed as superficial and lacking understanding of the problem by those circles which have been so fulsome in their praise of the percipience revealed in Mr Durrell's book and, by implication, of the lack of percipience of anyone else in Cyprus except Mr Durrell.' [FCO Archive 141/4456] In *Bitter Lemons* Durrell had written 'In the operations room on the top floor the Colonial Secretary sat at a desk tapping a pencil against his teeth; he was wearing a college blazer and trousers over his pyjamas, and a silk scarf ... At the Secretariat all was silence and emptiness. The Government by tradition spent the summer in the mountains and it would have been deemed loss of face to concede the necessity of staying in the capital for the trifling crisis of the moment.' In the island within an island of colonial Cyprus, the scars were open wounds.

Flaming Cassock was also friendless in Whitehall. It drew incoming fire from the Foreign Office, in the form of a memorandum from the Permanent Under Secretary Sir Frederick Hoyer Millar: 'What disturbs us ... is that the book not only fails in its objective which is "to do full justice in public to the work of the Cyprus security forces", but also gives the impression that something is seriously wrong with HMG's Cyprus policy'. (Actually there was a great deal wrong with the policy, or policies, for as Jim Callaghan of the opposition Labour Party pointed out at the time there were two different sets of policies, one hawkish and the other dovish, one for hanging on and the other for getting out, consistently out of synch and at odds with each other.) The Director of Intelligence added: 'The book does not seem to me to deserve the status which, having been commissioned and foreworded by Field Marshal Harding, one might think it might acquire. I therefore feel bound to advise against its publication.'

Officialdom was unanimous. The blizzard of paperwork about Campbell's book lies uneasily in the Colonial Office and Foreign Office files. It casts a revealing light on the end of Empire that so many senior officials spent so much time and effort in suppressing an authentic and truthful account of it.

Field Marshal Harding, by then ennobled and in retirement in Dorset, described himself as 'definitely hostile' to their arguments. He had a professional interest in a tribute to his security forces and a defence of his record and reputation. He asked for and was granted a personal interview with the senior civil servant at the Colonial Office, Sir John Macpherson, on 8 January 1959. It was frank and futile. Harding wrote to Macpherson afterwards 'Of course I would not do anything to make Hugh Foot's task more difficult, but I do not think appeasement is likely to help him any more than it has ever helped people in the past in dealing with personalities like Makarios.' Harding of course had dealt with Makarios extensively.

It was the independence agreement between Britain, Greece and Turkey, and the return of Makarios to the island in triumph on 1 March 1959 ('We have won!' he announced to a cheering crowd in Nicosia) that finally did for *Flaming Cassock* and laid it to rest. Campbell's arch-critic in the Colonial Office, J. D. Higham, noted 'The book blackens Makarios ... It is doubtful whether it is opportune to revive public memories of the black side of Makarios.' Macpherson added 'The fact that we must expect to put up with a great deal of glorification of Grivas and the "heroes of EOKA" does not diminish – indeed it rather increases – the need for extreme care to avoid reviving the vendetta.' The Deputy Governor stressed 'the even greater undesirability of the publication of the book in view of the London agreement on Cyprus'. An unnamed Colonial Office official administered the *coup de grâce*: 'This may be a convenient way of burying *Flaming Cassock* ... The Secretary of State assumes that any question of publishing *Flaming Cassock* is dead'.

And so it remained, dead and buried, until March 2014 when I applied to disinter it under the Freedom of Information Act. Even after so many years, the request touched sensitive nerve-endings in London and Nicosia and set off a series of manoeuvres by the Foreign and Commonwealth Office, initially citing Section 27 (1) of the Act exempting information 'that, if it were released, could set at risk relations between the UK and any other state'. The Government of Cyprus perhaps? After fifty-six years? And how could it serve the national interest in the twenty-first century that Britain's colonial record in the mid-twentieth century should remain as a state secret? Even to this day, the FCO is sensitive to contemporary criticisms of the founding fathers, Makarios among them, of independent states which once were British colonies.

After ten weeks of deliberations, surely including input from the British High Commission in Nicosia, the FCO then asked for another four, on the grounds that the book's publication might raise 'complex public interest considerations', including even *health and safety*. Section 38 (1) of the Act exempts information which, if disclosed, would be likely to endanger the physical or mental health of any individual. I wondered, what would the straightforward and humane Arthur Campbell have made of that? His book remained obscured behind the smokescreen.

Almost four months after the request was made, the FCO finally agreed to it, with certain passages edited out – or, in the official term, 'redacted'. One of these was a section which, in the diplomats' view, 'would harm British interests in Cyprus'. The other was a section which 'contains information about two individuals, the release of which would cause mental distress to their families'. These related to Greek Cypriots who had cooperated with the British. The original pages were removed and replaced by photocopies with the identities of the individuals left blank. The changes were understandable and relatively minor. The force and thrust and merit of *Flaming Cassock* were unaffected. The interesting postscript to this is that not only was the book redacted, but so were some of the files about its suppression. It was encouraging, on sifting through these formerly Top Secret documents, to learn that the British are disarmingly useless at wielding the blue pencil. Two copies of the 'killer memorandum' from the Cyprus Local Intelligence Committee in 1958 exist in separate folders and under different reference numbers. One is substantially redacted on five of its six pages. The other is completely untouched. I am grateful to the FCO for finally agreeing to expose *Flaming Cassock* to the light of day. After its long years in the darkness, it was officially declassified on 8 July 2014. It is the literary equivalent of buried treasure.

I persisted for three reasons. One was that I was an MP when the Act came before the House of Commons in November 2000: the publication of public-interest documents like *Flaming Cassock* was precisely what it was intended to enable. The second was to honour the memory of one of the Suffolk Regiment's finest soldiers. The last was that I had seen the mysterious third copy and was determined to reveal parts of it anyway. (This could have had awkward consequences, since I was obliged to sign the Official Secrets Act when I joined the BBC in London in 1964.)

Chapter 23

Flaming Cassock

The book runs to more than 300 passionate pages of typescript. It is an historical kaleidoscope, a truth-telling way-we-were account of the conflict, full of the most vivid anecdotes and incidents, and written from the heart. It has a measure of political innocence about it, as is often the case with military memoirs, and should never have been conspired against by the pin-striped suits in the first place. In its original draft the preface, almost certainly written in Berlin, is in Arthur Campbell's copper-plate hand-writing and looks back on a golden age before the troubles:

'As the story unfolds it will be seen early on how much the citizens of that beautiful, peaceful and friendly island suffered from the murderous machinations of the terrorists, and the many miseries necessarily imposed on them by government security forces. And yet no single Cypriot, whether of Greek or Turkish ethnic origin, benefitted one iota from the ugly betrayal of the island's beauty, from the convulsive disturbance of the peace or from the final harvest of hatred where, before, only concord had prevailed.' And it was not only hatred between Greeks and Turks. Campbell added 'As I write these words, one Greek Cypriot is being murdered every day by another'.

In the original version, Field Marshal Harding himself contributed an eighteen-page foreword to the book about the island's history and its people, which is absent from the edited text available in the National Archives. This is not surprising. After leaving the island he was under strong pressure to dilute, or withdraw altogether, his endorsement of *Flaming Cassock*. The first draft includes the following: 'In some strange way your heart goes out to a Cypriot even before you speak to him, though you know he will kill you as soon as you turn your back on him. In the darkest days of a bitter campaign many examples arose of this love/hate complex.'

Arthur Campbell intended *Flaming Cassock* to be both a history of the campaign and a tribute to the soldiers who served in it. In Malaya as in

Cyprus his loyalty was to them. After he left the island, and when he knew of the book's probable extinction, he told the *Daily Express* in February 1959, 'I want to tell the story somehow because I think the terrific behaviour and discipline of the troops should be known to everyone'. The *Express* headline was 'Lord Harding and the Book They Won't Publish'. Harding had to assure the Colonial Office that he was not the source of the news story.

The book begins in Metaxas Square, Nicosia, where a crowd of Greek Cypriot youths attacks the British Airways office before turning on the soldiers sent to disperse them. 'Helmeted British troops stood behind barricades in Luna Park, silent witnesses of this tumultuous scene. They were awaiting orders to move in against the rioters. They had nothing except their steel helmets to protect them against the stones and bricks, the bottles and the lengths of iron which the rabble hurled at them through the barriers. Yet they stood immobile, all 25 of them.'

The ringleader and flag bearer, 17-year-old Yiannakis, is arrested. The police inspector asks him 'Why do you lead your school mates into riots? Why do you incite them to violence? Why do you tell them to rebel against their legal government?' Yiannakis answers 'For one reason, Mister Inspector, to further the cause of *Enosis*'.

Arthur Campbell writes with regret of the subsequent vilification of a Governor who reformed and reorganised the security forces and insisted on their disciplined behaviour. 'Into this island of fear,' he writes, 'on 3 October 1955, flew Field Marshall Sir John Harding, the new Governor and Commander-in-Chief'. The day after his arrival an EOKA raiding party led by Grigoris Afxentiou attacked the police station at Lefkoniko in broad daylight and made off with its armoury of nine rifles and three other firearms. The timing was deliberate and Harding took the challenge personally. He ordered his security forces to mount a combined offensive and to close with the enemy whenever and wherever possible. Harding eventually got his man. Afxentiou was cornered and killed in March 1957. Campbell tells the story of how in the first six months Harding's forces turned from defence to limited aggression, though hampered still by inadequate intelligence. He imbued his soldiers, according to the book's pro–Harding narrative, 'with determination to free the island from fear'.

Harding was a controversial figure, but the poet and aesthete Lawrence Durrell concurred absolutely with the soldier Arthur Campbell in his assessment of the Governor. 'Upon the disorder and dishevelment of an administration still wallowing in shortages and indecisions he turned the pure direct eye of a soldier with a simple brief – the restoration of public order, the meeting of force with force; and he was followed swiftly by his soldiers, whose splendid professional bearing and brown faces – still smiling and kindly – brought a fresh atmosphere to the dusty purlieus of five towns ... one's heart went out to the patient and truly lion-hearted little man who had chosen once more to rake about in the dirty dustbins of politics for fragments which might be joined together before they were irretrievably thrown out and lost.' I wrote at the time:

> I am surprised to find Durrell as benevolent as he is towards the Army. If I were a resident of the *bon viveur* type, I should very much resent having noisome vehicles and trigger-happy troops infesting the island.

Durrell's view of Harding, like Campbell's, bordered on hero-worship: 'Secure in the mastery of his craft, the Field Marshal sat before the great wall map in Government House ... Absolutely composed, contained and with his eye (that fresh francolin's eye) upon the invisible enemy in the mountains.'

'Firmness with courtesy' was Harding's slogan long before it was Foot's. Here is Campbell again: 'It was tragic that this good and gifted man should find himself in a position in which his name was stigmatised by unscrupulous men who persuaded the Cypriot people whom he had come to govern and lead into peace and happiness, that he was a tyrant, a despot and a tough and brutal soldier. So far did this propaganda go that a child of six was heard to pray in church "Oh God, please kill Harding"'. The Field Marshal who started out as a Post Office clerk was regularly described as a blood-stained ogre guilty of shameful excesses and murderous colonialism. EOKA supporters were encouraged to send him hate mail.

Flaming Cassock is a treasure-trove of captured documents which show why he thought that he was winning. One is a letter dated 22 May 1956 from an EOKA fighter, Aloneftis, to Grivas, whom he addresses by his *nom de guerre* of Dighenis. 'My esteemed chief, I kiss your hand. It is with a degree of emotion that I write to inform you they have found all the hideouts. They had a traitor whom they took up in a helicopter and he pointed out all the hideouts … We are in very grave danger. Be careful of all roads – they control them all – do not make use of any roads. They are watching all roads and heights.'

It was the nearest that the Cyprus campaign came to a Malayan style victory. Of the killing of EOKA's Markos Drakos by his soldiers of D Company, Arthur Campbell writes: 'They tied his hands and feet to a stake and carried him down to their headquarters at Kakopetria. Drakos had at last met his end at the hands of soldiers better trained and more cunning than he.' The next day they were personally congratulated by Governor Harding. Campbell concluded 'It has been clearly demonstrated to the people that the forces of law and order are capable of mastering the forces of terrorism and intimidation.'

Like many senior officers, including Harding himself, Arthur Campbell was hostile to the stormy petrels of the press, especially the international press corps, some seventy strong, whom he saw as the terrorists' accomplices. Here he is at his most animated: 'Let there be no doubt in anyone's mind that the journalist and reporter, together with their editors, are the terrorists' best friend. The killers, the bombers, the robbers, the hijackers, the blackmailers, the racketeers must of necessity remain anonymous for as long as possible. How rewarding it must be for them, how uplifting for their morale, to see their activities portrayed before the world! Every apparently successful action of the EOKA terrorists against the security forces or against civilian targets was reported in depth and often in heroic terms, eliciting sympathy for the terrorist as underdog. The successes of the security forces, if reported at all, were made stories of by questioning their activities in terms of denial of human rights, resorting to torture, of indulging in unlawful practices and the like.'

Flaming Cassock also tells the inside story of the deportation of Archbishop Makarios from Cyprus on 9 March 1956, together with the Bishop of Kyrenia, a priest and the editor of a nationalist newspaper. After futile negotiations on the island, which Campbell describes as 'five months of wasted words', Makarios was on his way to talks in Athens when the British intercepted him at Nicosia Airport, which they controlled. After his abduction, and on receipt of the code words 'Banana', 'Pear' and 'Strawberry', the security forces raided a number of targets, including the Archbishop's office and the home of his secretary. He was flown in an RAF Hastings to Mombasa, where he was escorted onto the armed trawler HMS *Rosalind*, 40 miles off-shore. On the evening of 10th March, the deportees were transferred by launch to the frigate HMS *Loch Fada*, which would deliver them to the Seychelles. Only then did they learn of their destination.

Campbell quotes from the report by Inspector Arthur Taylor who was on board the ship as part of the security team to ensure the deportees' safe arrival. (One of them had threatened to throw himself overboard.) The Archbishop visited the bridge every day at noon to listen to the BBC news, in which he featured prominently at the time. He occupied the Captain's cabin and the others had a cabin in the officers' quarters. Meals were served in the Captain's cabin by the Captain's steward. When they reached the Seychelles on 14 March, the Archbishop wrote a cheque for £5, drawn on the Westminster Bank in London, which he gave to his steward as a tip before disembarking.

Exactly a year later, EOKA offered to suspend all operations if the Archbishop were released. Campbell writes 'The truce offer was sent to Sir John Harding but he quickly saw through the hypocritical and carefully chosen wording. He knew that for some time at least Grivas and his organisation would be unable to undertake operations whether or not the Ethnarch was released ... The Governor knew that peace had come to Cyprus as a result of the efforts of his security forces, but he fully realised that it was an uneasy peace, because fear still ruled the hearts of the people.' It is one of Campbell's constant laments that the people were too easily intimidated.

Arthur Campbell, fiercely loyal to the Governor, denies that the deportation was a heavy-handed over-reaction to the EOKA campaign. He writes that evidence had accumulated that Makarios was directing organised violence: 'The Archbishop was deported for his part in the terrorist conspiracy and because, for as long as he remained on the island, he constituted a major obstacle to the defeat of terrorism. There was no doubt in the minds of anyone in authority in Cyprus that it would take longer to break EOKA and restore peace, and some lives would be lost in so doing, if his inspiration and leadership were allowed to continue.' But the deportation of the Archbishop was counter-productive and had the effect of solidifying support for him.

Campbell also defends the jamming of Radio Athens, describing it as 'the infernal machine through which unscrupulous men incited youth to all sorts of violence, and through which no word of truth was spoken ... The Athens press and radio surpassed themselves in lies and falsehood designed to poison the minds of Cypriots with hatred for the English.'

The press spoke of Cyprus as 'terror island'. Murders were commonplace – 254 of them during the period Campbell is dealing with. The murders of political opponents or alleged 'traitors', in the streets, churches or even hospitals, were like public executions. One of the victims, Savvas Mekonikos, was tied to a eucalyptus tree and stoned to death in the Lefkoniko village square in May 1958. Grivas defended this as a punishment in the ancient Greek tradition. Like Lawrence Durrell before him Campbell contrasts the beauty of the island with the brutality of the campaign. He writes with eloquence and partisanship of an EOKA offensive in the autumn of 1956, when the organisation took advantage of the diversion of troops to Suez to resume its offensive. 'The tale of death continued throughout the dreary month of November; death in ambush and sudden raids in the mountains; death from bombs and electrical mines; death from shooting in the back in narrow streets of untidy towns. No member of the security forces, no Greek or Turkish Cypriot whom EOKA thought should be executed without trial as a traitor, could walk or drive out of his camp or house without the shadow of death hanging over him'. Harding called this phase of the campaign 'a serious setback'. One of his brigadiers conceded 'a temporary loss of initiative by the security forces'.

Campbell then describes the dramatic turn-around of the security situation that winter: the first insertion of special forces, the use of troop-carrying helicopters for lightning raids, the fruits at last of effective intelligence gathering, operational successes in the Troodos Mountains, the deaths of Drakos and Demetriou and the breaking of the EOKA organisations in Nicosia, Famagusta, Limassol, Kyrenia and Paphos. The number of its operational groups was reduced from sixteen to five, all of whom had gone to ground. Campbell concludes that these events isolated Grivas and left him impotent in his hiding place as 'a commander with nothing left to command'.

My admiration of the Arthur Campbell whom I knew does not extend entirely to his political analysis. In Cyprus as in Malaya it was very much of its time and place; but it derived from a visceral love of the island and its people; he did not believe in a military solution and he understood that the final answer had to be a settlement acceptable to the majority of the Greek Cypriot community. Campbell spoke eloquently for Harding and served faithfully as his master's voice. His narrative is a compelling account for many reasons. It is written from classified documents, viewed at first hand and which have long since disappeared from the record. It reflects the style and substance of Harding's governorship. It articulates the colonial mind-set, which was mistaken about the outcome. EOKA was sometimes subdued but never defeated. Campbell observes: 'A powerful and extremely brutal terrorist organisation had been fought to a standstill, but it is in the nature of such an organisation that it can never be irretrievably defeated or destroyed'. He chafes against 'the handicap of fighting fair within the provisions of British justice against an enemy who acknowledged no rules'. He laments 'There is in the island a generation of young people who have been reared in crime, who have been taught in church and school that subversion and violence, riot and murder, and disregard of law and the Christian code of life are right ... Those who long for peace and harmony in Cyprus are faced with the responsibility of leading these young people towards the Christian way of life. May God give them the courage they will need.'

Arthur Campbell wrote two remarkable books. The first, *Jungle Green*, was a best-seller. The second, *Flaming Cassock*, has been gathering dust under lock and key for more than half a century. We have much to learn from it about the history of Cyprus, the end of Empire and the unintelligent application of force. It deserves to take its place beside Durrell's *Bitter Lemons* as a classic account of the conflict. The decision to place it in the public domain was justified and long overdue: for how can we learn from our history if we imprison it?

Chapter 24

The Harding Memorandum

O ne of the oddities of the Cyprus emergency was that, while Governor Harding commissioned Arthur Campbell to write a history of it, he also wrote a substantial account himself. It consists of two overlapping and lengthy documents, classified Top Secret and not released until July 2012. The first runs to 222 pages and concentrates on the period between April and October 1956 when he was trying to break the deadlock between Greeks and Turks over the island's future. The second is more than 400 pages long, broader in scope and entitled *Sir John Harding's Memorandum on Cyprus Policy: an account of his term of office as Governor.* He signed off on it on 3 November 1957, just after leaving the island, and obviously still with all the records to hand. As a former Chief of Staff to seven successive generals in North Africa, he had a talent for paperwork and detail. It was only because he was wounded there that he never achieved high command in wartime himself. Both memoranda are self-justifying, soldierly and lacking in Campbell's literary gifts and graces. But they reflect his character and are a gold mine of the feisty and forceful cables with which he bombarded the Colonial Office and its Secretary of State over the two years of his governorship. He is clearly on unfamiliar ground and used to being obeyed by those he deals with: no one should second-guess a Field Marshal, not even a Secretary of State. Another distinguished soldier and contemporary, Lieutenant General Sir Brian Horrocks, said of him in 1955 'Many of us thought that Harding's main difficulty would lie in the political field. He was a stranger to the ways of Whitehall'.

Indeed he was. In the memorandum he issues peremptory warnings to Her Majesty's Government: 'I must, at the risk of being considered tedious, emphasise again my view that to embark on a constitution-making exercise to be followed by self-government without having frozen self-determination for at least ten years will be worse than useless from our point of view

... I must utter again the most solemn warning to HMG against getting manoeuvred into introducing a constitution without first having frozen self-determination for at least ten years.'[Colonial Office Archive 926/2084]

Some of the messages from London to Nicosia are also recorded, including a personal note to the Governor on 6 July 1956 from the Prime Minister Anthony Eden who had appointed him: 'It remains of course our intention not to introduce any constitution until law and order have been restored'. Harding agrees: 'We must now give over-riding priority to the defeat of terrorism and the restoration of law and order'. Which is just what he did: the iron fist inside the iron glove.

Like Arthur Campbell, the historian alongside him in Government House, he begins at the beginning, with the fatal feebleness of the response to the EOKA attacks on 1 April 1955. Harding describes an intimidated police force and a demoralised Special Branch after two of its key figures were assassinated. These were the wasted months. 'The audacity of the terrorists and the apparent inability of the forces of law and order to get to grips with them persuaded even those who deplored violence that they would be wise to take up a "wait and see" attitude and await the outcome of the struggle ... As the government found itself pushed into more severe counter-measures against the terrorists, and as these bore more onerously on the general population, the myth of alien oppression acquired a plausibility it had not had before ... By September a pall of fear had settled over the Greek Cypriot community, stifling not only public expression but even private thought.' Lawrence Durrell, who served Harding for a while as his press adviser, also described this process: 'The spirit of resistance itself gradually spread, igniting the sleeping villages one by one.'

The Governor was infuriated when such villages were visited by Labour MPs like Richard Crossman, who assured the people of Kythrea, a hotbed of support for EOKA, that the British never gave up their colonies until they were forced to. The use of force, both ours and EOKA's, was changing the realities on the ground.

For the first time it seemed to ordinary Cypriots, both Greek and Turkish, that the end of British rule was in sight; this in itself exacerbated the tensions between them, with fatal consequences. They realised that they might have to fight for their futures. Nor did it help that the new Governor was a soldier, who on 26 November 1955 declared a state of emergency, with all the coercive and punitive powers that went with it. The emergency measures were prepared by the Acting Governor before Harding's arrival 'to be introduced forthwith, should circumstances require this'; the Field Marshal introduced them six weeks into his term of office and consequently bore the opprobrium. Civil liberties were in abeyance. As the number of troops available to him increased, the colonial regime became inevitably more repressive. Harding even admits in his memorandum that it was repressive. The British were accused of seeking a military solution to a political problem.

Harding deals with this perception in his memorandum: 'I have no desire to enter into argument on this matter, and am content to allow the record of my actions to speak for itself. But, at the outset, I think it may be as well for me to state, simply and unreservedly, that I came to Cyprus convinced that, although military measures might be essential towards creating the conditions for a just and lasting settlement, the basis for that settlement had to be found in the political field through negotiation and compromise.'

So, within hours of arriving on the island, Harding plunged into talks with Archbishop Makarios. They ran to eight negotiating sessions while the pace of EOKA activity increased and more lives were lost. Makarios of course never condemned the violence which the British believed he had significantly instigated. Harding declared 'I was impressed by the evidence which was now rapidly accumulating from a number of different sources revealing his deep personal complicity in terrorism'. The talks were thus a dialogue of the deaf. The Field Marshal called them 'fruitless and frustrating' and wondered later whether he should have embarked on them in the first place: 'Had I known that the discussions with him were going to drag on for five weary months ... I might have decided that the price was too high to pay for such meagre prospects of reaching a settlement as were offered.'

Harding's assessment of Makarios is the only chapter of his account that has been partly 'redacted' by FCO officials, but with touching and typical inconsistency. They censored one version of the memorandum to conceal some of its source material, but not the other which is outspoken about his dislike of the bearded Beatitude on the other side of the table: 'Archbishop Makarios is an implacable and unscrupulous antagonist. His aims and character are incompatible with genuine compromise'. The scenario that comes over is that of simple soldier versus devious priest. 'He possesses neither depth of intellect nor breadth of understanding, but he is certainly shrewd, quick-witted and smooth-tongued ... In discussion he is elusive and a master of evasion ... He is first and foremost a politician, secondly an ecclesiastical administrator and only last and least a pastor and religious teacher.'

Since the talks were going nowhere, Harding then decided that the island would be better served if Makarios was no longer on it. So the Archbishop was deported, as described in Lieutenant Colonel Campbell's vivid and parallel history, *Flaming Cassock*. According to Harding, careful and anxious thought had been given to the decision; another option would have been house arrest in Nicosia, but 'nothing else can symbolise with equal effect our determination to stay in Cyprus and to withstand *Enosist* pressure ... If Archbishop Makarios had remained in Cyprus for the rest of that grim year [1956], who can say how many young Greek Cypriots he would have sent to their deaths in conflict with the security forces, possibly even in some frenzied attempt to launch a general uprising against the government? ... If his pernicious influence in support of terrorism was to be neutralised ... it was essential that he should be held *incommunicado*.'

It was felt at the time that the deportation of Makarios strengthened the Governor's hand. He could later be released in exchange for concessions by the other side. The same applied to the imposition or relaxation of the emergency powers. Yet without the Archbishop there was no one with whom to negotiate. It was a constitutional dead end.

After the deportation the Field Marshal believed, by his own account, that a great weight was lifted from him. 'For the first time since taking up my governorship I felt free to examine the problem on its merits ... As for HMG's own position, it seemed to me that that would be far stronger vis-à-vis world opinion if it could be shown that we had, on our part at least, made a thorough and imaginative effort to find a solution.' There was a world of difference between self-determination, which in practice meant *Enosis*, and self-government which did not.

Harding's ideas included a scheme – some might call it a pipe-dream – to turn around public opinion on the island, which he thought would take at least five years. This could not be done by press censorship which was already as tight as it could be. The further means he proposed included the revamping of the government's lacklustre information service, a closely co-ordinated overt and covert propaganda campaign, the indefinite jamming of Radio Athens and the take-over by the colonial authorities of the secondary schools 'sufficient to remove the present menace to internal security'. The schools were the engine of rebellion. They were in a ferment of support for union with Greece. The girls would gather the missiles and the boys would throw them. Colonel Grivas wrote in his captured diary 'The use of children for nuisance value disturbances must continue.'

But Harding convinced himself that support for *Enosis* was not as strong as it seemed. 'There is no doubt that under the surface of solidarity the Greek Cypriot people have considerable doubts and reservations about *Enosis* even in their present inflamed state ... In Cyprus as in Greece it is the irreconcilable extremists who call the tune on the *Enosis* issue ... The habit of years, a natural timidity and the real vitality of their Hellenism render the Greek Cypriots extremely susceptible to the uncompromising advocacy of *Enosis*.'

The Field Marshal believed that he had to shatter the widely-held perception that *Enosis* would be the inevitable outcome of the end of British rule. To this end, and ominously in the light of what followed, he was the first of the British decision-makers to play the Turkish card. The most revealing – and some would say downright cynical – passage in his memorandum is the cable in which he suggests how this should be done: 'There is only one way of shaking their [the Greek Cypriots'] belief in the inevitability of *Enosis*. That is to convince them that, if pushed too far, we will bring Turkey back into Cyprus in one way or another ... They realise that if that should happen *Enosis* would be doomed.' Harding's Turkish card next surfaced in the House of Commons in the form of a statement by the Colonial Secretary Alan Lennox-Boyd on 19 December 1956: 'I cannot see how it is anything other than logical to grant a community with such close interests to Turkey – and only 40 miles away – the same rights as we are prepared to recognise should go the Greek community'. [*Hansard*, 19 December 1956]

The central issue of sovereignty was wrapped in a double negative: the British Government had not said they would never relinquish it, but that was as far as they were willing to go. In Harding's view, a conditional form of self-determination should be conceded by the British only in their own time and on their own terms. The time frame would be ten to fifteen years. 'The terms should be dictated mainly by the need to assuage Turkish fears and anxieties.' The Greek Government should be presented with a new initiative, 'a combination of tough diplomacy and forgiving generosity ... An unmistakable warning that further Greek intransigence would be countered by our associating Turkey with our administration in Cyprus in such a way as to preclude *Enosis* for ever ... The warning of our readiness to bring Turkey back into Cyprus must be given in terms which, while unmistakable, would not appear to be too blatantly coercive.'

Harding's proposal for an interim tripartite state was a classic colonial exercise in 'divide and rule'. Greek Cypriots would not even be consulted about it. Makarios was in exile and had in the Governor's view 'queered the pitch' for any other spokesman for his community. 'Nor at the moment would we want to run the risk of allowing the Greek Cypriots – cowed by terrorism, insular by nature and habituated to intransigence by their own extremists – to exercise a veto of any such imaginative attempt to settle the international aspects of the Cyprus problem.' Through Harding's narrative there runs a red, white and blue thread of imperial hubris which was commonplace at the time – and to my regret as a young soldier I seem to have shared it – that the people of Cyprus were too easily misled and intimidated by extremists, but the benevolent British would wisely decide what was best for them and act accordingly.

To Harding's dismay, on 28 June 1956 his ideas were rejected by the Turkish Government, who would settle for nothing but partition, which Harding opposed. 'I have always regarded it as a counsel of despair,' he said, 'and still do so.' His gloomy conclusion: 'Looking back more than a year later on this unsuccessful attempt to tackle the problem of self-determination, it is clear to me that I under-estimated the strength of Turkish reaction.' And of course in the end the 'Turkish card' went wild. The Turks asserted themselves in Cyprus by force of arms. One lesson of the debacle is surely that diplomacy is usually best left to diplomats rather than field marshals. We should no sooner allow soldiers to negotiate for us than diplomats to fight for us: each to his own.

Much of the island's later tragedy is inadvertently foreshadowed in Harding's memorandum. Because it charts the colonial thinking of the time, it should have been declassified much earlier than it was. Apart from the courage and stoicism of our soldiers, we British have little to be proud of. I look back at us now in the old photographs of the 1st Battalion of The Suffolk Regiment being addressed by the Governor who was its commander-in-chief. We were just kids in khaki drill with batons and shields and steel helmets. Some of us look as if we were barely out of school. My own role on riot duty, which fortunately I never had to put into practice, was to shoot the roof-top bombers. We had hardly the least idea – certainly I didn't – of what we were doing or why we were doing it. We were innocents abroad.

In neither his memoranda of 1957 nor in his memoir dictated to his great niece in 1974 does the Field Marshal address the moral issues involved in his application of the emergency powers and in signing the death warrants of the nine EOKA convicts who were executed on his watch. True to his record as a soldier, he seemed more concerned about the strategic value of Dhekelia and Akrotiri, the British sovereign base areas, than about the impact of his policies on the people. And he may have been mistaken about the value of the bases. In a letter published by the *Sunday Times* in December 1956, Field Marshal Sir Claude Auchinleck wrote 'Cyprus as a military base has none, or practically none, of the requisites of an efficient base for the deployment and subsequent employment in military operations of either land, sea or air forces, or of all three.' The naval operation in Suez was launched from Malta.

There are two versions of the Governor's departure from the island in October 1957. One is that after two years he had done all he could and asked to be relieved of his duties: he recalled that the Government reluctantly agreed. Another is that his repressive measures had made him a liability and an obstacle to the settlement he had been seeking; and an experienced diplomat was needed to take his place.

At the end of his memorandum, Field Marshal Harding ventures a typically impatient criticism, in which he accepts his share of the blame, of the way in which the EOKA challenge was met: 'It is that our machine has been too slow and erratic to achieve results in the context of rapidly changing and developing situations. With respect I submit that we have been far too slow in making decisions, too hesitant in putting them into effect and too much distracted from our purpose by other business and events.' He concludes: 'I doubt if the effect for good or ill of the decisions reached and actions taken during my tour of duty as Governor will be apparent for some time to come'.

That time has surely now come. After more than half a century and with most of the Top Secret documents now in the public domain, a reckoning of his tour of duty can be made. Its first phase was diplomatic: its second phase was almost entirely military. The conclusion of the ever loyal and most unmilitary Lawrence Durrell who served him was that 'the Field Marshal performed a feat which would have done credit to a master of diplomatists'. But Durrell's was a lone voice. The record showed otherwise, that he failed as a diplomat, but was close to success as a soldier. Honoured by some and reviled by others, Field Marshal Lord Harding died in 1988.

In attempting the virtually impossible his record was mixed. The *Independent* concluded 'He never got the credit he deserved for being master of a difficult situation. And much of the criticism – due to the British Government of the day – fell on him'.

Chapter 25

Retrospective

I know so much more now than I did then, which casts a new light on the years of soldiering.

Failing the officer selection test was by no means unusual, or as calamitous as I supposed at the time, and I learned much from it. Six young soldiers from the draft that followed ours took the War Office Selection Board and all six failed it. ('Very consoling,' I wrote at the time, 'if I need to be consoled, which I don't.') Others who fell at the same hurdle included the TV newsreader Michael Aspel of the King's Royal Rifle Corps and Tam Dalyell MP of the Royal Scots Greys, who should have been a shoo-in for a commission, since the Regiment had been founded in 1681 by his ancestor, a Scottish royalist known as 'Bludy Tam'. But as a new recruit he was reputed to have lost a tank on manoeuvres. Tanks were smaller then, but it was still a considerable achievement. He remained intensely loyal to his Regiment and its successors. We served together in the House of Commons from 1997 to 2001, and were both marked down as 'awkward squad'. I took to him immediately. His book was called *The Importance of Being Awkward*. The Army's loss was the House of Commons' gain.

At a road block in the summer of 1958 a group of Greeks were penned behind barbed wire while their identities were checked. They were causing no trouble. One of the subalterns in Support Company, on his own initiative, fired shots over their heads to intimidate them. This should have been a court-martial offence. The CO knew nothing of it. But the other junior officers, when they learned of it, dealt with the offending lieutenant in such a way that he never did it again. The soldiers of Suffolk, both officers and men, were decent people and the best of British. Even at the time of the EOKA offensive in 'Black October' 1958, I noted:

The sum total of incidents was confined to roping in the curfew breakers – a task which was done with great humanity, considering the reputation which the brutal and licentious soldiery of Cyprus seem to have acquired.

Some units were less restrained in their behaviour. The operations of the security forces had a darker side to them than I knew from my vantage-point in the first floor of the Central Police Station. Indiscipline was exceptional but irrefutable and stands there on the record. Evidence of brutality was covered up and lay hidden in the National Archives for more than fifty years, until being revealed in 2012 in relation to a court case involving the suppression of the Mau Mau rebellion in Kenya. In one incident in Cyprus in July 1958 a patrol of soldiers shot and killed a blind man in a crowd of stone-throwers. In another a young British Army officer recorded seeing 150 soldiers indiscriminately 'kicking Cypriots as they lay on the ground and beating them in the head, face and body with rifle butts'. The officer described how he 'forcibly restrained several such groups of soldiers who had completely lost their heads. Many of them were screaming abuse and the whole area resembled a hysterical mob ... Several [Cypriots] appeared to be unconscious and bleeding profusely.' [*The Guardian*, 27 July 2012]

This conflicts markedly with both Governors' mantra of 'firmness with courtesy'. Harding insisted 'It is perfectly possible to combine firmness with good manners, and that will always be the guiding principle in dealing with the general public. Particular care will be taken to avoid imposing any unnecessary inconvenience on individuals ... Any indiscipline or breaches of this instruction will be severely dealt with'. On Harding's watch two army intelligence officers were court-martialled for 'exceeding their duty in obtaining evidence on murderers'. Radio Athens had a field day: 'The minutes of the trial speak of blackmail, torture and atrocities not seen since the days of the Nazi era.' [*Flaming Cassock*, p. 180] General Darling wrote of detention camp staff and interrogators 'In view of the harm that can be done, particularly in the political field, through excesses of zeal or absence of supervision, great care must be exercised in the selection of individuals for these groups'. [Colonial Office Archive 926/1077] In 1958 Governor Foot was so concerned about reports of the ill-treatment of suspects that he and the Director of Operations mounted unannounced raids on intelligence-gathering operations to assure themselves that the rules were being observed.

Something else I was unaware of was the degree of animosity between the younger officers, the regulars on one side and the conscripts on the other. The national servicemen tended to think that the regulars were as thick as two planks for having signed on in the first place. The regulars knew this and resented it. Much later Brigadier Charles Barnes, my former Intelligence Officer, confessed to me that he was rather impressed by the academic qualifications of some of the soldiers he led as a subaltern. I assured him with great conviction that he never let it show. 'Why,' he would ask, 'am I always blessed with idiots in my Section?' One of my predecessors in the Section went on to captain Oxford University at golf. We idiots were college boys with civilian ambitions: he was a soldier who had signed on for a lifetime.

The search for a negotiated settlement was hindered in 1957 by a blood feud between Sir John Harding and the EOKA leader Colonel Grivas. Each was trying to the best of his abilities to have the other killed. In late 1957 the security forces were ordered to conduct massive cordon and search operations in the foothills of Troodos, where Grivas was thought to be hiding. (He wasn't: having narrowly escaped capture in the mountains, he was living in a bungalow near one of the British bases in the south of the island.) Grivas, for his part, twice tried to have Harding assassinated, once in the Ledra Palace Hotel and once in the Governor's mansion, where a time bomb was planted in his bed, between the mattress and the springs, by his Greek Cypriot valet. It was found by two soldiers in a routine search and carried away on a dustpan by the Officer of the Watch to a bunker where it exploded safely. The Officer of the Watch was decorated for bravery. The Governor's wife was writing letters at the time. One of the soldiers shouted out:

'Lady Harding, there's a bomb in your bed.'
'Don't be silly', she said, 'I'm writing letters.'

And the Governor said later, 'That's funny, I slept unusually well last night'.

EOKA also tried to assassinate Major General Kendrew. He was unhurt but one of his escorts was killed. Of these feuds and conspiracies we humble foot-soldiers knew nothing at all. We did as we were ordered and counted the days to do. We should have asked more questions, but did not.

The same applies to the treatment of men arrested on suspicion of terrorism. We were also unaware of the use of torture, which seems to have been widely applied in Cyprus, as in other colonies in revolt. The historian Piers Brendon has written 'This was standard practice during the interrogation of suspects, who were beaten on the stomach with flat boards, hit in the testicles, half suffocated with wet cloths and otherwise abused. At least six men died under questioning and others were shot "while trying to escape". Yet some officers privately justified torture as a means of "defeating terrorism and saving human lives."' [*The Decline and Fall of the British Empire*, Vintage 2008, p. 621]

We also know now that when Sir Hugh Foot was Governor of Jamaica in 1957 and his transfer to Cyprus was first mooted, he objected on the grounds that the wrong policy was being followed. A Colonial Office official wrote 'Sir Hugh said that although he would like to have gone there if the policy had been one that he favoured, it didn't look that way'. He offered instead to reorganise the Colonial Office, which was the Foreign Office's poor relation and the despair of many who worked in it. If the Foreign Office was the Rolls-Royce of government departments, the Colonial Office was the Trabant. The official told him that it did not so much need to be reorganised as to be saved from disintegration. Its Cyprus desk appears to have been especially dysfunctional. The official also reported back 'My own conclusion from our conversations is that he would not be an ideal choice for Cyprus'. [Colonial Office Archive 967/321]

The savagery of the Cyprus campaign is now remembered only by those old men on either side who were young men at the time. When Governor Harding ordered the executions of two EOKA gunmen to go ahead, he also in effect signed the death warrants of two of his soldiers, a lance corporal and a private, who were abducted and executed by EOKA. An EOKA leaflet announced that they were hanged the same day. Colonel Grivas authored another leaflet in January 1956 while Harding was still negotiating with Makarios: 'We declare that *we shall not accept any decision* unless the abominable criminals and torturers are punished and that we shall continue our struggle despite any agreement until we punish the criminals with our own hands'. Both sides saw it as a fight to the finish.

The lack of a bipartisan policy on Cyprus was a constant handicap throughout the four-year campaign. The Conservatives accused Labour of abetting terrorism. Labour accused the Conservatives of pursuing a policy of futile repression – 'the height of folly and madness' as Jim Callaghan described it. From the start to the end of the emergency Cyprus was a parliamentary dividing line. The pages of *Hansard* reeked with acrimony.

I had no idea when I was a soldier how much time I would spend in later years with the soldiers of other armies, whether the Americans in Vietnam, the Serbs in Croatia or the 'Arrow Boys' in South Sudan. I was even back in uniform in 1991 alongside the Queen's Royal Irish Hussars in Gulf War One. Because the serial number of my accreditation card was 001, I can claim to have been the first embedded journalist, or 'embed'. It was helpful as a war reporter to have been there before and to know about weapons systems and orders of battle and chains of command, and the difference between a brigade and a battalion, or a Commanding Officer and an Officer Commanding. It meant that you started off on the front foot.

I had no idea either of the part that road blocks would play in my later life, mainly from being on the wrong side of them. In Cyprus I was setting them up on main roads, impeding the traffic and stopping people from going about their lawful business. In subsequent war zones, from Vietnam to Bosnia, I was among those being blocked. Stopped at a rebel road block one day in El Salvador in 1982, I was held at gunpoint in a ditch and lectured in Spanish on revolutionary Marxism. It served me right, I thought.

Whether we liked it or not (and most of us did not), National Service delivered certain benefits. It speeded up our transition from boys into men. It made us more confident. It bound us to each other in solidarity and comradeship. It gave us a sense that we were serving our country and not just ourselves. It taught us survival skills in a hostile environment. It bequeathed to us a short but exceptional passage of life to look back on.

Much later I fell into two highly-competitive professions, journalism and politics, in which the ambitious sought to succeed at each other's expense. National Service provided a better model – the Army's renowned 'buddy buddy system' – of living and working together.

So should we not bring it back? The answer is no. It may be that we need somehow to reinvent it, in a civilian form, as a disciplined outlet for the energies and idealism of the young. But National Service as we endured it was acceptable only to a generation as deferential as ours. Not even my RSM at the height of his powers would be able to tear today's young people from their text messages and i-pads. The human rights lawyers would have a field day. There would be thunderous editorials about the barrack room ill-treatment of the young. A well-meaning charity would campaign on their behalf. The truth is that our two years in uniform were good for us but not so good for the Army. Its ranks were stuffed with mavericks and days-to-do wallahs like myself. It wasted manpower training young men for very short-term service. By the time we were half-way useful soldiers we were within sight of our demob. It cannot be good for any army to have in its ranks a disaffected majority. Besides, today's Army is better than the Army I served in, not least because it no longer has Corporal 23398941 Bell M serving in it.

The serving soldiers of today should also know that the disciplinary system has greatly improved. If I thought I had any rights back then (which never occurred to me), it would not have been wise to mention them within earshot of the RSM. Forty years after call-up, I became a Member of Parliament in unusual circumstances. One of the committees I served on was the Standing Committee considering the Armed Forces Discipline Act 2000, intended to bring the system into line with the European Convention on Human Rights. As a result, commanding officers were stripped of some of their powers to impose summary field punishments. I thought of my time in the Regiment when I spoke in the debate ('We are trying to protect the rights of serving men and women … ') and voted for the Act in the division lobby. [*Hansard*, 6 April 2000] It struck a balance between justice and military efficiency – a balance that was lacking in the Army of the late 1950s. This may be a subversive other rank's view, but I don't remember that we were all that efficient either. In March 1957 the Cyprus Intelligence Committee estimated that half of EOKA's mountain fighters were escapees from British prisons and detention camps.

The counter-insurgency was actually a war. It was a small war, but the names of 371 British servicemen who died in the course of it are recorded on the Armed Forces memorial in Wayne's Keep. Most of them were national servicemen, the last to die in the service of their country. Not all of them were killed in action. No fewer than forty-nine were the victims of accidental discharges, in camps or on operations. (The generals were rightly alarmed.) One drowned. Some committed suicide. Many died in traffic accidents – seven during a single operation in the mountains in June 1956. Others ran into their own side's ambushes. Only 105 of them were killed (and 603 wounded) by EOKA, which regularly promised to shed British blood: 'The more troops you bring to the island, the greater your losses will be.' According to the record, the Suffolk Regiment lost only one man in three years, Lance Corporal R. Fermor who died in November 1957; he was not of the 1st Battalion but attached elsewhere. The Lancashire Fusiliers lost three, the Ox and Bucks lost three, the Royal Horse Guards eight and the Headquarters Staff ten. Five young soldiers of the Royal Army Service Corps were killed in a single attack in Ledra Street in December 1955. The death toll in the capital was higher because it was easier for the EOKA hit-men to find their targets and make their escape in the maze of the city's streets. As Lawrence Durrell observed, 'The labyrinth of warrens in the old town could hide a veritable army of bomb-throwers'. With the strength of the Battalion around us, the duty did not seem particularly dangerous at the time; we welcomed the hazards as relief from the boredom and we came through virtually unscathed. We had no idea how lucky we were. It was active service without too much risk of ending up with one's name engraved in stone. Apart from Lance Corporal Fermor, during my time on the island I cannot remember, and the letters do not mention, that the Regiment suffered a single serious casualty. We were counted out and counted back intact.

It has not been like that for our successors. As a leading formation in our hard-pressed and over-stretched armed forces, The Royal Anglian Regiment completed no fewer than four tours of duty in Afghanistan, and one in Iraq, in the decade between 2002 and 2012. The reservists served as well as the regulars. Eleven of its men have fallen, three in a notorious 'friendly fire' incident in Helmand Province on 23 August 2007. Many more have suffered life-changing injuries. And an unknowable number are the victims of PTSD (post-traumatic stress disorder), the most deniable of war wounds. Compared to their experience, ours was as nothing. We were the 1st Suffolk Sunbathing Battalion (Cyprus) 1956–59. Britannia's imperial ambitions came at a cost. By the time of the twilight of Empire, which this was, there were British war graves in no fewer than 152 countries around the world. Cyprus was one of them.

The lessons of the small war in Cyprus prefigured those of later and larger conflicts in Vietnam, Iraq and Afghanistan: military solutions fall apart, and the application of force in wars among the people does not win their hearts and minds but more often alienates them. As General Sir Rupert Smith has observed, 'You can have the biggest infantry in the world and the most super kit. Go in amongst the people, and every time we use our strength we fail to achieve our objective. We often reinforce our opponent's ability to achieve his objective, because his strategy is always to get us to overreact.' [*Iraq: the Futility of War*, Channel 4, 13 January 2006]

And so it was with the British and EOKA in Cyprus. On 19 September 1958 Major General Kendrew, the outgoing Director of Operations, issued an instruction to his soldiers (and I was one of them): 'Indiscriminate roughness, discourtesy and collective punitive measures have no place in IS (internal security) operations and merely make the task of the security forces harder by playing into the hands of the other side'. [FCO Archive 141/4493] His warning was unheeded. A little over two weeks later, there was a serious breakdown of discipline among British troops in Famagusta.

Operationally Governor Foot was in a minority of one. He was an Excellency to be ignored or over-ruled by his advisers. He had no control over operations. The decision-makers around him acted more like a military junta than a forward-thinking colonial administration. They had the support of the Macmillan government, under pressure from the Tory right to keep Cyprus as another Gibraltar. (Lord Salisbury resigned from the Cabinet over the decision to release Archbishop Makarios from his banishment.) The Governor wanted holding operations while he sought a political solution. Most of his military commanders preferred the big push or knockout blow, thus stiffening the resistance they were trying to overcome. General Darling, our Director of Operations from 1958–9, concluded in his final Top Secret report 'The lesson of Cyprus, therefore, is that a subversive yet nationalist organisation is not destroyed by an assault on the ordinary people.' [Colonial Office Archive 926/1077] The inefficacy of force is beginning to be recognised. Our armed forces are down-sizing yet again. Expeditionary warfare has not delivered the results expected of it. Campaigns in Iraq and Afghanistan have both been strategic failures.

The techniques of pacification which were employed in Malaya and Cyprus were tried again in Aden and, closer to home, in Northern Ireland by many of the same soldiers. The methods used included internment: Operation Matchbox in Cyprus was reinvented as Operation Motorman in Belfast. They were tried also in Vietnam. Eight years after leaving the Army I was reporting from South Vietnam for the BBC. Villagers were resettled in fortified compounds on the Malayan model. American artillery was pounding the Central Highlands. I flew on a defoliation mission as the US Air Force poisoned the ground with Agent Orange: a sign in the operations room said 'Only you can prevent forests'. (The British had used Agent Orange in Malaya.) None of it worked. The war was lost. One of the lessons of history, surely, is that we don't learn the lessons of history.

I would also argue from personal experience, having served abroad as both a soldier and a broadcast journalist, that the campaign in Cyprus provided the first example of the impact of television news on government policy – what later came to be known as the CNN effect. The emergency began long before there were rolling news channels, but only a year after the establishment of TV news services by both the BBC and ITN. Their crews were active in the streets and the villages, shooting black and white film with a magnetic sound track on the side of it. I worked with some of them subsequently. They were sharp characters, fiercely competitive in seeking out the most impactful stories of the day. There were no satellite uplinks of course: the news film was air-freighted to London and broadcast the next day, when it still had raw immediacy. It was a new dimension of news-gathering, which quite literally brought the conflict home to people. Claims by the Government of Cyprus to be dealing only with terrorists and criminals were undermined by images of British soldiers baton-charging schoolboys. The Secret documents of the time are full of references to the need to reassure public opinion at home and abroad. I believe that the presence of the TV cameras was one of the forces that in the end made the campaign politically unsustainable. It was because we could not go on as we were that we got out when we did.

There was also the issue of morale on the home front. A field commander's most important constituency in modern warfare is the families of the soldiers serving under him. The letters I sent home tended to be reassuring and deal lightly with the dangers and hardships of active service. Until the early months of 1959 I actually believed that we were winning. We dismissed what we read in the newspapers as exaggerations and had little access to television. Back in Britain, the TV coverage told an alternative and perhaps more credible story. So in due course the campaign ended, the deal was done, the flags were lowered and the regiments embarked on their troopships.

All that remains of Gibraltar Barracks today is the Keep, the citadel which is home to the museum and the headquarters of The Royal Anglian Regiment. In recent years its flag has been flying too often at half-mast. All that remains of The Suffolk Regiment is B (Suffolk) Company of 1st Battalion The Royal Anglian Regiment. All that remains of the square, the RSM's beloved parade ground, is being encroached on year after year by West Suffolk College. Just enough of it is left for The Suffolk Regiment's few hundred surviving old soldiers to march past – shuffle past would be a better term – every year on Minden Day. The youngest of us is 76. The band plays our quick march *Speed the Plough* and puts a spring into our step. *Speed the Plough* is also the second (and better) half of the quick march of The Royal Anglian Regiment. No other regiment does it quite this way. They envy us our solidarity. We never thought when we were actually soldiering that we would think so fondly of our time in the Army. In due course I became President of the Suffolk Concert Band, whose uniform of course is red and yellow. I conducted *Speed the Plough* in one of its concerts. In 1996 I opened the Museum of The Royal Anglian Regiment in Duxford. I wear the tie that binds us together, which is that of the Suffolk Regiment. And on the centenary of the Battle of Le Cateau I laid a wreath at the Menin Gate in Ypres on behalf of the people of Suffolk.

The Regiment amalgamated with The Royal Norfolk Regiment in Germany on 29 August 1959. The colours of The Suffolk Regiment were laid up in Bury St Edmunds on 26 March 1960 without having Cyprus emblazoned on them as a last battle honour. Nearly fifty years later the Regiment was again in the news. In May 2008 President George W. Bush, in a speech to the Israeli Knesset, referred to the British withdrawal from Jerusalem in 1948, when a company commander in the 1st Battalion was alleged to have handed over a key to the Old City to the Jewish community with the words 'Now, for the first time in over a thousand years, the Jews have a key to Jerusalem'. The story cannot be confirmed. Neither Lieutenant (later Brigadier) Bill Deller nor CSM (later my fierce RSM) Jack Gingell of A Company the 1st Battalion, who were there at the time, could recall anything like that having actually happened; though the Company Commander Major R. M. Allen of the Royal Norfolks, who was described as both a religious and difficult man, may have done it on his own initiative. The men of A Company were certainly the last to leave, as the Mandate ended on 15 May 1948 and the 2nd Royal Warwicks, 2 Brigade HQ and 1st Highland Light Infantry passed through their lines. It was the Suffolks more than any others who were manning the ramparts at the end of Empire. The Last Post was our defining bugle call. We folded the flag and took it with us from one conflict to the next.

The last of these was Cyprus. I visited the island in 1972, two years before the Turkish invasion, and returned to the site of Kykko Camp, my home for twenty months. It had reverted to the wild and was grazed by goats as if we had never been there – not regimental goats but wild ones. Nothing remained of the mighty monument erected by the outgoing CO, Bertie Bevan, the Ozymandias of Cyprus. The regimental photograph shows him, the RSM and the Adjutant standing proudly beside it in March 1959. It was engraved with the regimental badge and an inscription proclaiming to future generations that the Suffolk Regiment had served in Cyprus from 1956 to 1959. Instead, the monuments are elsewhere. The city which we had once patrolled abounds with statues of EOKA fighters, including Markos Drakos whom the Suffolks killed. The 'Kokkinotrimithia Concentration Camp' which we once guarded has been preserved as a memorial to those who did time in it.

I paid a call on my friend Sami Hifzi, the former army interpreter, at his home in the Turkish Quarter. His car was resting on blocks of wood. It was without spare parts or petrol. The Independence agreement had collapsed and the Turkish Cypriots were under an economic blockade which, together with a *coup* against President Makarios, led to the Turkish invasion in July 1974. The island has been partitioned and conflicted ever since. Its divisions are the second most insoluble problem in the Middle East.

None of this we knew, or could have known, when we were soldiers. What we did know was that the constitutional agreements reached between

Britain, Turkey and Greece in 1959 provided the Government with cover for withdrawing the troops, first from operations and then from the island, except for the sovereign base areas. In Cyprus, as so often in our history, most recently in Iraq and Afghanistan, we were declaring victory and leaving the field. It is one of the British Army's lesser known traditions that when the soldiers retreat the buglers sound the advance. They did it again in Basra in 2007.

National Service was a life-changing experience. One of the things it changed for me, and I believe for many others, was our attitude to authority. We started off acquiescent but ended up quite 'bolshie'. If ordered to jump, instead of asking 'how high?' we were more likely to answer 'Why?' Blind obedience had not worked for us – nor, I would argue, did it work for the Army itself. We suppressed a revolt, extinguished fires and underpinned a house of cards, the Independence settlement, that in due course collapsed. The decolonisation of Cyprus was not a success.

Except in one sense – that for us the conscript soldiers, individually and collectively, it *was* a success. We had come through. We had a medal to show for it. We had not let each other or the Regiment down. We had (as the old sweats put it) 'got our knees brown'. Most important of all, whether on operations or on parade, *we were indistinguishable from the regulars.* We were not weekend warriors but full-time soldiers and took a certain pride in it. And we had, if not the time of our lives, a time unlike any other. We did what was expected of us. We look back on it even today with a sense of achievement.

Not so many old people remember so vividly what they were doing when they were 19 or 20. We national servicemen do. They were high-impact years. We left the Army but the Army never really left us. I know that is the feeling among many of us.

There are things in life that you do not enjoy doing but enjoy having done. One of these in my case was four years in the House of Commons. The other was two years in the Suffolk Regiment. I would not have wished it otherwise. The soldiers of Suffolk were very special people.

And we who served can be proud that we served – the last who ever did – in the 12th of Foot.

Postscript

It isn't wise in matters regimental
To be too much in awe of the brass and braid
And the colonels in the great parade
With glittering gongs in rows and rows
Of OBEs and DSOs.
The Army's run by its NCOs:
The officers are mainly ornamental.

Note on Sources

The passages in display quotes are from my letters sent home from Cyprus between October 1957 and May 1959.

The claim that the security forces knew where Grivas was hiding (p. 56) is in *Burdened with Cyprus* by John Reddaway, Weidenfeld & Nicolson 1968, p. 70.

Paul Foot's report from the Central Prison (p. 85) is in *Oxford Opinion*, 31 January 1959.

Kenneth Robinson MP's criticism of Governor Harding (p. 142) is in *Hansard* 21 December 1956.

Allegations of brutality by the security forces (pp. 193 and 195) are in *The Guardian* 27 July 2012 and *The Decline and Fall of the British Empire* by Piers Brendon, Vintage 2008, p. 621.

The recently declassified government documents are held in the National Archives at Kew. The file numbers are as follows.

The Deputy Governor's concerns about the security situation in November 1957 (p. 22) are in FCO 141/4422.

Governor Foot's cable to London about Turkish Cypriot fears (p. 24) is in FCO 141/4422.

Governor Foot's arrival in Cyprus (p. 30) is in FCO 141/3939.

Governor Foot's letter to Grivas (p. 30) is in CO 967/346.

Governor Harding on the execution of Michael Karaolis (p. 34) is in FCO 371/123885.

General Darling on the final phase of the emergency (p. 55) is in CO226/1077.

Administrative Secretary's advice to General Darling (p. 55) is in FCO 141/427.

General Darling on new tactics against EOKA (p. 56) is in FCO 141/4459.

General Darling on the lessons of Cyprus (p. 56) is in CO 926/1077.

Governor Foot on the lessons of Cyprus (pp. 57 and 75) is in FCO 141/4233.

Governor Foot on Operation Matchbox (pp. 71, 75 and 103) is in FCO 141/4216.

Troops' indiscipline in Famagusta in October 1958 (p. 71) is in FCO 141/4493.

Governor Foot on troops' indiscipline in Famagusta in October 1958 (pp. 71 and 135) is in FCO 141/4493.

Governor Foot on EOKA smear campaign against security forces (p. 75) is in FCO 141/4218.

Governor Foot's message to the security forces (p. 85) is in FCO 141/4451.

General Darling on the slowness of the judicial process (p. 110) is in CO 926/1077.

Iris Russell's column in the *Sunday Dispatch* predicting disaster (p. 125) is in FCO 141/4422.

Governor Harding on the Grivas diaries (p. 132) is in FCO 141/4353.

Arthur Campbell on Makarios in *Flaming Cassock* (p. 180) is in FCO 141/4456.

Governor Foot on being muzzled by the Colonial Office (p. 134) is in FCO 141/4451.

Governor Foot on information policy (p. 134) is in FCO 141/4233.

Army Chief of Staff on the European Human Rights Convention (p. 135) is in FCO 141/4459.

Departure of Colonel Grivas from Cyprus in March 1959 (p. 154) is in FCO 141/4493.

Arthur Campbell on the training of soldiers in *Flaming Cassock* (p. 168) is in FCO 141/ 4456.

The suppression of Arthur Campbell's *Flaming Casssock* (pp. 171–6) is in CO 126/1106.and FCO 141/4456.

Arthur Campbell's redacted *Flaming Cassock* (pp. 177–84) is in FCO 141/4456.

Governor Harding's *Memorandum* (pp. 184–91) is in CO 926/2084.

General Darling on interrogators and detention camp staff (p. 193) is in CO 926/1277,

Governor Foot 'not an ideal choice for Cyprus' (p. 196) is in CO 967/321.

General Darling on the campaign as 'an assault on the ordinary people' (p. 109) is in CO 926/1077.

Index